Our Happy Hours: LGBT Voices From the Gay Bars

S. Renée Bess
and
Lee Lynch
Story Collectors

Flashpoint Publications

2017

Cover Design AcornGraphics

Edited by Patty Schramm and Nann Dunne

ISBN: 978-1-63304-813-3

First Printing 2017

Published in the United States of America

Published by

FLASHPOINT
PUBLICATIONS

Table of Contents

Renée's Acknowledgments

I am grateful for my spouse Vivian, who always listens to my ideas, asks me great questions, never shoots a hole through my dreams, and very lovingly makes a life with me.

I send a huge "thank you" to my friend and sister-writer, Lee Lynch, who didn't hesitate to join this project. Through her labor, she shared her skills, patience and devotion to writing. In many ways she is my teacher.

I appreciate all the support and work Patty Schramm provided as she navigated us through the publishing process. Patty, who experiences life six hours ahead of me and nine hours ahead of Lee, was available 24/7 to answer our questions and soothe our anxieties.

I thank Cathy Bryerose for giving me permission to fly without Regal Crest Books beneath me. Kites may soar through the air, but they always return to earth, usually near that place from which they're flown.

Thank you, Lori Lake, for your generosity to the publishing process of our anthology.

I have so much gratitude for the writers who never hesitated to offer us a contribution of their work. Each one expanded my thinking. Many challenged some of my pre-conceived notions.

I admire and appreciate the selfless work accomplished by the staff of the Attic Youth Center in Philadelphia. It will be my pleasure to donate my share of this book's royalties to that organization.

I thank my sister Stephanie who always shows me she's interested in my work.

I am eternally greatful to my parents, Thomas and Lorraine Bess, who encouraged my love of reading, even during those post-bedtime curfews when they caught me huddled in my bed sheet tent, a book in one hand and a flashlight in the other, discovering the adventures of Nancy Drew or the Hardy Boys.

Lee's Acknowledgments

Ann McMan for her cover and all around geniusness.

Patty Schramm, for her authoritative professionalism, creative ideas, organizing skills, and willingness to answer our questions, even when we emailed them six or nine hours behind her time zone's clock.

Nann Dunne for her patient, careful editing.

All of our talented contributors for building a strong body of LGBT literature and raising funds for community-based centers for our kids.

The Ali Forney Center, The Attic, and all the LGBT youth organizations worldwide for making safe spaces and providing essential services to queer kids in need.

Every writer in this collection knows exactly how vital that support is.

Elaine Lynch for pitching in whenever we needed technical help and for keeping Lee whole and healthy.

Vivian Lotz, who always listens to Renée's ideas, asks great questions, and very lovingly shares her life with Renée.

Our respective publishers, who permitted Renée and Lee to fly independently in order to assemble this collection of poetry and prose.

And thanks to Renée Bess for conceiving this project and asking me to sign on. It's been an honor and a privilege.

Foreword I

Renée Bess

A book is a journey down new paths. This anthology's particular journey began years ago, wrapped in the drumbeats of disco and house music, and poured from bottles of beer, wine, and liquor. It traveled alongside lust-filled glances and hopes for a connection, be it for one night, a few months, or perhaps that difficult-to-find "forever."

This book's expedition grew during the pre-dawn hours of June 13, 2016, when so many of us watched the media's coverage of the massacre at the Pulse Nightclub. That mass shooting pierced the soul of every LGBTQ person who knew the experience of finding safety, joy, and personal validation in a space where it was okay to slow drag with your same gender partner, or hold her/him/them lovingly in your gaze. For a moment we'd all been in that Orlando club, or we knew we could have been there.

We writers took to our desks and wrote poems, essays, and blogs about our collective pain. One such writer whose blog captured my attention was Lee Lynch. Lee described the essence of the important role the gay bar plays in our culture. Her words compelled me to wonder how other writers would respond if they were asked about the significance of gay bars and clubs in the lives of LGBTQ people.

This anthology offers some answers. There are as many different responses as there are writers who contributed to this book. Indeed, there are probably more. Pride, self-discovery, and joy exist in tandem with fear, anxiety, and the hurt and anger that accompany rejection.

LGBTQ voices from the gay bar span the width of a piano's keyboard. They jump and glide from one octave to another. Readers will see their own experiences in some of the work. They'll discover also some of the circumstances experienced by the "others" who must walk down different trails to find self-acceptance and tolerance within the mainstream gay community.

I wish all our readers an enjoyable time as they listen to our LGBTQ voices from the gay bars.

Foreword II

Lee Lynch

Freedom Clothes

So here I am, donning men's dress pants for the Golden Crown Literary Society Awards ceremony, and I keep thinking of the photos of our people in Orlando. They dressed up too in their best freedom clothes, also anticipating an evening of togetherness. I'm grateful to be alive and able to gather with other gay women, while I can barely take in how many of us were killed, wounded, traumatized and experienced losses because of our gender preferences.

I've been reading about NYC Gay Pride. When I attended the early NYC marches, there was some security—mostly to control us, I believe. In 2016 security is for our protection. Blocks and blocks are closed to parking. There will be thousands of officers on the streets, on rooftops, in the air and in boats. My biggest fear in the early 1970s was that my mother would see me on T.V. and find out for certain I was going to burn in hell.

Yet ever since the 1980s, when the right wing decided it would be politically expedient to build their power base by turning us into a featureless symbol against whom multitudes of non-gays could unite, I have expected mass killings. We're natural targets for people taught by their religions that their deities find us an abomination.

The horror of that Central Florida night brought back the general horror of gay bars for me. Like whole neighborhoods that house other minorities, the bars pen us in one place where we are queer ducks—queer sitting ducks. Orlando was a pogrom, "the organized killing of many helpless people,"* in this case organized by a stealth enemy that turns people like the deeply conflicted, unstable shooter into murderers.

I think affectionately of some gay bars—I got to wear freedom clothes there too—but I also remember the horror of them. They were a nightmare then, they're a nightmare again. Yet I thought of them as fun. Didn't we all? I loved being with other gays, but drank to tolerate the demeaning conditions of our loud, cold, dirty, dangerous pens.

Truth be told, I'm a wallflower by nature with seldom enough self-confidence to ask a woman to dance. Even with the drink in me and a cigarette going, the bars bored me silly. Any excitement came from dancing with my partner and being surrounded by our kind.

The gawking het couples on dates who came to laugh and stare at what to them was a grotesque sideshow, the ones who always managed to get tables because they knew the owners of the joints while we stood around without a place to set our drinks, degraded, intimidated and antagonized us, their very presence a warning that we danced to their fiddle. My rage at them continues to this day and fuels some of what I write. It's due to the gentle nature of our people we are the victims of violence and our tormentors get off scot-free.

I expected such an attack on LGBTQ people at least since the night, in the mid-1970s, when my friend and co-worker Dino was shot outside Partners Cafe in New Haven, Connecticut. Dino was walking to his car when out of nowhere, someone started shooting from a moving vehicle. Young, handsome Dino got a bullet in the arm. Now I'm only surprised at the infrequency of the attacks.

I *am* surprised that a gay bar has been designated a National Monument. This is only one of many such dichotomies. We're central to the frightening divide between U.S. voters, which only confirms how powerful we really are.

It's fitting that our monument should be a bar. Human communities form where they can, spontaneously, and eventually develop traditions. Hellish as they can be, at times they were glorious, glorious! The music may have been loud past bearing, but we danced all night. Under the glitter balls we saw ourselves reflected in our peers like nowhere else. I was not the only shy one and eventually a few strangers would become friends, friends grew to circles. With a gay bar nearby we never needed to be totally alone.

A night at the bar was always a celebration. Angry, estranged, alcoholic, festive—companionship was there for the taking. Danger united us, as it does still.

There will be increased security at venues and events like the one I'm headed to. I'll be wearing my dress-up pants, shirt, vest, pocket square and tie. Others will be in alluring frocks, and a number in their full-dress U.S. military uniforms. Day by day, more and more people condemn atrocities against LGBTQ people and other minorities and we are stronger for every changed mind.

I will remember the beautiful, proud and daring men and women who were attacked that nightmare night in Orlando, every time I don my glorious freedom clothes.

*www.merriam-webster.com/dictionary

ROCK 'N' DYKE ROLL:
A Fable of Memory

by Ann Aptaker

Subway ride's behind me. I've got plenty of quarters for the juke. My jeans and white tee are still crisp. My hair's slicked and side-parted. My black loafers shined—honey, I can even see my face.

Sipping a beer. Looking around. Cute eyes and red lipstick catch me hard. Well helloooo, wanna dance?

Hey sweetie. Hey darlin'. Hey sugar. Hey let's twist and shout. Let's boogaloo. Let's fast dance. Let's slow dance. Let's rock 'n' roll. Let's kiss. Let's grind. Let's forget about the workplace, forget about the boredom, the hiding, the wrong clothes, the forced smiles, the lies told. Let's have another beer. We're safe here, safe to slide tits to tits around the dance floor, safe to slide our hands along a feminine back, feel her skin, feel *her*.

Hey buddies in suits 'n' ties 'n' tees, hey sweeties in stockings and skirts, hey barkeep set 'em up; another beer, a scotch, a rum and coke, a seven and seven. We'll drink, we'll flirt to juke tunes booming with freedom and romance and lust. Sweet drinks, sweet talk, sweet woman hiding inside your glow, sweet honey in the sweet rock.

So sweetie? So darlin'? So sugar? So whaddya say? So you live around here? Are we gonna fall in love or just into sex? Hell, I don't know. But meantime, the music's blasting, the room's buzzing, the dance floor's shakin', the cigarettes glow through smoke. The blue jeans swagger, the skinny ties fly, the blouses stick to sweat. Everybody's talking or laughing or boozing or strutting or primping or romancing or trying to score, because tomorrow it's back into the boredom, the hiding, the wrong clothes, the forced smiles, the lies told, the hate.

Tomorrow.

But tonight we'll feel our lives, we'll *be* alive, shout and dance and love and sex our lives. Lets hop, let's stroll, let's rock 'n' roll, rock 'n' roll, rock 'n' dammit roll, let's rock 'n' dyke roll.

My Unexpected Sanctuary

by Dontá Morrison

The Black gay club is a collection of hits and misses. If one is unclear on what type of "gay" they are, it can become an overwhelmingly confusing ride through a myriad of experiences. Before settling into one of the various subcultures, it is important that a detailed understanding of that vein is achieved. Afterward, it is up to the individuals to mentally nurture themselves to a place where they feel comfortable with self and those around them. But once that stance is found, the Black gay club becomes a safe haven for those who need a place to escape to and twirl without judgment.

Even as a child I knew I was gay. Let me clarify: I did not know that I was "gay" per se; I just knew I was different from the other young boys on the playground who loved to play hide-and-go-get-it, a game which led to them being able to feel up the girls and steal kisses. During those times of recess, I found other things to get involved in that would take the pressure off of me having to "fit in with the boys." I didn't really have a social circle, but I wasn't a loner either. In other words, I knew how to blend in more than stand out.

That skill carried me through much of my teenage and early adult years: basically, the pre-sex era of my life. All of that changed once I discovered male-to-male intimacy. After that introduction, I realized how different my life was. It opened a desire for community and connection. Although I didn't feel alone, I longed to be a part of something more inclusive and understanding of the sexual journey I was on.

Then, in the summer of 1996, something wonderful happened.

After I reconnected with some childhood friends, they shared with me their newfound interest in same-sex relations. I was both shocked and intrigued. I had never assumed this set of acquaintances shared my desires. When they invited me to a gay club, I honestly didn't know what they meant by that. Was there actually a place where Black gay men congregated and danced together? My ignorance was obvious, and they chuckled at my lack of knowledge about the existence of a Black gay club scene. I explained that the only imagery I had was what television displayed: White men wearing tight jeans, white T-shirts, and leather jackets who idly stood around in a smoky bar making obscure facial gestures toward one another. To say the least, my perception was very one-sided and stereotypical.

In the Black community, being gay is taboo, a blatant insult to those who live within a heteronormative mindset. I never wanted to disappoint those I admired, so I suppressed my desires and avoided long-term physical and emotional relationships with men. My involvement was purely sexual and anything outside of that was clearly unwelcome. The thought of going to a place where I would be recognized as a part of a bigger and broader collective terrified me.

But curiosity got the best of me, and one Saturday night I agreed to accompany them. I said I couldn't stay long because I had church in the morning. I grew up in a religious family that was fully involved in church, and I was in no way missing a service due to this experience. I opted to drive myself versus carpool. I didn't know what to expect, nor did I want to be stuck when ready to leave. Filled with anxiety, I drove down Crenshaw Avenue toward Pico Boulevard.

What am I getting myself into? I have no business going there. I'm a child of God. Despite these thoughts circling through my mind, I continued on the path.

I made the right turn on Pico and instantly noticed a sign ahead that read, "Jewel's Catch One Disco." I laughed. A place that had *disco* in the title couldn't possibly be current. As I drove closer, I saw a crowd of people. I slowed down and stared at a diverse array of Black men waiting in a long line in front of the club. I was floored. I waited at the red light, and more men crossed the street in front of me. They weren't stereotypical gay men dressed in gaudy attire that brought attention to their sexuality, but men who looked like everyday guys going to hang out. I was now more intrigued. After circling the block for a frustratingly long time, I finally found a place to park. I popped a stick of gum in my mouth and took a deep breath. The time had come. I wasn't quite ready, but I wanted to see and meet more like me.

Standing in line was an experience in itself. A piece of me was praying that no one I knew would drive by and see me. I wasn't quite ready to be completely "out," nor did I want to lie about why I was there. However, I felt a strange sense of connection. I had yet to go inside, but I found the sidewalk conversations entertaining. Stories of bad dates, bad sex, gay scandals, catty comebacks, and who better not show their face in the club, were all a part of seemingly normal banter.

A few unapologetically stared at me, the "new guy." I smiled, so as not to appear shady or unapproachable. This was their environment, and I was but a visitor.

While the security guy checked my identification and patted me down, my gaze fell on the long staircase that led up to the club. I had no idea what waited at the top. He waved me inside and I started the ascent. I heard the beginning bassline of a song I recognized followed by loud cheers. My excitement intensified. At the top of the stairs, a cashier booth sat in front of a collage of Catch One Pageant winners. The black-and-white montage highlighted the history of the club. I gave my $10.00 and entered a venue that would forever change my life.

I crossed into a world of transparent behavior that allowed the Black gay community to be fully expressive. Jewel's Catch One Disco, also known as the Catch, wasn't just a club. The massive, two-level space housed two dance floors and three bars, an overwhelming sight for any first-time guest.

As everyone busied about, I found the nearest corner and buried myself into it. My fight to look comfortable clearly wasn't working; I resembled a nervous child on the first day of school. The friends I came to meet could quite possibly be in the next room, but I didn't have the intestinal fortitude to venture out alone.

Music from some of my favorite artists resounded through the speakers, and I couldn't help but move to the beat. Anthems recited by Lil' Kim, Foxy Brown, Missy Elliott, Snoop Dogg, and all the other West Coast all-stars set the tone and created an atmosphere unlike any other. Nervously, I forced down my anxiety and casually strode through the crowd in search of my compadres. I caught eyes with a few men who were definitely my type. One beckoned me to come closer, yet despite the temptation, I refrained. It was too soon. I was too new.

Men lined the opening to the dance floor, eyeing everyone who passed. It reminded me of the senior hallway in high school. Freshmen dare not enter, and those who did were at risk of being persecuted for no reason outside of simply being freshmen. Keeping my head up and my gait confident, I glided by them and into the main room. First I noticed strippers on platforms doing acrobatic acts similar to a Cirque De Soleil performance. I was mesmerized. I had never seen male strippers live and in person. The way they rhythmically gyrated to the beat, all the while going up and down a steel pole, fascinated me. The amount of money being thrown at them was enough to make me temporarily rethink my current vocation. As bad as I wanted to, I still didn't get too close. I didn't want to be perceived as a pervert ogling their perfectly sculpted bodies. So, I stood afar and lustfully watched.

Finally, a familiar face approached. My friend drew closer with a smile on his face and a drink in his hand. He explained he had spotted me earlier but got caught up in conversation with a guy he had been wanting to meet for quite some time. He grabbed my hand and escorted me through the crowd. I felt awkward publicly holding another man's hand. I wanted to pull away, but if I did, we might get separated. As we walked, he exchanged head nods with those he knew. Each looked at me with what could be suspicion, but gave a nod nonetheless. We entered into an open space where those who weren't dancing casually stood around and mingled. I saw our other friends, as well as a few I didn't know who huddled close. My friends and I exchanged embraces, and I stood with this circle and observed all that the Catch had to offer: the music, the freedom, the camaraderie, and even the drama.

Eventually I became a regular at the establishment. I no longer had to stand and wait for security to check my identification and—sometimes—was even allowed free admission. I attended the special events and celebrations, especially those following Los Angeles Black Gay Pride that occurred every Fourth of July weekend. Over time those I met at the Catch were not merely my club and party friends; they became my family. Through our shared experiences, challenges, and triumphs, these confidants knew me on a level unlike so many before.

Because of my openness and willingness to visit, I'm now a more confident Black gay man. Yes, the gay club had a life-lasting, positive impact upon me. When the church called me an abomination and *suggested* I leave, the club provided refuge. When family members shamed me and made me feel less than worthy, the club validated my presence and allowed me to be the person God created me to be, without judgment. The Catch gave me an opportunity to meet and network with some remarkable Black gay leaders. Some wouldn't believe that to be true, but many Black gay men in positions of power have a connection or story that leads back to the gay club.

There are many hubs in the Black community. The church is the most recognized one, but for the LGBT community, our hub is the club. The safe haven we call home. Life changes and we age out of it as a weekly routine, but none of us can deny the way it shaped our lives. I'm proud to say the Catch is a part of my history. I proudly share memories and do my part to ensure that its legacy doesn't die.

Regrettably, Jewels Catch One Disco closed down in 2015. The closure was a devastating blow to the Los Angeles Black LGBT community. For over 40 years, this venue housed us, supported us, and promoted us. Its era may have ended, but its roots in the community run deep. It shall be remembered by those of us whose lives it impacted. I hope the up-and-coming generation will have the same opportunity to be a part of a club environment that is more than music and dance, but is a sanctuary. A refuge from the homophobia and hate. A place where everyone can come together in unity to celebrate life, showcase love, and for a few hours just dance all their cares away. In essence, a gay club is a beautiful form of church.

Frank Jeffrey's

by Rae Theodore

Third date.
I invite the woman who will be my wife
To a hole-in-the-wall called Frank Jeffrey's.

That night, we belly up to the old wooden bar,
Plant our elbows like settlers claiming territory out west.

The bartender knows my name,
Knows my usual—
Miller Lite,
Even though I feel it should be something harder
To match the way I am
On the outside.

I think I'm scoring points with my girl,
Racking them up like a human pinball machine.
Ka-ching,
Ka-ching.

We talk with the bartender about labels.
Gay, straight, bi, who the hell cares?
And laugh about that time I got hit on by a dude.
"Am I sending the right signal?" I had asked
In my flannel shirt with brown boots
Fat and heavy on the bottom bar-stool rung.

She follows me to my place
Where we sit on my black IKEA couch,
Watch *Kinsey* from a DVD.
I freeze like an ice cube when it's time to make a move.
"I thought you were asexual," she will later confess.

Frank Jeffrey's closed ten years ago.
Gone the way of fountain pens,

Phone books,
Typewriters,
Film.

Still, when we pass the building that birthed a shiny new pub
That serves Blue Moon on tap and burgers on brioche,
I remember:
The faded rainbow flag plastered in the window.
The doorknob smooth and cool in my hand.
The wooden floorboards creaking under my scuffed boots.
Sitting Michael Jordan tall on the vinyl-covered stools.
Bringing my girl home for the first time

The Zoo Bar

by James Schwartz

Politically progressive Kalamazoo lies an hour north on US-131 from the Amish farm I grew up on in southwest "river country" Michigan.

The Zoo Bar opened in the late '70s Disco Era (Tiny Tim was there!) and closed in 2005 as did Kalamazoo's other LGBT watering hole, Brothers Beta Club. Located on Portage Road, The Zoo was a small ramshackle bar with a dance floor, a jukebox, and a patio out back where all manner of decadence occurred.

Nightly cabaret shows, pageants, male dancers, DJs, and Leather Night brought out Michigan's gay community and occasionally international visitors. On House Night, I was one of the few white faces sweating under the strobes to Chicago and Detroit house and techno (Kalamazoo lies halfway between the two cities).

My constant companion in those days was a short, buxom, self-proclaimed "fag hag" with a liking for glitter, drag queens, and alcoholic beverages.

We attended all the drag shows, of which I performed in several.

I sometimes worked the door, and on one slow Monday night, I filled in for a no-show DJ.

In the late '90s, Chelsea Del Ray, Carmen San Diego, Amber Foxx, Jamie Hunter, Goddess, Monet St. Croix, Brianna Fest, and so many others ruled the drag scene. Kalamazoo being a college town, there was no shortage of male dancers.

April and I made it our business to know everyone, and we never missed the legendary Cedar Street "after" parties.

****

On a rainy night, I was at The Zoo filling in for the DJ. A guy eyed me all night and finally asked me to dance only after he got drunk. He was from Africa, with a friend headed to Chicago.

He was dressed like me, in jeans and a T-shirt, but his face was decorated with tribal scars, his left ear half gone, a mound of scar tissue. We made out on the dance floor.

Men cruised, flicked through the bar's newsletter and *The Rainbow Gazette*, published by P-FLAG and featuring gay news, events, my early poetry, and Lee Lynch's "The Amazon Trail" column.

Several drag queens made a late, dramatic entrance and were soon at the bar matching a party of lesbians shot for shot.

My lover-not-to-be and I untangled ourselves; our goodbye kiss caused the room to come to a standstill followed by appreciative cat calls and wolf whistles from the lesbians.

****

Brothers Beta Club burned down, and The Zoo closed soon after. Ten years later, Kalamazoo's sole gay club, Metro, announced the end so, as of 2017, Kalamazoo will have no gay bar or club despite the large LGBT community and annual Pride event.

It seemed like the end of an era in many ways. As an honorary founding father of LGBT Amish.com, I was proud to march alongside CARES and Miss Kalamazoo Pride 2014 LaDonna Divine at Lansing, Michigan, Pride in 2014, the first time Amish were represented at a Pride event.

As an artist in the "Age of Trump," I plan to resist. With or without a local gay bar. I know my community is resilient and can withstand the coming winter. Local drag diva Chanel Hunter recently went viral wearing a "Fuck Trump" frock while miming the National Anthem, which segued into "Born This Way."

However marginalized, we're going to be okay.

Knickers

by Jennifer Morales

Mat took a chance and invited the dean's wife out.

"Hey, do you want to go dancing sometime?"

"Yes," KC said. "I love dancing, but it's been awhile. Where?"

"There's a place I found that's just outside of Des Moines."

"Really? What?"

"It's this gay place—a lesbian bar, believe it or not." Mat was keeping an eye out for signs of queer life since her exile in rural Iowa began, almost four months ago. There weren't many. A few on the Grinnell campus where she was a visiting professor of poetry, but elsewhere, not so much.

"Oh." KC took a deep breath. "Do I have to be gay?"

"It's not technically a requirement." Mat shifted the phone from one sweaty ear to the other.

"When?"

"How about this Saturday?"

"Let me check my calendar." She drifted away from the phone then back again. "I can do that. Who else is coming?"

"Nobody else. Just you and me."

"Oh?" KC's voice dropped an octave. "Oh."

"Will you come?" Mat held her breath.

"I will..." Some uncertainty flickered in her voice.

"You will, but...what?"

"But on one condition." A note of playfulness entered KC's tone.

"What condition?" Mat didn't care what it was; KC would have it. She wanted her there, close, disentangled from their lives on campus. KC had been Mat's anchor the past few months, charged as she was with helping new faculty settle into life in Grinnell. But Mat wanted to shed that officious arrangement and find out what, if anything, KC wanted from her.

"You'll have to protect me from the lesbians." KC laughed.

Mat laughed, too, a cool relief easing through her tense body. "I will. I won't let anybody get to you."

****

Knickers was on the edge of town, in a hunter-green pole building with a couple of neon bar signs in the small, high windows near the door. It could have been any bar in any tiny Midwestern town, a dream in sheet metal thrown up in a weekend by some enterprising family hoping to profit off selling bad beer to farmers after their long days disking the fields and arguing with the bank. The gravel parking lot was filled with pickups illuminated by a barn light stuck high on a pole. The American flag waved from a shorter pole near the entrance. From the outside, nothing gave it away except for the rainbow sticker on the door.

Mat settled into a bar stool right on time, 8 o'clock. She was happy, finally, to be in queer space, but the feeling didn't last long. A couple minutes after she ordered her first drink, a bride-to-be and her entourage of six twenty-something girls shimmied in, dancing through the door to a song only they seemed to hear. The preternaturally tanned bride wore a tiara with blinking lights that spelled out "Last chance!" She and her entire crew were wearing necklaces of plastic penises. They had clearly been drinking somewhere else already. One of them made a beeline for the DJ to make a request while the bride and the others hugged and wobbled their way toward the bar on their high heels. Mat wondered how they had made it across the gravel parking lot without killing themselves.

She couldn't hear what the bartender said to them, but it was met with an immediate roar of approval from the entourage. The bartender gestured toward the DJ, and he gave a thumbs up. LMFAO's "Shots" tumbled out of the speakers from every direction. The bartender, a curvy woman in tight jeans and long black hair, climbed up and over onto the edge of the bar, a bottle of something tucked under her arm. With a practiced hand, she pulled the bride into the space between her legs and tipped her head back. She made a show of adjusting her position, grinding her crotch into the bride's back until a blush deep enough to be visible in the rainbow light crossed the bride's face. With the bride's head in her lap, the bartender began to pour from the bottle into her open mouth. One by one the bridesmaids assumed the position, each as eager to be fed as baby birds.

When they were all through, Mat got up to study a poster near the door. It was for a fundraiser for a local softball team coach. There was a photo of the coach wearing a yellow Hawkeyes jersey. No insurance. Breast cancer. Spaghetti dinner.

It was 8:20. No KC. Mat began to worry she had scared her off. Their on-campus flirtations, the not-so-accidental running-into-each-others, the daily text messages—these seemed to be leading somewhere, as vague and possibly crazy as that destination might be.

But maybe Mat had misunderstood. Maybe inviting her out to a gay bar was a step too far. KC was married, after all. But she didn't act like it, not when the two of them were alone together. With her children grown and just recently out of the house, KC was asking questions about herself and her identity. Mat wanted to be part of the answer.

A short butch with a white-blonde crew cut made a line for Mat, working the small crowd for the bartender.

"She says you're next."

The bartender had scooted her way down the bar to a point just opposite them and fixed Mat with a determined stare.

Mat raised her glass in salute, adding what she hoped was a winning smile.

The butch grabbed Mat's coat collar. "She says you're next. Don't make me pick you up."

Mat doubted that the woman could lift her an inch off the sticky floor, but she wasn't letting go of Mat's coat. Mat went along.

The bartender turned Mat to face away from her with a swift grip of the shoulder and grabbed her chin. "I'll be nice," she said, gripping Mat between her thighs and laying a firm hand on Mat's face to wedge the crown of Mat's head between her breasts. Mat felt her warmth beneath her jeans.

"She'll be nice," the blonde butch repeated, watching Mat with interest in the second before the sweet, watermelon liquid started pouring into Mat's mouth. Mat forgot to swallow, and the booze started running out of the corners of her mouth and onto her shoulders.

"Ugh." Mat wiped her mouth. "Gah."

The blonde offered a handful of napkins and said, "I'm Freddie."

Mat wiped the rest of her face and dug into the corners of her shirt to sop up what she could of the watermelon liqueur.

"You gotta swallow." Freddie laughed and held out a hand for the wet napkins, which she balled up and threw into the trash bin behind the counter. "I think Rosie did you extra because you're new."

"That obvious, huh?"

"This town is so small, we can smell new blood coming in from fifty miles away." She smiled and her prominent incisors seemed vampire-like. "Let me buy you a drink, and you can tell me how in hell you ended up at Knickers."

Freddie gestured to Rosie, who brought Mat another gin and tonic and Freddie a beer.

Mat asked Freddie, "Do you work here?"

"Naw, just good friends with the bartenders. I keep them company when things are slow." Freddie scanned Mat from top to bottom. "So, what brings you to this corner of the world? You sure aren't here for the scenery."

"I don't know, the scenery's not so bad." Mat let Freddie notice her checking Rosie out. Mat was remembering the grip of her thighs, the feeling of drowning in her lap.

Freddie did notice and said, "Hey, watch yourself there, tiger. She's taken and I don't think her boyfriend will like that look on your face."

"Her boyfriend?" Mat turned back toward Rosie, whose low-slung black jeans revealed a pair of angel wing tattoos between the pinnacles of her hips. "She had me fooled."

"Yeah, me, too, once. She's a flirt, makes good tips for it. But believe me, she doesn't know what to do with a woman."

"There's a story there, huh?" Mat looked at Freddie over the top of her rocks glass.

"Maybe, but I already know that one." Freddie took out a pack of cigarettes and lit one. "What's your story?"

"I'm Mat Rodriguez, from Milwaukee. I'm teaching over at the college."

"Which one?"

"Grinnell."

"Pay must be good to get you to move out here." She offered Mat a cigarette from the pack, and Mat waved it away. "Or do you like the country?"

"Neither, actually. I'm getting divorced."

Freddie's eyes narrowed and a bright smile crossed her face. "I knew it." She shouted to Rosie, "You owe me twenty bucks, Rosie. I won that bet."

"A bet?"

"Yeah, back when Iowa made gay marriage legal, I bet Rosie that gays would be coming back to Iowa to get divorced not two, three years later, even with that one-year residency requirement. I think I just made some money off you." Freddie hit Mat on the shoulder and called out again, "Rosie, bring your wallet!"

Rosie was serving the bridal party and didn't hear her. One of the bridesmaids had her nose nuzzled up into Rosie's neck. Rosie was trying to ease her onto a barstool.

"Eh." Freddie waved her hand. "I know where to find her later."

Mat took out her phone. No call or text from KC. 8:45.

"Waiting for someone?"

"Yeah. She's late."

Freddie looked toward the door as if she were waiting for KC now, too. "Bitches."

Mat laughed. In Freddie's world, that's probably how things broke down. Either the woman was there and she was golden, or she wasn't and she was a bitch. Mat raised her glass to Freddie and drained it.

The bachelorette party was off dancing near the DJ booth, and Rosie was checking on her other customers at the bar. Freddie signaled to her.

When she arrived, Freddie said, "You owe me twenty bucks on that bet. Remember you said nobody was going to come to Iowa to get divorced, with the residency requirement?" She put a hand on Mat's shoulder. "Well, old Mattie here is living proof of what I said."

Rosie studied Mat with new interest. "You moved here? For a whole year? To get divorced?" When Mat nodded, she added, "Gay divorced?"

Mat shrugged. "Yep."

"Wow," Rosie said to Freddie. "Next couple are on me,

okay?" as if that settled their bet.

"You're kind of embarrassed, huh?" Freddie asked when Rosie stepped away.

Mat shrugged again. "Yeah, I mean, wouldn't you be? What kind of loser can drop her entire life for a year to move to someplace just to get divorced? And then divorce is like its own kind of failure, on top of that."

Freddie rubbed Mat's hair, like they were buddies on the softball team. "Aw, don't feel bad."

"But I do." She combed her hair back into place with her fingers.

Freddie leaned in close. "Naw, man. You're like a hero to me."

Mat snorted.

"No, for real. It's like this. Everybody wanted to be the first to get married, right? All the TV cameras following you around. The waiting in line in the rain with your rainbow umbrellas, and strangers bringing you flowers and cake. All the stroke-of-midnight weddings in city hall as soon as it became legal. The borrowed dresses and shit, right? But you," she said, poking Mat in the chest with her short finger, "you, my man. You're not here because it's exciting. You're here because you're human."

Mat took a breath and settled into her reasoning. For all her barfly ways, Freddie was a philosopher.

"Look, gay marriage"—Freddie stretched out the word "marriage" to a full three syllables—"doesn't prove we're as normal as the average Dick and Jane. But gay divorce sure does." She took a swig of her beer and howled, "We're just as fucked up as anybody, right? We're finally normal!"

Freddie was indeed fucked up, in more ways than one, but Mat took what she said to heart. She was right: Mat was a pioneer. As Mat sat there pondering this, she felt the door open behind her, letting in some cool evening air.

She turned. KC, her dark eyes skipping from side to side and her fingers clamped on her purse, stood in the doorway. Mat stood up right away to go to her.

"Cute," Freddie said. "That's your friend? She's really cute."

When Mat reached KC, she clutched her elbow and pulled her in close. "You made it. I'm glad."

KC was still looking around the place. The bridesmaids had long since cleared out, but new people had arrived, clusters of women with the occasional gay boy in tow. The DJ cranked the music up, and the spinning lights from the ceiling began a more frenzied swirl.

"I guess you brought the party." Mat pointed to the spiraling disco ball above their heads. "You want a drink?"

KC nodded. "I'm sorry," she said into Mat's ear as they worked their way between the bodies that were starting to fill the floor.

"For what?"

"I'm late."

"That's okay." Mat studied her face. "Are you all right?" KC still hadn't taken off her coat.

Mat ordered KC a gin and tonic while she took in the scene from the safety of the barstool. Mat stood close, shielding KC from whatever she thought might be out there.

"I've never been to a gay bar before," KC finally said.

"Not much different here than a regular bar." In the spotlight, an emaciated young drag queen, in a tight white dress with cutouts along the side, balanced on her stiletto heels, while a guy in torn jeans and a plaid, sleeveless shirt danced around her knees in adoration. When he turned his face toward them, his white baseball cap tipped back, Mat wasn't sure anymore if it was a guy or a girl.

"A little different," KC said, smiling at Mat.

"Does Charles know you're here?"

"No. Are you kidding me?"

"I don't know." Mat searched KC's face. "I don't know what kinds of things he expects from you."

"Not this. But maybe that's okay," she said, brightening. "If we don't do something once in a while to keep our husbands—or wives, as the case may be—on their toes, things can get pretty boring."

Someone bumped Mat from behind and knocked her in between KC's knees. They were face to face, warmth radiating up between them. Mat tipped her head toward KC, toward her beautiful lips.

KC's hands flew up to Mat's shoulders, and she laughed. "You on *your* toes, there, partner?"

"Yeah."

A woman in a Harley Davidson jacket got up from the stool next to KC and went to hug a friend who had just come in. Mat sat on the stool, spinning it in quarter circles from side to side.

"Sometimes you remind me of my son," KC said.

"Oh?" Mat tried not to sound disappointed.

"Yes, he's the same way. Can't just sit there, has to keep moving, even while he's in a chair." She sighed.

"I guess I've always been that way. I probably could get a diagnosis of adult ADHD, if I wanted one."

"Who would want one?" She turned her seat to face Mat. "Anyway, I like you the way you are."

"Oh, yeah?"

She pursed her lips. "Yeah. I do."

"I'm glad, KC. I really like you, too." Mat grabbed the edge of KC's checkered shirt, sticking out from under her coat, and tugged.

"Thanks for straightening me out."

"Never. I will never, ever straighten you out."

A Katy Perry song came on and Mat asked, "Do you want to dance?"

"I guess that's why I'm here." KC took off her coat and draped it over the seat. "Isn't this the 'I Kissed a Girl' singer?"

"Yeah," Mat said into her ear. "But this isn't that song."

"Hmm. Too bad." KC pressed her mouth dangerously close to Mat's neck.

Freddie came by on the next song, a bottle of beer in hand, and attempted to dance with KC, who made a grimace of surprise at the attention.

After three or four songs, KC dragged her hand across her throat and gestured back toward the bar.

"God, I'm old," she said, laughing.

"You're just getting good," Mat said.

A new bartender, a girl with tattooed sleeves of flowers covering her muscular arms, was taking over for Rosie. She brought Mat and KC glasses of water, and Mat ordered them another round.

They watched the crowd for a while. Freddie and the drag queen were dancing together.

KC asked, "How do we know when we're done?"

"Done? What do you mean?" Mat's breath snagged.

"Done with a relationship?"

She looked at Mat askance. "No. Done with adventures, with playing at being young. When are we supposed to give up and settle down?"

Mat leaned back with both her elbows on the bar. "I was figuring on when I'm dead. Like what Warren Zevon said, 'I'll sleep when I'm dead.'"

"And 'Enjoy every sandwich.' He said that, too."

"Sounds about right."

Mat dragged KC back to dance a few more times. The dance floor was getting more packed as it got on toward midnight, and Mat liked the feeling of not having any choice about how close the two of them danced. Occasionally KC's hips would touch Mat's and Mat would put a hand there or on her waist. KC didn't seem to mind.

Just after midnight, the DJ put on a slow dance, and just like in middle school, the floor cleared out, leaving only those intrepid couples who really wanted to let the world know they were together.

Mat gestured toward the door, and KC said, "I'll get our coats."

Freddie was in the parking lot smoking and hanging out with a circle of other women. When she saw them, she called, "You leaving?"

"Yeah." Mat turned and waved. The group of women Freddie was with didn't look any different from the assortment of dykes you'd find outside a bar in Milwaukee—wide butches in cargo shorts, polo-wearing sporty bois, the occasional baby dyke in a tank top and Converse, a few mini-skirted femmes. For all of Mat's resistance to rural life, it really wasn't much different, here or there.

Freddie said, "Hey, your girlfriend's cute."

KC cocked an eyebrow at Mat.

Mat called out, "She's not my girlfriend."

"I'll keep that in mind," Freddie yelled, now waving to KC.

"You have an admirer."

"Not my type." KC kept her eyes on Mat as she said it.

"Good." Mat dug into her pocket for her keys. "You want to sit in my car for a few minutes?"

"Yes, let's do that. And then I've got to go. I'm feeling

old." She blew a puff of air up into her bangs. "Old and sweaty."

Mat opened the passenger door for KC and settled herself in the driver's seat. "So that's Queer Iowa. Now we know."

"Whatever it was, I had fun. Thanks."

"So did I." Mat was aware of KC's nearness, of her breath infiltrating the chilly space, so Mat focused outside. In spite of the barn light behind them, there were stars sparkling above the field across the road. "You want to do it again sometime?"

KC reached for Mat's hand across the stick shift and squeezed. That was all it took. Mat leaned over and kissed her, and KC kissed her back. Suddenly all the pent-up feeling, all the wondering if KC felt the same way, rushed to the surface of Mat's skin in the form of heat. Her lips tingled and her hands went to KC's face, stroking her cheeks and pushing into her with her mouth.

KC pressed with an open hand on Mat's shoulder, and Mat fell back into her own seat. "Sorry."

KC touched her own mouth, as if to check if everything was in order. "No, it's okay. It's fine." She was breathing fast. "I'm just surprised, is all—at myself, not you."

"What's that supposed to mean?"

KC ran her knuckles up and down Mat's sternum, a mixed gesture Mat didn't know whether to interpret as comforting or distancing or both.

"I don't mean anything. I mean, you're wonderful. But I'm, I'm me."

"You're you, right. That's the whole point. I like you."

"I like you too, Mat." She looked out the passenger window. Freddie's friends were drifting apart, some going back into Knickers, some to their cars and trucks.

"Hey, are you crying?" Mat asked.

"I should go." She leaned across the space to kiss Mat on the cheek, smudging her with tears. She grabbed her bag and got out of the car.

In a minute, KC was gone, pulling onto the gloomy frontage road without a look back, leaving Mat alone with the cornfield stars.

LACE

by Cheryl Head

Washington, DC

LACE on the Avenue was a new concept in the menu of entertainment for the region's lesbian community. Developed, owned, and operated by Linda McAllister Mah, it boasted a sophisticated atmosphere, with high-end design elements, and a dress code which nodded to its elegance. Seating at mother-of-pearl-tiled counters, and restrooms with European fixtures added to the mystique, but LACE wasn't just a lounge. A full-service dining area under an oversized chandelier, included chef-created food offerings. The dance level featured sculptured walls, a state-of-the-art sound and video system, and an elevated VIP section.

LACE was all that and a bag of chips, but for McAllister it was mostly a dream come true.

A life-long entrepreneur, and a licensed social worker, the North Carolina native was drawn to the power and promise of the nation's capital and was shocked to find that lesbians in Washington, DC had such limited social options. So, she set about building a comfortable space where, as she said in a 2010 interview with Metro Weekly, "...women can come together and just be able to engage with each other."

After buying and selling one commercial property, McAllister came across a building with a workable footprint and location and began the 18-month process of acquiring permits, licenses, certificates, permissions, and "thumbs ups" from DC regulators and area neighbors. It was a rocky course, but Linda used her business and listening skills to negotiate the process.

When the doors of LACE opened on November 15, 2008, the line of patrons wrapped around the corner. Women of all labels, curious about the buzz, including the pink, save-the-date cards, wanted to be the first to experience the club whose slogan read: Where Every Night is Ladies Night.

LACE remained open for five years before succumbing to

personnel changes and a trend toward a changing patronage. To keep the bills paid, Linda accommodated requests to host more events for men and for the neighborhood. But, ultimately, it was an iteration of her dream she couldn't support, and LACE closed in August of 2013.

On October 29, 2016, Linda passed away, after a fight with cancer. In a Memorial Service, she was celebrated by family, friends, former employees, customers, and community leaders who recalled her tenacity and optimism. A resolution from the Center for Black Equity (the administrative arm of international Black gay pride events) credited LACE for its work with LGBTQ community-based organizations and for being "the first, woman-owned lesbian lounge and restaurant in Washington, DC, securing a safe space for women of all ages, races, and ethnicities for socializing, dining, and dancing."

COSTING

by Heather Jane

Blue Curacao

We were young.
looking for adventure.
My Blue Curacao met the challenge.
1001 ways to ask the wrong question,
to take a wrong turn,
to get lost for a night.
We swore we'd never meet again.
But she is citrusy sweet,
and is the prettiest at the bar.
I can't resist, again and again.
Night after night, we're lost together,
until eventually I realize,
My Blue Curacao,
has lied to me.
I find her once
in the clear light of day,
and the dazzling blue is gone.
She confesses it was a lure
to draw me
and others
into her trap.
Betrayed,
I resolve to leave the blue beauty on the shelf.
I will admire her from afar,
if at all.

Kir Royale

We made it Ladies' Night
whenever we went there.
I followed your lead.

You had style,
aspirations of grace,
and elegance.
You couldn't be Kir.
You were Kir Royale.
Doors opened for you.
(I opened them.)
Chairs were pulled out for you.
(I did that too.)
Kir Royale, you spoke to me
as if I had something to say.
You called,
and asked me to go out.
You made me feel special.
And when you bottomed out
I knew what to do.
You were wise
and had me chosen from the beginning.
You could spot
the experienced caregivers,
the experienced codependents.
I had to give you up, Kir Royale.
I lost Ladies' Night with you,
along with style and any hope for grace.

Apple Cider

I was so thirsty.
I needed a refreshing drink.
I walked right up to the bar
and asked for what I wanted.
Apple Cider quenched my thirst.
Bubbly and sweet,
my style this time.
I wasn't trying to pretend with apple cider,
to aspire to an unattainable goal.
Apple cider didn't lure me down a dark path.
We had a good time, I won't lie.
When we first met
she tasted so delicious.

I may have had a few too many.
But now I've learned
some drinks,
the temptress especially,
are best had at home.
Apple cider is that drink for me.

Cranberry and Soda

I am Cranberry and Soda.
All this time,
along for the ride.
Safety is more important to me.
I don't get to forget.
I remember
what you told me.
I watch your phone,
your purse,
whatever you left behind at the table.
I am tart.
My bubbles are sharper,
and I go down fast.
But I'm a cheap date.
I'll drive you home
at the end of the night.
First though,
let's sit back
and enjoy this time out together.
Our glasses are filled,
the people are talking, laughing, and flirting,
and I like to watch.

A Night Out

by Beth Burnett

The man at the door had a bushy beard and moustache that covered most of his mouth and made it difficult for me to understand when he spoke to me.

"Howwo ya?" I thought I heard and I must have looked confused because the guy behind me said, "She's twenty-one, Fred. I saw her at the Mix last night."

How old are you, he had apparently asked. I was grateful to the guy who spoke up because I was afraid I'd start blushing when I lied. Truthfully, I was eighteen and terrified. I looked at my rescuer. I had never been at the Mix, and I had never seen the guy before. Either he had mistaken me for someone else, or he felt sorry for me. I smiled slightly at him before slipping into the door of Legends nightclub.

The woman behind the counter at 7-11 had told me about Legends. I'm not sure how she pegged me as different, but whatever she saw in me was enough to make her say, "You need to check out the gay bars in Cleveland, kid. My brother is a homo and this is where he goes." I fled in terror, but later I looked at the piece of paper she had slipped across the counter.

There was no one like me in the small town of Bay Village, Ohio, at least none that I knew of. I didn't have a word for what I was, not then, but I knew there was something off about me.

I had once found a book called *Curious Wine* in a used bookstore, and I was shocked that it was about women loving women. It gave me hope that I might not be the only one, and that hope kept me from turning tail and running back to my car and the relative safety of Bay Village.

I blinked in the darkness of the club and scanned the crowd, looking for something familiar. All I saw were male bodies, some dressed in nothing but bikini underwear, dancing in a pulsing throng on a dance floor surrounded by mirrors.

Stunned, I stepped into the crowd around the bar, convinced I was the only girl in the place. Anxious, I pressed my hand against my stomach and tried to quell the rising panic in my gut. I focused on making my face blank. I wanted to turn around and leave, but my legs propelled me forward. At the bar, I asked the guy for a beer. I hated the taste of beer, but I didn't know what else to say and I suddenly felt the need for something in my hand, something to look at.

I leaned back against the bar and tried to look nonchalant. I had dressed in what I figured a girl like me might wear to a gay bar, which meant I was wearing my brother's jeans and a flannel shirt unbuttoned over a tight tank top. I had slicked my short, shaggy hair back, and I was feeling several shades of ridiculous.

The men next to me smiled, but no one talked to me. I decided that I would finish my beer and head out. As I drank my beer, I couldn't help but stare at the dance floor. The men were grinding against each other, some of them reaching around to touch each other's crotches. I saw one man slide his hand down another's pants. Dumbfounded, I nearly choked on my beer.

I looked away quickly and into the eyes of the man who had stepped up to the bar next to me. He was tall, taller than me, and I was the tallest girl in my class. He was wearing a tight T-shirt and a jean jacket covered in patches. His hair was cut short, but spikey in the front. He was handsome but pretty, like Rob Lowe in *The Outsiders*, and his green eyes were fascinating. He winked at me but didn't say anything. I nodded and turned back to the bar, looking down at my beer. I wanted to ask the man if there was a place where I could meet women, but I was afraid my voice would shake and I didn't want to seem new.

A soft, sweet voice interrupted my anxious thoughts. "Are you new?"

I looked around. The voice belonged to the man next to me. I coughed, spilling a bit of beer out of my mouth. Blinking, I gaped. "I'm sorry," I blurted. "It's just—I thought you were a man."

Her mouth tightened. She turned away from me and stared at the wall behind the bar. Looking at her more closely, I don't know how I mistook her for a man.

"I'm sorry," I said. "I didn't mean it like that."

She glared at me. "I expect that in the outside world. But this is my space and I expect better of other dykes."

"I'm sorry," I said again. "I'm sorry. It's just... when I first saw you. That's all. I've just—" I swallowed hard. "I just have never met a woman who looks like you." I paused, blinking so as not to cry. "Except for me."

Her face softened and she reached over to pat my hand. "You are new, aren't you?"

"Brand new," I whispered. "I've never been to a gay bar before."

"Well, you picked a hell of a place to start." She laughed as two men in speedos ran by shooting each other with water guns. "Why didn't you go to The Rose?"

"I've never heard of it," I muttered, still blushing. "I only heard of this place because the clerk at the 7-11 told me about it."

"See? We're everywhere."

I shook my head. "I don't think she was one of us." It felt good to use the collective, as if I somehow had equal status with this strong woman next to me.

The woman laughed. "I'm Sue," she said and reached out to shake my hand.

I put my hand in hers and tried to think of a cool name. I debated telling her my name was Luke. It sounded tough. Luke felt like a costume, but it felt safe and cool and a million miles removed from who I really was. I opened my mouth to say it and found myself telling the truth. "I'm Ellen. But I wish my name was Luke."

Sue laughed again. "Just be yourself, kid. That's the only guaranteed truth in the world."

"But I'm not even sure who I am," I spluttered. "And I don't know how to find out."

Sue shook her head. "I'm twice your age, Els, and the only thing I know for sure is that I don't know shit. Come on, let's go to The Rose and find your people."

I followed her to her car, and we drove for a few minutes in silence. Finally, I worked up the nerve to ask a question. "Why were you at that bar?"

"I like to hang at Legends sometimes," she replied. "It's fun to get out on the dance floor and get a good workout without having to worry about seeing ex-girlfriends or being hit on."

I must have looked dubious because she laughed. "Believe me, Els, there will come a time when the idea of not getting hit on is actually a relief."

I rubbed my chin. "I've never even been on a date, so I can't imagine a time when a woman hitting on me would be a bad thing."

She smiled and pulled into the parking lot of The Rose. It was a plain brown building set back from the road a bit. We were in a kind of industrial area of Lakewood, but there was another bar across the street and what looked like a diner a few buildings down. "The Barrel," Sue said. "The best place to get steak and eggs at four a.m."

"The men at the bar were crazy," I said. "Is it going to be like that here?"

Sue had already gotten out of the car, and she turned to look back at me. "They aren't crazy, Els. They all have lives, many of them in the closet. They work with people who make gay jokes. They overhear conversations about how disgusting the gay menace is and how it's going to harm children. They worry about getting kicked out of their own homes, or being denied housing. Out there, out in the real world, they aren't safe. They're in costume all day, every day, just to stay alive. Why shouldn't they get a little crazy when they're finally in a safe space?"

I got out of the car silently. I wasn't that different from the men in the bar, then. I was picked on by my classmates all the time. Most of them have called me Ellen-Allen for years, ever since Roger Briton said, "Is it Ellen or Allen? Is she a boy or a girl? Who can tell?" Graduation couldn't come fast enough, but I feared college would be more of the same. I hadn't told my parents that I was gay. I thought my mom might be okay with it, but my dad hated gay people. I cringed every time I heard him yell "faggot" when he was pissed off about something. Is that what he would think of me?

Sue put a hand on my shoulder as we neared the door. "Just remember to be yourself, Els," she said, smiling.

I smiled back. I could do this. I wasn't Ellen-Allen here. I was Els and I was on the edge of a cliff. I was ready to jump over and see if I could fly.

We stepped through the door, and I stood for a moment and surveyed the scene. A few women looked up at us and a couple waved. Sue waved at a group sitting around a table in the corner. "Come on," she said. "We'll get drinks and join my friends."

I barely heard her. There were women everywhere. Some were like me, young, and trying to look cool. There were women in long skirts with long hair flowing freely or wrapped in ponytails. I saw women in jeans, in suits, in a full-length red dress. A lot of women looked to be my mother's age, some were even older than that. A woman near me smiled and I smiled back. She looked like my grandmother with full white hair twisted into a bun and a button-front, floral-print blouse. I tugged on Sue's sleeve. "I didn't know there were old lesbians," I whispered.

She grinned. "What the hell do you think you'll be in forty years?"

My head was spinning and I placed a hand on the bar to steady myself. I don't know what I thought. I didn't know any old lesbians. I didn't know any young lesbians. Reading about women making love to each other was one thing. Actually meeting real-life lesbians was quite another. It hadn't really occurred to me until just this moment that I wasn't alone. Suddenly, everything I had ever thought about myself was called into question. Looking at the women in the room, the overwhelming thought was that they were all so real. Women were laughing, talking, smiling, crying, dancing. Some were singing along with the music; others were playing pool. The woman who looked like my grandmother was holding hands with another white-haired lady, only that woman had cropped hair and was wearing men's trousers and a striped dress shirt. I wondered if they were lovers or sisters or friends.

Sue knocked my arm with her elbow. She was holding a beer and a cocktail. "Come on, Els. Let's go meet my friends."

"Sue," I whispered. "Is everyone here a lesbian?"

She looked around. "Maybe not everyone, but I imagine most of them."

I followed her to the table, breathing deeply to keep from passing out. Women smiled at me as we walked by. A woman in a short dress with a lot of cleavage twiddled her fingers at me from across the room, and I felt the blush shooting across my face.

We pulled up chairs at the table in the corner, and the women scooched over to make room for us. I sat down between Sue and a woman wearing jeans and a Cleveland Browns sweatshirt. Sue put her hand on my shoulder. "Everyone, please welcome my new friend, Els. You are the first lesbians she's ever met, so be on your best behavior."

The women at the table laughed as they introduced themselves one by one. I knew I had no hope of remembering all the names, but I smiled at each of them. The woman in the Browns sweatshirt was Joanne. She put her hand over mine and smiled widely. "Is this really your first time meeting lesbians?"

I nodded, not quite trusting myself to speak.

She nodded back. "Well then, welcome home, kid. Welcome home."

The Saints:
Wasn't That A Time?

by Cindy Rizzo

There was a brief time in the late 1970s when three women's bars occupied a small, one-and-one-half-block area near Boston's waterfront, on the edge of the financial district. It was a somewhat dangerous neighborhood after dark, not yet overtaken by the well-lit clubs and restaurants that would later bleed into the area from the nearby Quincy Market. Back then, you had to pay close attention to your surroundings as you walked over from the T stop or from your parking space on a side street.

But the short distance from The Saints on Broad Street, down Franklin Street to Somewhere, and around the corner to Club 76 on Batterymarch was a well-worn path for lesbians. My friends and I would walk from our home base at The Saints, stroll into Somewhere and get the once-over from the well-dressed, preppy women leaning against the railings on the upper level and likely identifying us as the rag-tag "political dykes" that we were. We didn't stay long.

The crowd at Club 76 was equally foreign to us—older women we never ran across in our usual haunts. The lesbian generation gap was definitely a thing back then as it is now.

Eventually, our curiosity satisfied, we returned to our comfort zone, The Saints.

I would venture to say that there never was and probably never will be a women's bar like The Saints. It was run by a collective of proud, working-class dykes who took it over at night from a daytime staff that catered to the business-lunch crowd. The place had a standard layout with small tables in the barroom (plus pinball machines where I spent a lot of my time), a side room with the requisite pool table and booths, and a back room for dancing. Because it was open day and night by people who cared about it, The Saints was clean and well-kept, its oak fixtures shiny and smooth.

But truly, there was nothing standard about The Saints.

The Collective, as they were known, ran the place as a true "women's space," the term we all used back then to signal lesbian. While men could wander into the other two clubs and gawk if they were straight or dance if they were gay, The Saints' managers never let a man get past the front entrance.

I can still hear Merry or Sandy in their strong Boston accents saying, "This is a women's club. No men allowed."

They were polite and quiet when they did this unless the guy mouthed off or was drunk or both. Then they double-or triple-teamed him, escorting him out of the doorway and back onto the street.

And yes, there were public accommodations laws, and yes, a few complaints were filed against them over the years. But as a twenty-two-year-old lesbian living in a new city trying to find community, I never felt safer than I did at The Saints.

By the time I moved to Boston in 1977, I was already out as a lesbian. My first encounter with a gay bar had been in upstate New York during my sophomore year of college when I went with a group of other students to a small, dark place where a large man in a suit took our money at the door. It was the quintessential mob-owned bar, the intimidating bouncer right out of central casting.

That night, I wound up slow dancing with an older student from another college who invited me back to her apartment to spend the night. Even though the drinking age was eighteen back then, I decided I wouldn't touch any alcohol that night so I could remain alert and fully remember my first sexual experience with another woman.

What was I thinking? I was nineteen years old, and I was going to have my first lesbian sex with a strange woman I'd just met in a sleazy bar!

To cut to the chase, that particular story ended with the woman freaking out that it was my first time and with me insanely thinking I was in love. Clearly, and contrary to the song, I had not found love in a hopeless place.

But a few years later at The Saints, I found something better—community.

This was an era when radical lesbian feminism as well as lesbian separatism was in full bloom. All of us were in the throes of deciding how much, if any, "male energy" we wanted in our lives. We lived together in groups of four or more, with chore wheels on our refrigerators and the inevitable roommate hook-ups and break-ups that disrupted households in spite of our firm commitments to "non-monogamy" and in opposition to "couplism."

But what united us during those times was a fierce dedication to our politics and to the thriving lesbian culture. In addition to the three bars downtown, there were ongoing women's music concerts that filled large college auditoriums and well-attended book readings for classics like *This Bridge Called My Back*. We heard Adrienne Rich and Pat Parker read poetry and attended conferences on fighting racism where activist sisters Barbara and Beverly Smith spoke.

All of this energy, political and cultural, found expression at The Saints. It was a place where you could plan demonstrations and organize conferences. It was a place where I could sit by myself and quietly read that week's *Gay Community News* or that month's *Sojourner* without anyone thinking I was strange or unapproachably nerdy. And of course, it was a place where you could dance to songs like "I Will Survive" until closing time.

The Collective welcomed us while also remaining loyal to their working-class-dyke base. They were a bridge between these two worlds as well as guardians against a kind of classism that often infected the careless actions of many a middle-class, political dyke. Anyone who might still have had ties to the men in their family or to white neighborhoods like South Boston or Charlestown was automatically suspect. It was unfair and it was hurtful, but it was also a time when there were limited notions of what it could mean to be a lesbian, and the political version felt so right to many of us that, at times, we colluded in a damaging kind of tunnel vision.

While there was much to appreciate from those days, there was a lot I'm happy to see fade away. Our lesbian feminism, and especially our lesbian separatism, was viciously transphobic. I remember one particular concert I attended (also attended by members of The Collective) in which a lesbian separatist performer began her set by declaring she'd heard that there was "someone with a penis" in our Boston community pretending to be a lesbian.

I knew the person she spoke of. Her (and I emphatically say HER) story was well-known to many of us. She was an outspoken activist for many of the same lesbian and feminist causes we all favored. She worked tirelessly organizing protests and other actions. She did more than most of us, but to many in those days, she was a pariah and someone who could be condemned by a performer standing before a lesbian audience.

Of course, these things still go on from time to time, but now there's a movement and many allies who will speak up and fight back. In the late 1970s, there were just a few brave individuals, who made little headway.

I have no idea whether this transwoman or any others were ever turned away from The Saints. The sick feeling in my stomach makes me wonder if I really want to know.

If you go onto Google Maps now and look up 112 Broad Street in Boston, you'll see an Irish pub with a lovely outdoor seating area on one side. The elevated highway that functioned as a northern boundary for the address is long gone, replaced by a beautiful greenway that has reinvigorated the area. I look at that picture and wish that The Saints could have held out into the present so that we'd be able to enjoy that lovely outdoor area with the round umbrella tables and benches. In this era of openness, so different from that of 1978, we'd have been able to sit outside on warm summer evenings, flirting and laughing and kissing the cute girl we just met.

But the changing lesbian landscape and the unforgiving economy were no match for The Saints. In my early twenties, I must have visited that bar at least three times a week. I remember Wednesday nights were packed, and Thursday nights were filled with those of us who'd attended the lesbian rap group at the Women's Center. Plus, as always, there was Saturday. A few years later, for me and many others, that wasn't sustainable.

We tried to help The Collective. I remember we started eating meals there at night and people sold pies and other baked goods to try and make up lost revenue. The Collective held fundraising dances in an effort to buy the building. When they weren't able to do so, they found a place in a more residential neighborhood but couldn't get approval for a liquor license. In the end, none of it worked out and The Saints that we knew and loved was gone for good.

Club 76 didn't last very long, but the other bar, Somewhere, later renamed Somewhere Else, hung on a while longer before it closed. And soon there were more upscale places with fancier décor and well-dressed women who didn't live in group houses with chore wheels. Some of us were now them.

The members of The Collective regrouped, and a few of them opened a café in Cambridge. For a while, they traveled each August to the Michigan Womyn's Music Festival and sold food there.

It's almost forty years later, and I still haven't forgotten The Saints. I know I'll never see its likes again, and I deeply regret that young queer women never will. But my time there will always be with me as one of the most formative experiences of my early lesbian life. Although I've grown and changed and evolved over the years, at my core, I'm still that young dyke sitting by myself at The Saints with the current issue of *Gay Community News* spread out in front of me.

Connected Community

by Steven Reigns

I had been on that dance floor.
Met a man, made out,
never got his name.
The news of Pulse
made me think about him
and all of the men
I've met on dance floors
and what we shared
for a song, a night, a few months.
Through romance,
community gets built,
connections forged
from Ft. Worth to Seattle
to Orlando to Los Angeles.
We are a network, feeling
the flutters of butterflies
in Kyoto but also of
gunmen in Orlando.

Omar Mateen's Shirtless Pic Makes Me Sad

by Clay Kerrigan

Most of Omar Mateen's mirror selfies are pretty bad. One might conclude that the kid gleaned very little from the other photos around his profile on Jack'd and whatever other apps he may have been using. But there's one picture that stands out from the rest. It's the one that seems to be circulated the least, because it's the picture that makes Omar look not like an awkward loner, not like a mass-murdering terrorist, not like an authority-loving weirdo in an NYPD shirt and a bad haircut, but actually *hot*.

This is the image that Jay Michaelson used for his *Daily Beast* article wherein he cites Mateen's homosexuality as the cause of his homophobia. While this isn't exactly a revolutionary idea, it's an important one to remember after a terror event caused by a man whose demons took on so many faces—closet case, social pariah, wife beater, ISIL allegiant—that media sources can pick and choose which root cause conforms to their narrative.

Amy Goodman of *Democracy Now!* made the connection between mass shooters and their common history of spousal abuse. Jay Michaelson says that, so far, claims of Mateen's sexuality are based mostly on loose evidence and conjecture, that mass shooters are often framed as gay soon after a shooting—a homophobic tactic of conservatives to reframe the shooters as weak and insane.

At the time that I write this, it hasn't even been a week since the Pulse nightclub shooting and we're still scrambling for answers. But when I see that picture of Omar shirtless, I know what I'm looking at. When I hear stories of Mateen getting drunk by himself at Pulse, I know who that man is. Omar is us. We are Omar. Or, at least, I have been.

It's unlikely that we'll find out what other apps he was on, what other pictures he has taken. It is in the best interest of the FBI, the media, and politicians to control the narrative about him. What the public believes or does not believe about him will enact shifts in culture and policy. Additionally, straight people don't know what they're looking at when they read through profiles on gay dating or, dare I say, hook-up apps. Ours is a world of coded imagery and language that straight people don't know what to do with, and because the powers that be don't know what to do with it, they will assume most people won't know what to do with it, so what is to be gained from releasing such information?

To be fair, there *is* little to be learned from Omar's repressed sexuality, or double life, for the world at large. How does it help or change anything to find out he had a secret gay life? That frustration with gay culture led him to this heinous crime? Who should change their behavior? Intolerant Muslims? Maybe, but there are plenty of gay Muslims out there, many of whom were the first to speak out after the shooting in their own (rightful) attempt to control the narrative. Conservative families? Progressives have been trying forever to get them to budge on social issues, and it's taken decades. What about the patrons of the club that he frequented?

The world doesn't know about our internal politics, about how things work in those gay bars and clubs. They don't know how common it is for gays to go to the bars by themselves because they have no one else. They don't know how common it is to remain alone the whole night, changing positions around the bar, timing your drinks and cigarette breaks so as to build feigned structure into your umpteenth lonely night at a bar full of guys who seem like friends and lovers who have known each other forever. How do they know each other? Where did they meet? Certainly it wasn't here, where no one talks to strangers. We call these "safe spaces," but when does it become safe and familiar? Are there not those for whom it never becomes safe, just crazy-making?

One at this stage of their homosexual-social development wonders what secrets he has yet to learn. We aren't raised in families of our ilk like racial or religious minorities. We don't have elders to teach us the mechanics of the culture that awaits us. We must figure it out on our own or opt out of it, as so many str8 bros on Grindr and Scruff like to say they have. "Normal non-scene dude here who wants to meet another masc guy for hiking and lifting," etc.

But what if you aren't a hot masc white guy? What if you are a chubby, awkward, angry, Middle Eastern kid from a conservative family? What the hell do you do? The frustration of being unable to operate in the gay world is as frustrating as being gay and unable to operate in the straight world, if not more so. This is supposed to be your family, the people who understand the struggles you face out in the world. But it's never that easy. Both of these forms of loneliness could and do drive people to suicide. Or just back to the bars, waiting for something to happen. And as he waits, he drinks. And drinks. And drinks.

We have accounts from patrons and gogo boys from Pulse claiming that Omar's been going to the bar for at least three years, getting so drunk that he'd have to be escorted out. In his drunkenness, he would rant about being married to whoever would listen. So sometime, along the way, to hedge his bets, he married a woman, as so many closeted gay men have done. But it's not to say he didn't try.

There are the accounts of him asking a boy on a date in college. He asked a boy on a date! The boy said no! It's happened to all of us.

Then there's the guy who saw him outside of Pulse the night of the shooting, who he recognized from social media after talking to him for over a year. How many of us have gays in the same city that we've never met, but spoken to for months or years? Those guys are, to me, some of my most intimate relationships. These are conversations that have never been, may never be, spoken out loud. We discuss relationships, hookups, frustrations, and triumphs, all while trading nudes and some sexts (or none at all). For some gays, this is the most interaction they get from their brethren. We're yelled at for being on our phones in the bar, but when we're alone, who is there to talk to?

Of course, none of this is an excuse to walk into a bar with an automatic weapon. Not to anyone in their right mind, that is. I think of the film *Falling Down*, wherein Michael Douglas treks through Los Angeles aiming a series of weapons at icons of frustration for the working class and city dwellers, venting the grievances of the audience in a way that is partly comedic and wholly tragic. It's a great film, but the reality would be anything but enjoyable. One doesn't have to look far to find real-world examples of the same thing.

Years of frustration led Omar to purchase an AR-15, the same weapon used by several other mass shooters, and he went out and did what the Columbine teenagers did after years of bullying, what Elliot Rodger did after years of being ignored by the women of UCSB. The difference here is that these two examples felt an entitlement to what they were being denied, that their supreme natures went unrecognized and so their lessers must pay.

Omar went another way. We don't know what Omar's upbringing was like or who he was. We know he was a wife beater, which can be a pretty good indication of the kind of person he was, but we also know that his father proclaimed himself president of Afghanistan on a public access television show. Things sound like they were pretty whacked out for him. Access to the kind of social currency and cultural knowledge required to move comfortably in gay spaces was likely far from his reach.

One hundred members of our queer family were torn down that Sunday night in June, and only half of them survived. It was the night before Los Angeles Pride was to commence on the opposite side of the country. My friends and I were unsure if we should have been going out to celebrate, but somewhere in our group texts, I said I was committed to going out, that I was "heartbroken certainly, proud absolutely."

The Los Angeles gay scene is divided in half, between the mainstream Weho gays and the arty/beardy Silver Lake gays. Pride is never a big deal on the eastside, but on this day every one of the three gay bars of Silver Lake was packed, indoors and on the patios, spilling into the parking lots. None of the bars expected turnout like this. And never in my life had I seen so many gays talking to each other en masse, no cliques or hierarchies, just one big conversation. It was, personally, a revelation to suddenly have zero fear of talking to whoever I laid eyes on, stranger or not.

I recognize the difference here. I'm a white gay dude with a mustache, I work out five times a week, and I get plenty of attention on the apps and have zero trouble getting laid. It looks pretty sunny for me. But at twenty-nine-years old, I've made most of my gay male friends only in the past year. I've had lovers and boyfriends aplenty, but friends? I'm only just learning what it means to have gay male friends.

And so on Sunday, when we collectively mourned and celebrated, it was something of a pinnacle for me to finally feel no fear in the walls of the gay bar. Everyone was my friend. Everyone was open. Everyone was family. I'm not sure if it was just the tragic magic of that day or if that's how Pride always feels (I haven't attended many).

But I do know that there are many gays older than I am who have never felt part of the gay family, have opted out or not thought about it at all. They live happy peaceful lives without this family, this brotherhood. I've dated plenty of them. But I also know that there are other gays who need it, yearn for it, and for all their attempts, will never have it because there's no one to teach them how to get it.

Having been barred entry from one culture, Omar looked to another that would readily accept him, one that had an ideology in place that would brand him a hero for enacting vengeance on the gays that rejected him. That he claimed allegiance to ISIL is not evidence that he was "radicalized" in the way that we know young people to be brain-washed by ISIL. Like a member of a cult, he claimed allegiance to Hezbollah and Al Qaeda as well, organizations in conflict with each other, betraying his misunderstanding of their inner workings. An ideologue would know the difference, would have ravenously devoured their literatures. This kid adopted a vague comprehension of a system of radical conservative values that were close to home. Had he been a white kid in an Evangelical Christian family, he would have committed the same act in the name of God.

Omar Mateen's picture makes me sad because he looks pretty good. I would have talked to that kid. He looks clean-cut and body confident. He's contoured his facial hair to his jaw, a trend that makes me crazy but is common enough amongst homos that I've got to let it slide. He's relaxed and shirtless on an ugly couch which gives the air of a sort of straight-unawareness that is kind of sexy. None of his other pictures are attractive, but in this one, he nailed it. That big, toothy, casual smile, his pretty eyes, the flattering angle of his head. Even his shoulders and chest look like they are kind of swole One would think this was a different person. I truly want to know what the rest of his app selfies were like. Why does this one stand out so much? Because the others are so bad, and it's likely that the bad ones are selected by the media and the FBI to make him look like the kind of ugly loner who shoots up public places.

In my own frustration with my community, I've considered violence, but never upon anyone else but myself. In seeking my brothers and coming up empty, I've imagined countless forms of suicide in my very loneliest moments. I was raised by kindly, upper-class, metropolitan people who don't enact violence on others for any reason, and so it's never been an option for me. But what if I had been brought up in a culture of xenophobic Texas gun collectors? What if Omar Mateen was the kind of guy that I see in that picture? Happy, confident, owning his sexiness. Would he have gotten more attention in that bar? Would he have made friends any easier? No one can say. But it takes much more than a good selfie or a good body to get by in these clubs. Something nameless but, for some, essential, affirming, life-giving.

It's 1927 and I Miss You

by Earlon Sterling

I didn't know Miss Florence had been making plans for me until Kitty walked in the door dressed in her party clothes. The two of them sat me down on the couch, and the lectures started.

"Look," Miss Florence said, "I know that you're worried about AJ, we all are. But you can't sit around here with that hangdog look on your face waiting for her to return."

"It's not good for your baby girl, you like this," Kitty added. "And you're making everybody in the house feel worse."

I looked up at the two of them staring down at me. Miss Florence, the closest thing to a mother that I'd had in a long time, and Kitty, my best friend. They were right. AJ would be disappointed if she knew that I was moping around the house like a lost soul, even if I felt like one.

"OK," I told them. "Let me get some clothes on. Kitty, call the cab and tell them to be here in half an hour."

Between the heat coming out of the kitchen and the heat coming off all the bodies, the place was jumpin' and hot when we walked in. The odor of fried chicken and fish mixed in the air with cigarettes and reefer. All the furniture had been moved into the back rooms, and rickety tables and chairs had been brought out for the party. You never knew if and when a fight would break out, and if you had good furniture, you didn't want to lose it.

The guys were upstairs doing their thing, and the first floor was wall-to-wall women. There were couples on the floor dancing to a little three-piece band. The singer hadn't started yet. The bid whist card tables looked like they were being held together with spit and a prayer. I spotted Kitty's partner, Josephine, at a table racking in the dimes. She looked real fine in the shirt I had sewn for her. She jumped up to give me a big hug.

"You owe me a dance tonight. I'm not going to let you

forget," she said. I let her know that I wouldn't forget.

Kitty and I each grabbed a plate of food and found a wall that we could lean on to eat.

"I'm glad we were able to talk you into getting out of the house," Kitty said.

"Kitty, I wasn't sure, shoot, I'm still not sure if I should be out, you know what I mean? You know how some folks think."

She laughed. "Yeah, good girls don't go out alone, or you're supposed to stay at home 'til AJ gets out of the joint. What a bunch of horse shit. You're grown, you get to do what you want. Folks act like every woman that's out by herself is on the make. Somebody needs to remind them that Lincoln freed the slaves, including women. Besides, folks that know you, know you. The rest, they can go to hell."

I looked around at all the women. A lot of them I didn't know; Kitty didn't know them either. I guess some had come in from Harlem, and a whole bunch came up from the South. You could tell the ones that came from Harlem; they dressed the flashiest. I think they spent all their money trying to look good.

Josephine sauntered over with a big smile on her face. She had cashed in her dimes and handed the bills to Kitty, who promptly tucked the money in her bra. Josephine took Kitty's plate and finished off her food.

"You ready for that dance?" Josephine asked.

We did a couple of turns on the floor before a slow one came on, and she didn't even attempt to hold me tight. She was very proper. But it was nice being out dancing and laughing again.

"You know, if you need anything while AJ's gone, just let me know. I feel bad that I wasn't able to get her out of there before the law showed up."

I looked her in the face. "You were there? What happened? All we got was that she beat up some white man."

"Shit, beat him up? She damn near killed him. She's got a real thing about men, especially white men trying to have their way with colored girls. He was trying to pull this girl into the alley behind The Plantation when we heard her yelling. AJ pulled out her little black club, aimed it and opened the back of the man's head with one swing. He was out like a light. But she kept on hitting him and knocked some of his teeth out. I tried to pull her off then, but she wasn't having it. She just kept beating on him. That boy ain't never going to be the same in the head. When the cops came, I just slid off in the shadows. There was nothing I could do to help her."

We walked off the floor. "It's probably for the best. It wouldn't have done for both of you to go to jail, but it sounds like he got what was due him. Thanks for letting me know what happened."

Kitty managed to snag a seat, and I took it when she got up to dance with her honey. I was surprised at what I didn't know about AJ. I didn't know before how AJ felt about race-mixing, but when I thought about her color, and how she got it, I wasn't surprised. I looked at Kitty and thought about the two of us. We were the color of milk chocolate. I guessed AJ did have a certain color woman that she liked. I was lost in thought when I noticed a woman standing in front of me.

"Hi," she said. "I saw you dancing. You look real fine out there on the floor. I was wondering if you'd like to take a turn with me. My name is Lane. I just got into town a few days ago, came in from New York to check and see what this little city is about."

She was very nice looking, a tall, honey-brown woman with hazel eyes. She smiled down at me, put her foot on the rung of the chair I was sitting on, and leaned in close, too close. She started talking again.

"If this isn't your scene, I'm sure we could find..."

"Tell me," I said, "do women from New York let you get all in their face like you're trying to do to me? If you like that foot, I suggest you put it back down on the floor." I was firm, not mean, but I wanted her to know that I wasn't the type you pick up for a one-night boogie, and I wanted Kitty and Josephine to know that I could take care of myself.

"Listen," she began again, "I saw you come in by yourself and thought maybe you were lonely or something, At least let me buy you a drink, I..."

"I came out to spend time with my friends," I told her. "I'm not out here to pick up anything, and I can buy my own drinks, thank you."

Another slow song came on.

"Are you positive that I can't talk you into a dance? I can show you how it really should be done." She still hadn't moved her foot, and it was like I was talking to a wall.

She didn't take no easily. "Look, I know how the dance goes. I have a girl, and she's the only one that I bump and grind with." That was a lie. AJ and I had never even danced that close.

"But she's not here, and you know what they say, what you don't know…"

I stood up. She was going to have to either step back or fall down. She stepped back, and I got in her face. I wasn't going to let her or anyone else disrespect me like that.

"Child, I've tried to be nice, God knows I have. I let you have a little fun, talk a little to see if you could get better, but now it's time for you to step off. I understand that in New York you're a back-breaker and a heart shaker. I get it. But let me tell you. I got a woman, and a daughter, and my daughter is the only child I play with. Now unless you want more than your feelings hurt, you need to leave me the hell alone."

I didn't know if she meant to say anything else, because Josephine walked up, and the look in her eyes could only be described as murderous. "Hey, Mattie, you want to dance again?"

"Yeah." I brushed by the woman as I moved to the dance floor. It was more of a bump than a brush. I wanted her to know that I didn't need Josephine to cover my back. If she wanted to push, I was more than willing to push back.

I saw one of the regulars go up and talk to her while we danced. She looked at me and turned a lighter shade of brown. I guess they told her who my woman was. But it didn't matter to me. I didn't leave Mississippi to come up here to be mistreated by anybody.

I did a few more turns on the dance floor with some of the studs that I knew, before the smell of all the cigarette smoke got to me. I liked going out, but I liked it better when AJ and I had true friends over. Kitty and Josephine waited outside with me until the cab came. I went home, curled up in bed, and dreamed of AJ.

The G Spot
San Francisco, CA

by Sallyanne Monti

In 1998, I shed my catholic-guilt ridden frock and burst out of the closet. In my newfound lesbian glory with a trail of rainbow stickers behind me, I was Out and Proud.

I was a resident of Alameda, California, an island in the San Francisco Bay. With a large LGBT population, us girls were the ALPS (The Alameda Lesbian Pot Luck Society), and the Boys were the GI Joes. Together we were all members of Out on the Island. Known as OOTI, this organization made great strides for equal rights and gaining recognition for our Alameda LGBT Community contributions.

While the world around me was on the cusp of launching the biggest Marriage Equality Crusade of all, I was a thirty-seven-year-old new dyke, seeking safe havens to express my recent realization that I was a lesbian, and to meet like-minded people. I initially found a virtual haven on the new Internet dating website called OneandOnly.com.

As I registered my online dating profile and uploaded the least dorky photo I had, I felt apprehensive. I'd been a willing participant in promoting my straight life anxious to make a name for myself as I grew my career and family. Why was I feeling fearful? Perhaps it was knowing there'd be no turning back from publicly labeling myself a single lesbian mother of four via this thing called the World Wide Web. The WWW was in its infancy. In the late 90's no one understood the magnitude of its reach or the blaring spotlight one might shine upon oneself by registering on a dating site. As I gained access to this cybernetic world of date seeking strangers I was shocked at the vast number of lesbians advertising for friends, partners, lovers and soul mates. I thought, where did they all hide during the day? A resounding answer echoed through my mind. The same places you hide; at work, in school, at home and in the fabric of our lives. My finger hesitated atop my computer mouse as I contemplated if I had the nerve to join the online lesbian dating community. With a deep breath and a long sigh, I pushed the submit button. There was no turning back. My apprehension accelerated, yet in the back of my mind hope was born. Hope that somewhere in my future there was joy, companionship and maybe even love. In light of past heartaches, rejections, and contradictions I was hoping I'd meet someone who meant what they said.

Each evening with the dinner dishes put away and the kids settled I opened my computer. In the hopes that someone would find me interesting enough to ping or ding or poke or whatever it is one is supposed to do to communicate their interest in the ever-evolving world of online dating.

After a series of odd first dates with a series of peculiar women:

In a coffee shop (with a gal who never stopped talking and then proclaimed post-latte we had nothing in common)

In a hospital parking lot (with a gal who was a security guard in their psychiatric ward who told me she aspired to be a corrections officer so she could tackle people to the ground legally)

In a trailer park (with a gal who introduced me to her step daughter who she'd had an affair with, which had ended her long-term relationship with the girl's mother)

I met someone special who seemed sincere and who said she wanted a relationship.

As it turned out, she was neither sincere nor did she want a relationship. Her response to our intense and immediate connection was to instruct me it was time for us to date around, and not with each other.

For the first time in my life, I was officially dating around. Given the peculiarity of the dating pool, dating around was not of my own doing, nor of my own choice. My on-again, off-again not-so-sincere ex-girlfriend who wasn't ready to be in a relationship, had prescribed it. In fact, she thought it was a brilliant idea that we date around. So like it or not I was single and dating around.

As a result, one July evening, I nearly had a heart attack, when my very nice, very sincere and not at all peculiar new date nonchalantly asked, "Sweetie? How would you like to go to The G Spot tonight?"

As her words sunk in, I felt my eyes open widely while the

heat of embarrassment turned my face crimson. Was I being propositioned right here in the middle of her living room? Maybe it was the giant zucchini I'd brought her from my garden that gave her the impression I'd be interested in a visit to her G spot. As I watched her, she burst into a hearty laugh. She had the kind of sultry voice you could listen to for hours. Her laugh was a culmination of the dulcet tones I would come to appreciate over the next two decades of my life, as our short-lived dating around with each other would evolve into a beautiful lifelong friendship. But on this night, when we barely knew each other I was embarrassed. Under other circumstances, I might have been annoyed at how quickly she burst into laughter at my expense, but the sound of her laugh was enchanting. I almost forgot what she was laughing about when she said, "Oh Sweetie, The G Spot stands for The Girl Spot and it's at The Endup Club at 6th and Harrison in San Francisco. Every Saturday night it's just for us girls."

I don't know if I was relieved or disappointed. Once I'd gotten over the shock of her G Spot comment I was sure I was being pursued and desired. In the wake of past rejection, it felt nice. Once I realized she was talking about taking me to a Lesbian Bar named The G Spot and not extending a personal invitation for intimacy, I felt foolish and a bit frantic as I realized I'd never been to a Lesbian Bar in my life. Tonight would be a night of firsts. And The G Spot would instantly become my temple of worship for the better part of the next five years.

The Girl Spot, widely known as The G Spot was founded in 1988 by prominent women's event pioneer Mariah Hanson (of The Dinah Palm Springs fame) as a weekly Saturday Night Girls Dance Club held at San Francisco's renowned Endup Club. The Endup is a favorite boys club, known as the place where everyone would end up. The G Spot was an instant hit that reached international fame and was the place for lesbians to be seen for fifteen years, until the boys took back Saturday night at The Endup in 2003.

On this night in July of 1998, we set off from my date's apartment in Marin County, south down the 101 Freeway over the Golden Gate Bridge on our way to San Francisco's The G Spot. She giggled as she drove and assured me this would be a night to remember. After parking, I followed her black leather jacketed back into the narrow space between the two red velvet ropes that would guide us to the club entrance. As we took our place behind a line of women of every shape, size, and character, I found myself thinking, where do they all hide during the day? As I shook my head in an attempt to chase that silly thought away, we reached the front of the line.

A large bald man with multiple face piercings said: "ID please." As I handed him my driver's license, I couldn't help but feel like I'd come home. As I turned around and looked at my date, my face now flushed from excitement, she smiled, shook her head knowingly and grabbed my hand. With her body pressed against my back, her arm around my waist, her thumb tucked into the front of my jeans, she led me just beyond the velvet ropes and through black drapes that split into a small foyer with a Cashier's Booth behind glass. I promptly proceeded to get us both tangled in the fabric of the black drapes as I reached for my wallet to pay our entry fee. I was anything but smooth as I entered The G Spot for the first time.

It was darker inside than I'd expected and it took a minute for my eyes to adjust to the dim backdrop lighting. Just beyond the entry was a giant bar that wrapped itself in a U-shape in what was the main room of the Club. There were women packed three deep waiting to order drinks. The music, still said to be the best sound system in San Francisco, hammered a thunderous beat that resonated in the middle of my chest.

With every beat I got more and more excited. I couldn't believe I was in an actual lesbian bar, the lesbian bar to be in. This was the place to go if you wanted to scope the scene, make new friends, feel included or simply date around. I shook my head as if to clear the confusion caused by my own adrenalin, the thudding club music and the bright flashing lights. The delirium was intoxicating and the sense of community was tremendous.

To the right of the U-shaped Bar was another room with a giant dance floor. The women were dancing to the loud booming music in the shadows of rapidly flickering strobe lights and a giant spiraling disco ball shooting sparkly diamonds and rays of colors across the dance floor. Just beyond the Bar was a small stage elevated about 3 feet off the ground, with a very sexy Go-Go dancer in a scant bikini. The dancer was blond and curvaceous and was gyrating her hips within inches of cheering women, as they surrounded the stage leaning in to stuff dollar bills in her bikini. As the women continued hollering, in a fluid motion the dancer spread her legs, deeply squatted and with her butt within an inch of the floor she leaned and rolled on her back. In all her sexy dancer glory with her come hither gestures, her back was flat on the floor with her feet in imaginary stirrups.

As I contemplated how she could possibly stretch her body into this position, she lifted her legs, threw them backwards over her shoulders and wrapped them around her neck. As she traced a seductive path down the inside of her thighs with her long red painted finger nails leading to the scantly clad center of her womanly being, the crowd went wild. She looked like some kind of wild sexy frog woman about to hop off into the abyss, as a frenzy of lesbians stuffed more and more dollar bills into her G-string, screaming her name over and over again, Ni-COLE, Ni-COLE, Ni-COLE.

I observed all of this as we waited our turn at the Bar and wondered what was happening in the other rooms barely visible from where we stood. As we lifted our drinks off the Bar, a Scotch for my date and a Vodka and Cranberry for me, my date grabbed my hand and led me into another room beyond the stage and dance floor.

This room had a series of dark leather clad booths lined up against the wall on elevated platforms that were accessed from a small set of stairs. From the vantage point in these cozy booths, you could cuddle up with your honey and watch The club scene and the sexy young dykes playing pool. To the right of the booth seating was a brick fireplace lit year-round, to warm the San Francisco chill and illuminate the two pool tables in the center of the room. Across from the pool tables was a smaller bar and beyond the smaller bar was a wall of French doors thrown wide-open that led to an outdoor patio, twinkling in white lights and alive with people drinking, chatting and smoking. It was 1998 and in those days, smoking was still permitted in designated areas.

As the night progressed a cast of characters would eventually enter the scene. These characters were The G Spot regulars and in my careful observance of them over the years to come I would name them and invent stories in my mind of who they were, what their lives were like and why they were here every Saturday night. They were the lifeline to my new community and the fodder for my growing imagination.

On this first night at The G Spot, I cuddled up to my date in a leather-clad booth and watched in wonder. As my date sipped her signature Scotch, we watched the club scene. Until we joined the host of women on the crowded dance floor letting the beat of that famous San Francisco sound system and spectacle of twinkling club lighting take us away. I was home and like any homecoming I felt like I finally belonged.

Each week we'd return to The G Spot to join our posse of people and peculiars. There was the UPS Driver, who always wore sneakers, khaki shorts, and a flannel shirt. She was your middle of the road lesbian, with short dark hair and a youthful face for her forty some odd years. She never danced, drank the same beer for hours and was relentless in her attempts to date me.

There were The Twins, two incredibly thin Asian girls who were barely of drinking age, who looked exactly alike, and never left each other's sides and stole kisses in between conservative dance moves and giggles.

There were The Pool Table Dykes, a revolving group of three to four incredibly handsome young lesbians with buzz cuts and baseball caps. In their Levi's and tailored men's shirts this group of twenty something's owned the pool tables and flirted relentlessly with any woman, any age, as they wooed competitor after competitor into their circle of green table felt and billiard balls. One by one the women would lose more than a game of pool to these outrageously gorgeous gentleman-ladies. They'd lose their minds as they stared into the crooked smiles and sexy come hither gazes of these blued eyed beauties incessantly rubbing their long shiny pool sticks into those little square cue-chalks in a haze of sputtering blue dust. In between challengers, they'd break into the coolest sideways-dipping-sliding-across-the floor-dance moves you've ever seen. They were the benchmark for cool and a mystery to all of us who couldn't stop starring at them no matter how hard we tried.

But nothing compared to five-foot tall Mirror Chick and her entourage of a half a dozen seven-foot tall gorgeous drag queens. Mirror Chick, as we named her, and her striking posse made their grand entrance around 9pm every Saturday night. Like clockwork an almost hush would ensue as the crowd parted and Mirror Chick entered. She was the biggest mystery of all and spent the entire evening shaking her one and only dance move in a rigorous left to right lower body shimmer, while watching herself incessantly in the mirrors surrounding the dance floor. She couldn't stop looking at herself and her stern expression never changed. This expression was counter-intuitive to the elegant flow of her long curly dark hair that always looked amazing no matter how many hours she danced and how much sweat would drip down her face.

With her entourage of high-heeled beautiful drag queens and their perfect bodies and amazing clothes surrounding her, she'd start her dance move slow and steady. As the beat continued and the evening wore on, Mirror Chick would work herself into a frenzy of movement. In her low hanging jeans, wife-beater tank tops, with her fists clenched and her large biceps flexed she'd shimmy until the tattoo on her lower back began to peak out of the top of her jeans.

For years I tried to read the writing on that tattoo, in the hopes of gaining a clue as to who this mysterious matriarch of my beloved G Spot really was. One day I got my answer. As I opened the latest edition of a leading magazine, I was shocked to find Mirror Chick's face staring back at me. I frantically turned the pages trying desperately to learn who she was and why she was in this magazine. I learned that she was an athlete earning awards in competitive events all over the world.

She'd sustained serious injuries that left her physically compromised. The article detailed how she was rehabilitating herself and building back her strength through rigorous and continuous dancing. The G Spot was her rehab facility, her posse of drag queens, her protectors, and the stern expression was her determination and motivation to get well in the face of extreme injury. This was nothing short of remarkable. I was humbled as all the pieces fell into place. I realized my fabricated cast of G Spot regulars were simply people just like me, all with their own lives, their own stories, their own challenges and their own successes.

During the years that followed my 1998 G Spot inauguration, until it's closing Saturday night in the summer of 2003, this club was my sanctuary. I would eventually bring my wife to this place. Together as we danced and romanced away our Saturday nights surrounded by our growing cast of G Spot characters, we were thankful for a safe place to go where we could openly express our love for each other and stand proud and out with our friends and community.

Week after week, everyday people would come out of their lives to seek refuge, healing, and community within the walls of The G Spot, during a time when being a lesbian was anything but cool. These were the days we held hands and marched endless miles together through The Castro in San Francisco bearing hand-printed signs with compelling messages on our quest for Marriage Equality. These were the nights when we pushed our way through the red velvet ropes beyond a tangle of dark drapes to the haven of The G Spot, we all came to love and count on.

It was September 9, 2000, the evening of my commitment ceremony to my beautiful Bride. Our guests had left and remaining was six of our best girlfriends who made up our bridal party. Still in their sharp black tuxedos, each wearing a bow tie and cummerbund in a color of the rainbow, they symbolized how far we'd come as a community and how much further there was for us to go.

As I stood next to my new wife, still in our wedding outfits, I heard the distinguishable laugh of my dearest friend resonate from across the outdoor deck that had hosted our reception. As I turned my head, still holding my wife's hand, I saw my best buddy holding her signature Scotch. As our eyes met she walked over to my wife and I and said as she raised her glass in a toast, "Well Sweeties, how'd ya like to go to The G Spot tonight, it is after all your wedding night?" We burst into laughter as our drink glasses met in a best friend triangle over our heads.

And so we did, in all our wedding attire, with all our wedding regalia, and our six best girlfriends, off we went to the one place we knew we could be ourselves and where we knew we'd be welcome, The G Spot. We danced the night away with the UPS Driver, The Twins, Pool Table Dykes and Mirror Chick and her Entourage. As we found our way to the leather clad booths in the glow of the crackling fireplace, my dearest friend once again raised her signature Scotch in a final toast. As we clinked glasses, in the dulcet tones of her sultry voice she toasted, "To The G Spot and to coming home."

"To The G Spot and Coming Home," we all echoed.

Conduct Becoming a Lesbian

by Karen DiPrima

About four years ago, Sisters nightclub, a friendly little pub tucked away on a side alley in the gayborhood, suddenly shuttered its doors after last call one Sunday. In the seeming blink of an eye, the city's only lesbian bar was gone.

When I read about the closing on the morning after, it felt like a punch to the gut. Sisters was my finishing school, an alma mater of sorts. It was where I earned a degree in Conduct Becoming a Lesbian.

You'll need to understand that, decades ago, I left a traditional marriage after falling in love with my now-wife, Margo. She was proudly out for years and had found her tribe. However, as a recent refugee from Planet Straight, I straddled both worlds. I was eager to throw off the old and embrace the new, but I felt like an oddity no matter where I turned. Desperate to fit in, I attacked my dilemma the way writers do—through research.

I found a dearth of material on the subject. My few references included *Claire of the Moon* and a handful of paperbacks from the sales racks at the adult section of the local video store, books whose salacious titles should have warned me their real audience was straight men. Most disappointing of all, Margo, my personal lexicon on all things gay and someone I considered a full-fledged lesbian, wasn't helpful. She insisted I just needed to "be myself."

Her stingy guidance wasn't enough for me. In my dogged quest for knowledge, I realized the one place to study lesbians *en masse,* and thereby uncover and emulate their secrets and behaviors, was Sisters, newly opened and conveniently located only a few miles away.

My first time at Sisters, my expectations were high. Margo was well-known among the ladies, having quarterbacked the flag football team to the championships a couple of years in a row. On her arm, I anticipated a warm welcome for me, too. Maybe even hugs. I was pretty sure lesbians greeted each other with full-body hugs. *Note to self: Confirm hugging etiquette by re-watching that monologue about lesbians and personal space from* Claire.

Shouts rang out acknowledging Margo when we walked in. I felt the scrutiny of a million eyes. There were no hugs for me, only curt nods and skeptical head-to-toe appraisals with hands on hips. Occasionally, eyes lingered on my better assets. *Note to self: Remember to thank Margo for discouraging that shirt with the plunging neckline.*

Someone called us over to a booth. I perched at the end of the bench while Margo went to get drinks. In her absence, someone made a comment (did she say "Maybelline"?) and everyone laughed. Furtive glances at me followed additional quips I didn't understand and more laughter. Obviously an inside joke understood only by full-fledged lesbians. These women don't wear makeup, so why all this talk about lipstick? *Note to self: Discuss lesbian definitions for common vocabulary words with Margo.*

An awkward moment ensued when Margo handed me a glass instead of a bottle. In the dim light I could see I was the only one grasping a Coke instead of a Miller Lite. Doesn't she realize, although I hate beer, I'd drink a keg if that's what the rules called for? *Note to self: Next time, instruct Margo to buy lesbian-approved beverages only.*

Margo pulled me to the dance floor. "Is it me, or is everybody staring at us?" I asked.

"Oh yeah, they're checking you out from every angle, you can be sure of that," she said. *Note to self: Dear God, I completely forgot to ask Margo if my ass looks fat in these jeans.*

There were new faces at the table when we returned. Someone asked, hadn't she seen me on the softball field last year? When Margo told her I didn't play, a look of confusion rippled around the table. A lesbian who didn't play? By choice, not due to injury? *Note to self: Find a sport to excel in. Immediately.*

Our ride home was quiet as I sorted out a barrage of impressions. *Random notes to self: Fish out pinky ring from jewelry box and wear next time. Future clothing purchases from LL Bean men's catalogue. Nail polish? What were you thinking?*

Margo chuckled and squeezed my hand. "That thing with Sharon was my fault. I should have told you about hair." I blushed, remembering how Robyn had bristled when I complimented Sharon's curly blonde hair and then stroked a lock of it.

"I just wanted to see if it was natural or a perm. I wasn't coming on to her. By the way, should I cut my hair?"

Margo roared at my plaintive tone of voice. "No, no, no! Or yes—if that's what you want. Just be yourself. That's good enough."

Needless to say, after a few more outings at Sisters, I declared my education complete. I did not cut my hair, buy cleats, or fill my closet with flannel shirts. I understood what "lipstick" meant and held my head high as a femme. As it turned out, the lesbian code of conduct is a universal credo, just as Margo had described. The secret to fitting in, on Planet Lesbos or anywhere else, is self-confidence. Be yourself, whoever you are.

Decades ago, Sisters was the one place outside of our own home where we felt safe enough to be ourselves, where a touch or a kiss wouldn't be (literally) life-threatening. It was where we celebrated or commiserated with women like us and recharged when the stress of a sometimes hateful world became too much. I'll never forget the exhilarating feeling of Margo's arms around me, when we slow danced for the very first time in public, at Sisters.

Some say mainstream acceptance has rendered gay and lesbian bars obsolete. I don't know about that. Margo and I have been around the world, but nowhere in our travels have I ever felt the "one human family" closeness I felt at Sisters. And, as recent events have demonstrated, hate can infiltrate anywhere, seemingly at will. Our new political regime has emboldened haters of all kinds—the homophobes, the racists, the misogynists. In this environment, perhaps it is in our community's best interests not to gather together as unwitting targets for the worst among us. I don't know about that, either.

All I know is this: I will miss Sisters. In the decades before Obergefell v. Hodges, for me, Sisters was a bright light beaming into the dark, uncertain future. I was grateful for her existence. And now, I wish I'd known the clock was ticking. I would have liked one last slow dance across her well-worn floor.

LONG STORY SHORT

by Renée Bess

One night years ago,
I sat next to my fiancé in a corner bar in North Philly.
Yes, North Philly. Yes, fiancé.
I was following the script
written for most black middle-class West Mt. Airy girls,
faithful to family rules, career-bound, obedient
and trying like hell
to remain hidden from myself.

The smoke-filled, beer-laden heavy air
reminded me of a poem I needed to write.
I watched the honey-brown barmaid glance at my male partner,
And take his request in short order.
She moved closer to me, her eyes able to read
what I thought was invisible.
Leaning over the bar, she put her hand atop mine
and breathed for both of us.
"What can I get for you, baby?"
Baby?
"A bourbon and ginger ale, please."
Baby?
I saw her return, a beer bottle in one hand,
my dark caramel-colored drink in the other.
The liquid flowed over my tongue
as smoothly as the barmaid had called me
something other than my name.
Baby!
Those voices closest to me rose above my head,
a word jumble needing no more than my nod.
 I held the barmaid within my gaze.
"Would you like another one?"
Yes, a second, third and fourth one if that means
You'll touch my hand and moan "baby" over and over again.
"No thanks," I answered

and promptly straightened my posture.
My empty glass had become a mirror whose reflection
I swore to avoid.

But the night I walked away from that North Philly bar
I knew there were other places
where I'd let myself be found.
Where I'd sit next to a woman
and sip bourbon and ginger.
She would touch the small of my back
or cover my hand with hers
as she asked,
"What can I get for you, Baby?"

ON THE SIDEWALK IN FRONT OF KELLER'S

by Richard Natale

It's 1975. You've finally decided to come out. Now what?

You don't know any gay people. Not personally. Your gaydar isn't set up yet, and you'll have to learn how to walk before you can prowl.

This being New York, you have spotted a few sore thumbs, but completely missed the subtler variety, boys with darting eyes who haunt shop windows waiting for someone to stop and give them the nod. Once, at a party with your then girlfriend, she complained "the nerve of that guy," and you were genuinely puzzled. "He was cruising you. Didn't you notice?" You hadn't noticed, and what's more, you found the claim highly dubious. You would know if a guy was putting the make on you, wouldn't you?

Or the time you were in Barney's and the shoe salesman stared at you a beat too long while slipping on a pair of Cole-Haan loafers, and you found yourself looking back at him wondering what was the matter? When he rang up the sale, he slipped you a note that read, "Would you like to have dinner?" You ran out of the store like it was on fire.

But you kept the note.

After much deliberation, you finally made the leap a couple of weeks back and already you're getting restless. You walk around the Village on a Saturday afternoon expecting the streets to be chock-a-block with men eager to offer you tea and sympathy. No takers. You return the following Saturday, and a young man smiles at you, but is quickly whisked away by a friend (boyfriend?). You decide to scope out a bar, but after standing in the doorway and peeking inside, you decide against it. Nothing but a handful of glum guys nursing drinks and staring off into space.

Disheartened, you wander around until dark, grab a bite to eat, and resign yourself to spending the rest of the night reading the early edition of the *Sunday Times* and watching

Saturday Night Live, that new comedy program.

Then your luck changes.

On the subway up to 72nd Street, you get off behind a trio of guys who are as giggly as schoolchildren and, on a hunch, tail them up to Columbus almost to the corner of 75th Street, where they duck into a place called the Wildwood. You've passed this particular establishment a hundred times without taking the slightest notice. A gay bar on the upper West Side? Is that so?

Deep breath. You step inside. It's crowded and many of the patrons are as high-spirited as the three guys you followed. They're clustered into groups, chatting, laughing, seemingly having a gay old time. Gay old time. That's a good one.

But you don't know a soul and feel awkward. You fail to notice the equally solitary men along the bar's perimeters, hoping and praying that someone, anyone, will talk to them. You're about to turn on your heel—nothing worse than being alone in a crowd—when the hunky bartender (as if there was any other kind) says, "What are you having?"

Well, maybe one drink.

You order a Bud. "On me," the bartender says with a big smile, and immediately, your longing button is pressed. The bartender's gaydar is pinpoint accurate, and he recognizes a neophyte when he sees one. You tip him two dollars, thanking him for the beer and, possibly, for saving your life. Scoping out the room again, you see a TV at the far end of the bar with a sign over it: "Mary Hartman, Mary Hartman" every night at eleven. You like that show. You don't always get the jokes, but it's fun in a weird way.

At one p.m., you go home alone feeling somewhat more upbeat. On Monday night, you return at eleven and the place is quite full and everyone's eyes are turned upwards toward the TV. Watching *Mary Hartman* with an audience is revelatory. The patrons enjoy even the most obscure bits of humor. You laugh along because that's what people do when they're surrounded by laughter. By the second commercial, your sphincter has relaxed enough that you begin to have a good time.

You return to the Wildwood the next night and the next. On your fourth visit, a guy named Clint introduces himself.

He's lanky, with a blond mustache, charming, and engaging, and a bit goofy. He's seen you a few times, he says. You swap origin stories. He seems interested in what you have to say, and you wonder if he's also "interested," and whether this is friendly chit-chat or a prelude. He mentions that he manages an antique store on East 60th and suggests you stop by sometime. Then he shakes your hand and leaves.

That Saturday you wander into the antique shop as if by accident. It's nippy out and there's no one else in the place and Clint is happy to see you. He offers you hot chocolate. There's a kettle in the back, he says, as he flips over the "Open" sign in the window. As you sip the hot chocolate and nibble oatmeal cookies, he says, "I find you very attractive and would like to have sex with you."

You want to tell him the truth. That you've never done this before, and you're quite nervous. But you're not about to scare away your first concrete offer, and you do things in the back of the shop that are new to you and yet feel familiar. On the way home, you're as pleased as punch. Not a single guilt pang.

You wish you had someone with whom to share the moment. But the only gay person whose acquaintance you've made so far is the one you just had sex with.

At Wildwood, you run into Clint again and take him back to your place. You both conclude that you like each other, but maybe not in that way. He asks if you'd like to go dancing with him and his best friend, Ralph, that Friday night. Your first gay disco is down on 12th Street and the Hudson. At the end of the night, Clint says he's going to the Anvil to watch a live sex show and maybe check out the backroom (which is actually downstairs). You panic. You're curious. You're just not ready. When you demur, he suggests Sunday brunch together and maybe hit the bars along Christopher Street.

The atmosphere in the Village is different on a Sunday afternoon. At the bottom of Christopher, where the street widens, it's as if someone smashed a gay piñata and hundreds of men poured out. Many have facial hair, wear plaid shirts, jeans, and Tony Lama boots. Others are dressed like you and Clint, preppie casual with sneakers. And there's a smattering of drag queens. You eventually wend your way to West Street and to a bar called Keller's where most of the patrons are standing on the sidewalk.

You don't realize it yet, but you're home.

It's at Keller's that Clint introduces you to Jose, a fifth-grade teacher. The wiry, dark Puerto Rican is wicked smart with a drier than dry sense of humor. He speaks as rapidly in English as in Spanish. You like him immediately. And he seems to like you. As a friend. Which is really what you're looking for at this point. You've picked up a couple of men at the Wildwood in the interim, but except for Clint, they were merely one-night stands who all but ignored you the next time you ran into them, which you found strange. Your hide still needs thickening.

In turn, Jose introduces you to his friends. Two guys who work in the fashion industry: Gavin, an elfin Brit with a giant mustache and mouth full of marbles, and his lover, Anton, a black man who, while American, speaks in a crisper English accent than his mate.

Gerry is a firecracker chorus boy who most recently danced in that "Gypsy" revival with Angela Lansbury you saw right after moving to the city. Gerry's use of the phrase "Sing out, Louise" varies from that in the actual show.

You are soon joined by Jorge, a *muy* macho guy from Havana, and you quickly learn never, not ever, to confuse a Puerto Rican for a Cuban, or vice versa. Jorge is beefy and humorless. The others take turns taunting him with feminine pronouns, which sends him round the bend. To prove his virility, he lowers his gym shorts and flashes his decidedly manly equipment, which only fuels the fire. You have rarely laughed so hard.

The only person who doesn't tease him is Steve, a puppy dog, playful, with the most infectious laugh and not a mean bone in his body. Clint mentions that Steve, in addition to being an opera and ballet aficionado, almost singlehandedly keeps the Mine Shaft in business. You ask what the Mine Shaft is. He tells you. Your eyes widen. Slings and bathtubs? Hmm.

Then there's little Jose, or Joey as they call him. Average height, perky, always smiling that crooked smile. You develop an immediate crush. Clint says he's been working Joey for months. He eventually succeeds but, uncharacteristically, offers no details. You finally seduce Joey and get your first taste of cock tease.

And lastly, there's Gil, who, along with Clint, becomes your closest friend. Gilberto Rivera says that he considers Catherine Deneuve to be his spiritual twin, despite the fact that he's billiard-ball hairless. Gil is fun to be around, grandiose and spirited, and you are neither. His energy is exhilarating.

Unlike the others, Gil loves to talk about himself, and you struggle to keep up. In between drags on his ever-present cigarette, which he holds high up in the air at an angle, he tells you that he works as a teller in a bank uptown. Lives in Washington Heights with his parents. His mother protects him from his homophobic father who would stab him in his sleep, given the opportunity. Or so Gil says.

Oh, and don't let the Catherine Deneuve thing fool you, he confides. Like Jorge, he's a total top. Not that you asked, or that you're even sure what that means.

Every Sunday afternoon from then on, you are part of the core group, which includes the occasional new boyfriend, none of whom seems to last very long. Except in inclement weather, you gather on the sidewalk with a beer to shoot the shit and laugh and talk about music and movies and the boys who pass by, rating them, berating them. The phrase "attitude for days" is frequently uttered.

But here's what's really important. For the first time in your life, you're part of a like-minded group. You accept one another at face value, embrace your similarities and your differences. No class distinctions, no judgment. They don't care whether you're straight acting or fey (except maybe for Jorge), a top or a bottom, into leather or chiffon, a slut or a cock tease. Life is too serious, and closeted, most of the week. Sunday is for hanging with friends in front of Keller's, having a few beers, talking, laughing, sharing (though sometimes, after dark, you wander across the street to the other bars and try your luck).

You run into the guys, alone or in pairs on Friday night at 12 West, which is now your official disco. You're either there with Clint and Ralph (who recently became your roommate) or with Gil, whose pre-disco regimen includes chilled vodka and half a Quaalude. He convinces you to give it a go. Much to your surprise, you don't fall asleep. The combination loosens you, especially on the dance floor.

Early one Saturday morning as the music is winding down, Gavin and Anton invite you to join them at the Anvil, and this time you say yes. You're not quite sure what to make of the pretty young contortionists on the bar, though you marvel at their muscle control. You try not to act too incredulous when Gavin swears that one weekend Mick Jagger came in to see the show, accompanied by Jackie O and her sister Lee.

He and Anton gradually make their way downstairs, and after careful consideration, you decide to pay a visit yourself. It's dark, but not pitch black. The immediate sensation is like moving through a car wash. Hands reaching, grabbing, holding. Your first anonymous experience proves satisfactory. Back upstairs, you find Anton bubbling all over Gavin. He tells you that the most wonderful thing ever has occurred. "I just got a blow-job from Givenchy," Anton whispers in your ear.

Your mind conjures up the image of a distinguished French gentleman in a designer suit on his knees. You don't dare question whether, in the compromised light, Anton might have made a mistake. Why burst his bubble? But if it's true, what a story to tell the grandkids.

The group buys a block of tickets to see Labelle. Sitting side by side, you pass a bottle of poppers back and forth, marveling at the space-age costumes and singing along.

That summer, the group lucks into a unique arrangement with Jeremy, their favorite bartender at Keller's. He's sharing a house in the Pines and has an extra bed in his room. Since none of you can afford even a half share, he lets you split it among yourselves, which works out to roughly two weekends apiece. If the weather's good, the rest of the group joins whoever has the share that weekend. You spend Saturday together on the beach, go to a tea dance, grab a bite, then spend the rest of the night at the Ice Palace in Cherry Grove. On the way back, just after dawn, you retrieve your beach bags from under the house and catch the first ferry back to the mainland, get a few hours' sleep, then meet up again at Keller's.

Good times.

New Year's Eve, you all make plans to attend a party in a Chelsea penthouse turned one-night-only disco. Shortly after the ball drops, Grace Jones, in full Cleopatra drag, is carted in on a litter supported by four muscular, barely clad Nubians. She's singing, "I Need a Man." The place goes wild.

The following summer, you marvel at the Tall Ships celebration in New York harbor to celebrate the bicentennial. At Keller's the following Sunday, you swap stories about your encounters with foreign sailors. Juan confesses he's become smitten with a Haitian seaman. His dour, virile façade falls away to reveal a lovestruck, gobsmacked romantic.

Shortly after ushering in another New Year together, you're offered a reporting job in Los Angeles. The position and the money are impossible to refuse. When you break it to your friends that Sunday, the reactions range from congratulatory (Jose, Steve, Gavin, and Anton) to indifferent (Joey and Jorge) to envious (Gerry, the dancer) to outraged (Clint and especially Gil).

"You're going to hate L.A.," Gil says. "I give it six months." You forgive him because his reaction is such a blatant cover for separation anxiety. His fear is that the group will start to split apart, and you're so much stronger together than separately. Whatever petty differences you have from time to time are quickly forgotten. You've come to accept each other unconditionally. And that's a rare thing, to be guarded, to be cherished.

Your last night in New York, Gil insists the two of you go dancing at 12 West despite your nine a.m. flight. "You owe me," he insists. "And you can sleep on the plane." Walking in, you see Clint and Ralph and the rest of the group. They yell, "Surprise." They've brought a cake, and like a deb at a ball, they line up for a turn on the floor with you. Towards the end of the evening, the DJ plays Oydssey's "Native New Yorker," and your friends form a circle around you and sing the words to the song, just for you.

The perfect send-off.

****

In L.A., the cars are close together and the people are far apart. You find the bar scene stratified and exclusionary. The manicured pretty boys congregate in WeHo, older, rougher-hewn dudes on the East Side, with some crossover in between.

You sleep with several men, but none of those encounters evolve into friendships and you're socked with the homesick blues. You concede that Gil was probably right. You're out of sync in L.A. Then one rainy night, you wander into the Blue Parrot in WeHo, which is virtually deserted. You hone in on the only promising prospect, an Iowa farm boy type with wheaten hair swept across his forehead. You try but fail to catch his attention. Just as you're about to give up, he introduces himself. Jack is his name. Two sentences in, you realize he's not from Iowa at all, but from Brooklyn. You hit it off immediately and spend the next twelve years of your life together.

You keep in regular contact with Clint and Gil, phone calls two or three times a week, each conversation lasting an hour or more. They bring you up-to-date on the others and what's changed at Keller's (nothing). You mention Jack, but not that the relationship is getting serious until you're sure it is, about two weeks before you move in together. Gerry, who has hung up his dancing shoes and become a florist, sends you a congratulatory bouquet. The card predictably reads, "Sing out, Louise."

Anton passes through town on the way back from a business trip in the Far East. You have dinner, and he tells you all about his new job as a textile designer. Steve decides to visit and asks to crash on your couch, which he does for exactly one night, since the following evening, at the Spike, you introduce him to one of Jack's friends, Gene. He and Steve have a weeklong affair. Other than Gene however, Steve finds L.A. a wasteland. No opera company? No dance company? No Mine Shaft? Barbaric.

A few months later, you travel to New York to spend the holidays with family. Jack stays behind for work and because he hates the holidays and his family. Anton and Gavin say that, because your time in Manhattan is limited, they've decided to throw you a party. This way you can see the old gang. They all show up, and you pick up the conversation as if you'd never left. You promise to make every effort to join them on Sunday at Keller's, but family obligations keep you in Brooklyn.

Gavin, a shutterbug, clicks away all night, and a few weeks later, you receive a thick packet in the mail. You show the pictures to Jack, who has heard all the stories, but except for Steve and Anton whom he's met, he's understandably disinterested.

****

In mid-May, you get the first phone call. It's Gil. Steve had a bad cold that developed into pneumonia. He went into the hospital and died. You're sure you've misheard.

The following February, Clint phones. Your old roommate Ralph has some rare skin cancer. Three months later, he's gone.

Clint comes out for a visit. You score tickets to the Golden Globes. Given how starstruck Clint is, you ask Jack if you can take him instead. He doesn't mind at all, because that's Jack. You rent tuxedos and are seated on either side of Natalie Cole, who repeatedly excuses herself to go to the ladies room to powder her nose. By the third time, you have to look away from each other to keep from laughing.

You drive him to the airport the next morning, and he's still buzzing from his brush with celebrity. One of the last things he tells you is that he's got "it." You never see Clint again, though you speak on the phone up until the day before he passes. Gil departs the following summer, and when you hear that his father refused to visit him in the hospital or attend the funeral, you cry the whole night.

Over the next several years, the losses mount. Soon your L.A. friends, many of them transplanted New Yorkers, start to perish.

And then Jack.

After Jack dies, while cleaning out a closet, you find a box containing the photos Gavin took at the party. As you look them over, you are dumbstruck. All gone. It doesn't seem possible. You've already given up trying to figure out why them and not you. There is no logic in insanity.

An entire swath of your life wiped away. No one left with whom to reminisce about those Keller's Sundays, the sidewalk where you shared being who you were without fear or judgment. Where you found acceptance and affection.

On occasion, you allow yourself to imagine what would have happened if those friends had been granted a normal lifespan, as you have. You are almost certain that, even if you'd lost touch over the years, at some point, maybe in the era of social media, you would have reconnected and picked up the conversations that you never quite finished.

AWOL to AWOL

by Mercedes Lewis

I have always been pretty much a loner. AWOL—A Woman of Longing—looking for kindred spirits but not knowing what or who they were, or what that might even look like. A woman longing for something but not sure what it was. A woman, surrounded by a multitude of people, yet so very lonely. A woman outside, looking in, wondering where she fit.

In every sense of the word, I am a late bloomer. I knew nothing about the Stonewall Riots; I had no idea who Harvey Milk was; and the only thing I knew concerning the rainbow was that it was God's promise after the flood, and later, that it was a symbol for Hawaii. In fact, when I joined the military, one of the five or six questions they asked was if you were a homosexual. Frankly, it was the Vietnam War era, and they weren't refusing very many people, so the instructor "cheated" and told us to answer all the questions no. Well, I didn't know what a homosexual was, and I didn't want to lie, or just answer, so I raised my hand and asked the sergeant what a homosexual was. He said if I had to ask, I wasn't one, so just answer the question no. Little did either of us know.

The first gay club I walked into, the music informed and shaped me, making me aware of who I really was, and who I could be. Me! I was a total ingénue. In fact, had I not come from the city, one would think I was a hayseed who came in straight from the farm. I was an eighteen-year-old running from something with no idea what I was running to. I signed up for Fun, Travel, and Adventure, although more days than not, FTA was referred to as "fuck the Army," definitely a passive-aggressive, love-hate relationship with Uncle Sam post the Vietnam War.

One evening, one of my sergeants announced that she was tired of me wandering around the barracks, and that she would take me out for some fun. I was to be ready at eleven p.m. Eleven o'clock at night. Going out. Already I thought she was crazy, but she explained that in Atlanta, the party didn't really get hopping until about that time. I had to take her word for it. She was, after all, the sergeant.

She drove us to what appeared to be a warehouse district. I was beginning to get a little concerned. We pulled into the crowded parking lot of a large, nondescript building. As soon as I stepped from the vehicle, I could hear the music thumping. Adrenaline began to course through my veins. I wasn't even inside yet, and already I felt more alive. I rushed to the dance floor to dance with myself. I didn't have to for long. Everyone was dancing, and sweating, and laughing. This must be heaven, I thought. Then someone handed me a little brown bottle and directed me to inhale. Being a good little soldier, of course I did. Then, my world exploded into bright, throbbing lights, and music I could feel in my very soul. Everything disappeared except me and the music. I later learned that the bottle was referred to as poppers, and I never did them again. I loved music and dancing. I found that the poppers didn't add anything to the experience that was worth the risk.

The floor cleared after a while, and I got to witness my very first drag show. Beautiful women, dressed to the nines, took to the stage and sang all the latest songs. I was in love. The sergeant was cracking up, as I gushed over those beautiful women, especially Rachel. Could this night get any better?

Then, the sergeant leaned over and whispered in my ear, "They're all men."

What? All men! No way. I couldn't believe it. They moved with such assurance. Such grace and such flair. And they handled those high heels like pros. I couldn't be persuaded. I was in love. "For the fifth time, I'm telling you. Those are men!" That was the refrain of the evening. She was right of course. I was both devastated and elated. Going forward, I don't think I missed another show, and I discovered that Rachel was so much woman she had a girlfriend. Or, to put it more accurately, he was a straight man who loved to camp it up and had found the perfect soul mate who not only stood beside him, but encouraged him. I got over it.

I wish I could say that I was more a part of that wave of activism. I'm still green and wet behind the ears, but I'm learning all I can about what was paid in order for me to be who I am today: out, loud, and proud. Able, more often than not, to live a fearless life. Able to live, able to love, able to *be*. Because of those that went before me. Because of the clubs. Because of the riots and the refusal to be marginalized any longer, the refusal to continue to die in silence. Because of the bloodshed and sacrifice of other brave souls. But, I can say, I'm a different AWOL because of them and because of the club experience. I will do better this time around. I am A Woman of Love: love for myself, love for others, and love for my community. This time, I will be on the frontline, and I will not be silenced.

I will stand on the shoulders of those that went before me and, I hope, make them as proud of me as I am to be a part of what they did as trailblazers. Like Sylvester, I, who have nothing, will stand proud. Like LaBelle, this Nightbird will fly by the light of the moon. For the past, for the present, for the future.

Motordrome Molly

by Martha Miller

The Crone's Nest was one of two gay bars in town; it opened in 1963 without the support of anyone from the town council, the mayor's office, the police department, parents, or registered voters. By the turn of the century, the younger crowd hung out at Tallulah's, but in 1967, young and old frequented The Crone's Nest.

In 1976, a country western bar opened across the street. Though the owner was a middle-aged man, the bar was called Dolly's. The patrons drove big pickup trucks, and as soon as they figured out the folks across the street were gay, trouble started. They let air out of tires, broke the front window, wrote "fag" with spray paint on the front door, and shouted insults after people as they came and went.

Word got around that the owner of Dolly's wanted The Crone's Nest to move.

"We'll outlast them," Tinkerbelle, a plump femme, said. "It's what people like us do. We'll deal with them for a while, then they'll get tired and move. We know how to take cruelty and keep going." Back then Tink worked in a coal mine, a job that the second wave of the women's movement won for her. She'd done other things, but Freeman Mine paid the best.

Everyone agreed to ignore the troublemakers, except Molly. She said, "Sometime or other, we got to take a stand."

Molly had come to town the August after Dolly's moved in, and when they shouted at her, she shouted back. She was a small, round woman with short graying hair and razory dark eyes. Without her leathers and helmet, she looked like a second-grade school teacher. Every summer she came to The Crone's Nest when the state fair was in town. She traveled in a 1964 Chevy pickup truck, and in the bed she carried two motorcycles, one for the show and the other, much nicer one, to haul around the pretty girls.

Dykes who took dates to the fair bought them corn dogs, cotton candy, lemonade shake ups, and took them to see the

Butter Cow. At seven and nine p.m. (two shows in one evening), they made their way to Happy Hollow where there were games, rides, colorful lights, and the Motordrome—a large cylinder shaped like a barrel. Viewers climbed up a set of wobbly, metal stairs to the top, and looking down inside, they watched the motorcycles start at the bottom and go in a circle. As the riders picked up speed, they started climbing up the wall toward the viewers.

As the only woman, Molly always was first to ride. She knew that a mistake could be deadly, but mindless circling and the women's faces up at the top of the dome sometimes distracted her. The summer that she broke her wrist on the first night was one of those times. Her distraction's name was Beth, who wore her long blonde hair in pigtails tied with pink ribbons. When the ambulance pulled up, Molly could see her in the crowd that had gathered.

Back then the motorcycle races were on a one-mile dirt track, at the opposite end of the fairgrounds, by the grandstand, and were always held the last weekend of the fair. The whole town was taken over by people with motorcycles. When hotels and motels filled up, the bikers would camp at parking meters downtown. The party lasted the whole weekend.

One year, some drunken bikers rode their motorcycles into the lobby of the Leland Hotel. They were arrested, but they were let out the next afternoon for the races, after which they headed home as agreed.

Tinkerbelle had spent one season with Molly when they were younger. She'd been treated like a queen by Molly and by the other carnival workers. The motordrome riders were among the most revered in Happy Hollow—more than the double Ferris wheel or the burlesque show. In the years that followed, Tink settled down with one butch after the next. If she was single in August, she and Molly would take up again. But the year of the broken wrist, Tink was living in a trailer out in the country with Jana and her dogs.

All week long, Molly had spent time with Beth. They rode together, ate at the best restaurants, spent time at the lake, and even more time in Molly's motel room. Beth told her friends several times that she was going with Molly to the next fair and the next and eventually they would winter in

Florida. Molly hadn't said a thing about that. But if she had some hard truth to tell the girl, right after the races was the best time.

The motorcycle races finished at about seven-thirty. The gates that led out of the grandstand and the infield were covered with people who, like lines of ants, were shuffling forward steadily and orderly toward the exits. Men and women mounted their bikes and headed out for the long trips home. By then, the carnival workers had the motordrome torn down.

The day of the races, Molly picked up Beth for what she thought was the last time. The wind was warm as it blew the blonde pigtails back and forth. Beth held her arms around Molly's waist, and the vibrations of the Harley's seat sent waves of pleasure up her thighs. Molly was used to it, but she liked it when a long ride would spark her passenger.

After the races, she parked the black Harley next to The Crone's Nest's door. With her left wrist in a cast, she could brake, but the clutch was iffy, and the wall would help her kick-start and get going without the girl behind her—she'd been thinking ahead.

Beth threw a leg over and skipped down off the bike. "You need me to help?"

Molly cleared her throat and said, "I got it. You just stand clear."

Beth, the taller and slimmer of the two, threw her arm loosely around Molly's shoulders, as they walked into The Crone's Nest.

Sunday was always drag show night, so the bar was crowded.

Across the street, the patrons of Dolly's were quiet. With the motorcycles up and down the street, they'd been too busy to make trouble. But on Sunday night, the bikers were gone. After nine o'clock, two pickup trucks pulled to the curb across from Dolly's and five straight men got out. The door to The Crone's Nest was propped open to clear out some of the cigarette smoke, and the men heard the music from Miss Pauline, who was on stage in a spotlight lip-syncing a rendition of Etta James's "All the Way."

They stepped inside and were immediately stopped by the dyke-at-the-door. They shouted insults and made obscene gestures toward Miss Pauline. Rachel, a thin guy with a moustache, was working behind the bar. That night she wore a pink tutu, matching tights, and a rhinestone tiara. No one noticed until the straight men were gone that Rachel had put a baseball bat on the bar, within her reach.

Almost an hour later, Tinkerbelle came in and said Molly's bike was lying on its side. Several customers, including Molly, ran out to see what had happened. The Harley lay there with the windshield cracked, the gas tank dented, and the back tire flat.

"Those sons-of-bitches," Molly shouted. She started to cross the street, and someone put a hand on her shoulder.

"Wait a minute." It was Rachel.

Molly turned toward her. "I'm not going to take this. Those assholes—"

Rachel put her forefinger to her lips and whispered, "Quiet." She jerked her head to the right. "Those are their trucks."

Molly said, "So?"

Rachel handed her the baseball bat and said, "Wait a minute, I have a tire iron in my trunk. Car's in back." The skirt of her tutu bounced as she ran through the bar. As she returned with the crowbar in her hand, someone from a table near the stage called to her, "What's going on?"

As loud as she could, Rachel shouted, "Bring your car keys out front. We have some dirt to do."

Molly had started without her. She was working on the windows of the first truck; the crack of the bat spider-webbing the windshield reverberated. Rachel went to the second and started on the truck's windows. Four people produced a nails-on-a-blackboard sound of keys into metal and paint. Tinkerbelle pulled a large pocket knife from her bra, and hard as it was, she punctured tires and left them hissing. She was on the fifth one when the crowd parted and four of the five straight men came toward their trucks.

One of them shouted, "You stupid fucking queers."

And then the battle started.

It didn't stop until a fat guy landed a lucky blow, and Miss Pauline, the six-foot-two-inch drag queen, got knocked out. She fell like a cut tree. All was quiet. With the noise stopped, sirens could be heard. People scattered. Some ran into the bar, others for their cars, and more still down the alley. Three people took hold of Miss Pauline, dragged her back into the bar, and shut the door.

Inside, Molly knelt over Pauline and kept repeating her name, but she was out cold.

Rachel approached with a glass of ice water. She hesitated and said, "Pauline will be upset when she sees the dirt on her only strapless gown."

"She's going to have a helluva shiner," Molly said. "Here, let's straighten her wig at least."

As they tugged on the red, shoulder-length hair, Pauline groaned.

Rachel held the cold glass against one temple then the other.

With a flutter, Pauline's eyes opened. "What happened?"

From behind them, Tinkerbelle said, "Did anybody see it? I just turned around and Pauline was lying on the sidewalk."

Molly shook her head. "I didn't see it, but I know you got the best of them."

Then Pauline asked, "Are my eyelashes all right?"

Before they could answer, the door opened and a policeman stepped in. "What's going on?"

Pauline sat up, kicked off her come-fuck-me pumps, got hold of a chair, and with the help of the others, stood. She turned to face the officer. Blood ran out of her nostrils; one eye was swelling.

She fanned herself with her left hand. "It got too hot. I fainted, that's all."

The officer raised his voice a bit. "There's blood out there on the sidewalk. Looks like somebody did some damage to a couple of trucks."

Pauline looked from Molly to Rachel to Tinkerbelle and shrugged.

"Mister, your dress is tore," the policeman said.

Pauline's dress, split open down the right side, showed her bra and panties. She burst into fake tears.

Rachel said, "Here, honey. Take a seat."

Pauline sat.

Beth emerged from the ladies room, filing a broken fingernail.

The policeman shook his nightstick at them. "Don't any

of you go anywhere."

As soon as he was out the door, Pauline wilted, sliding out of the chair to the floor.

Beth crossed the room to the middle of everything. She took Molly's hand—the one without the cast. "We need to get out of here."

Molly pulled her hand away. "You don't leave your friends in a mess like this."

Beth seemed to consider this, but before she could impart any wisdom, a noise came from behind the stage.

Rachel whispered, "Oh, shit."

All five straight men stood side by side blocking the back door, the only remaining exit. Though there were only four straight men outside, all five of them were there now. Four of them had torn shirts, scuffs, and bruises. One had a bloody knee. But the one who obviously hadn't been in the battle stood with the others. He was wearing a wife-beater and cutoff jeans.

They started toward the little group of women and female impersonators.

Molly said to Rachel, "You take the big one. I'll get the rest."

Rachel answered, "Might be safer to surrender to the cops."

Pauline's head rolled from side to side, and her red wig came completely off. She hollered, "Somebody help me. I'm going to need a cab."

Tinkerbelle knelt beside her. "You just lay here. I'll get you a ride."

Pauline nodded and closed her eyes.

The guy wearing the wife-beater called out, "I don't think you should let him go to sleep."

Rachel removed her tiara, set it on the bar, and stepped forward. "The cops are out front. Help me get him out of here before we all end up in jail."

The tallest, fattest one made some kissing sounds and said, "Baby, I'd love to get you in a cell."

"Clearly, that wouldn't be my first choice. But I've spent the night in jail before," Rachel said.

Wife-beater came toward them. He knelt next to Pauline. To Rachel, he said, "You got a car?"

"In back."

He called to the others, "Come on. Let's get him out of here before he dies and we get sent up for a long time."

"Aw," fat boy said, "he's all right."

"Come on." To Rachel, wife-beater said, "How'd he get his eyelashes to do that?"

Rachel shrugged. "It's a talent. A gift, really."

Wife-beater nodded. He tossed the red wig to fat boy, and between them, they lifted Pauline up and carried her to Rachel's car, then laid her down across the back seat.

The others went back inside.

Rachel opened the driver's side door, turned, and said, "Thanks."

"Listen, you guys got insurance?"

Rachel shook her head no. She started the car, rolled slowly down the alley, and turned left. Wife-beater walked away into the August night, just in time.

Back inside, the policeman came in with another officer. The guys from Dolly's went out the back door. They soon returned with their hands in the air, two more cops behind them.

Molly stepped forward. The front door was partially open, and she tried to get a look at her Harley. She could only see part of it, lying on its side. "I know this looks bad."

A voice came from behind her. "Jake?" Beth approached one of the officers.

He raised his nightstick, pushed back the bill of his hat, and said, "Goddamn. I knew this day was coming."

To Molly, Beth said, "My cousin, Jake. Our grandmas were sisters."

Jake said, "You all got a helluva mess out there. We've got Great Northern Towing to haul those big trucks away. Several tires were flat."

"Could you just report it as a big wreck?" Beth asked.

Jake turned around and the cousins watched a tow truck hook up one of the damaged trucks. "I don't think anyone would believe that."

The straight men were lying facedown on the floor. One of the policemen was putting cuffs on them.

Jake pointed with his nightstick. "You folks sit over there."

There were only the three of them remaining: Molly,

Beth, and Tinkerbelle. They sat and the men in back lay cuffed for what seemed like an hour while the officers conferred.

An officer with a clipboard finally approached them. "You gals want to press any charges?"

Molly said, "No, sir," obviously trying to sound as respectful as she could.

Evidently the guys in the cuffs were asked the same thing and also declined.

Jake came back to the women. "We got a lot of property damage out there. You ladies know how that happened?"

Beth said, "Vandalism?" like it was a question.

"That's what these other guys said."

Molly said, "Somebody vandalized those vehicles out there."

****

In the early hours of Monday morning, Tinkerbelle gave Molly and Beth a ride back to the motel to get Molly's pickup, which already had the motordrome bike loaded. The fork had been bent on the bike from the fall the first day Molly saw Beth. It was going to take awhile to get the bikes running again. The motordrome bike could be replaced because the owners insured Molly, but she was on her own with the Harley.

It was a rainy afternoon when the Harley was added to the back of Molly's truck, and Beth, who was still young enough to believe in true love, had what little she owned in a couple of green garbage bags packed between the wrecks.

Two weeks later, Miss Pauline was back on the stage. The swelling on her eyes had gone down. If one looked closely, beneath the makeup, one could see the purple and yellow semicircles beneath her eyes. She never did have her nose fixed. The small bump there gave her a tough look, but nobody noticed because her eyes were so stunning.

The motordrome show came back the next year, but Molly wasn't with it. One of the carnival guys told Tinkerbelle that Molly and Beth were resting in Florida, but they would be back next season and would both be riding in the show. But the following season, the show didn't come back. There'd been an accident where a man was killed when a motorcycle went too far up. The act was closed down.

As far as anyone could remember, neither Molly nor Beth returned.

The Remix

by Liz McMullen

"Girl, your face looks positively naked. I can't believe your mama let you leave the house looking like that." Tyrese brushed the air beside his head, as if he had long luxurious hair rather than a gleaming shaved head.

I loved this MAC store. It was on the corner of Christopher and Gay Street—it doesn't get much gayer than that. "I was sleeping when Mama left for work, and you know I can't be bothered with makeup. You're lucky I gelled my hair before I got on the train."

The boutique was well lit, had fourteen-foot ceilings, and was decorated with a simple palette of black and white. MAC was cosmetics wonderland with every conceivable eye shadow and silky lipsticks that defied the imagination. Whoever named the lip colors was a genius: Tendertalk Lip balm, Vamplify Candy, Vibe Tribe, and Velvetease. I shucked my messenger bag and assumed the position, or rather the perch, on Tyrese's makeup chair. "I did manage to wash my face before leaving work."

"You're lucky you're young, and I know you didn't bother moisturizing." Tyrese started off with face cream and a primer. "What are we going for tonight? Smoky and dangerous or femme drag?"

"A red dress that would make Marilyn Monroe proud and platform heels high enough to make the drag queens wonder if I'm one of theirs."

Tyrese's perfume was musky enough to make me smile in appreciation. "You smell divine. I wondered where that bottle of perfume had gotten off to."

He ignored me as he smoothed a layer of foundation over my freckles. "I'll give you a bold eye with David Bowie contouring. We can go nude with your lips or clear Lipglass."

"Ugh! Lipglass is way too sticky and ruined my bag last time."

Tyrese rolled his eyes. "You shouldn't have tried to fit the tube in the tight pocket of your cell wallet. Besides, your hair is too short to worry about snagging."

I snickered. "Lesbian remember? The girls I meet just might have hair long enough to get caught as we kiss."

There was a smile in his voice as he responded, but he was on a mission. "Close your eyes and stay still."

The glide of the blending brush was soothing, and I sighed in appreciation. "So how did the photo shoot go?"

"It went." Tyrese rested an angled makeup sponge where my cheekbone met the corner of my eye. This helped keep the line of makeup clean as he drew the color from my lids to my temples.

I opened the eye he wasn't working on. He seemed more sad than aggravated. "The models or the photographer?" I asked.

"He acted like he'd never seen me before. I worked morning to night during Fashion Week. Saw him every damned day. It was his idea to book me for the Cosmo shoot." Tyrese gestured for me to keep both eyes closed. I couldn't tell if it was out of necessity or to shield his disappointment.

"Is the dress matte or does it shimmer?" Tyrese asked as if he were broaching a subject of major importance, of the life-and-death variety.

I accepted the change of subject. "Matte, and it's synthetic so no wrinkles from living in my messenger bag all day." I had smartened up from my last packing job and wrapped the heels in a T-shirt so they wouldn't snag or stain the dress.

Tyrese's mouth formed a perfect O. "The one with the single red feather at the end of each halter string?"

My dress gave the impression that I had more curves than my boyish hips and barely there boobs normally allowed. The front draped over my cleavage and was held up by two strings, at the end of which were the lone red feathers that Tyrese admired. "You can borrow it for a date with Malcolm."

Tyrese's dreamy expression said it all. He was finally in love. "We're not at the vampy dress phase yet. He doesn't know I do drag."

I pursed my lips. This was a tough one, especially these days when personals specified "straight acting" or "no sissies or flamers." From the times I had met up with the couple, Malcom seemed really cool and smitten. Love, especially between young men, can be a fragile thing. I didn't blame Tyrese for his caution.

"Why don't we do a gloss with some shimmer? Gold or silver maybe?"

"The platforms have silver straps, but I don't need to be matchy matchy. What do you think?" The big question was what would Jade think. Tonight wasn't exactly a date, but she said she was working and I could hang out backstage if I wanted to. Jade made go-go dancing full-on burlesque. With all of her options and rapt fans, I didn't have much of a chance. This was probably wishful makeuping.

Tyrese fished out my dress and looked at the shoes himself. "Screw it. Since when do you need to look natural? I'll use an iridescent-red lip liner that will stay put all night. Then all you need to do is reapply this pale gloss. The pink will mute the red and is silky rather than sticky."

"Thank God." I wondered if Jade's lips were as soft as they looked.

Tyrese made some final touches then urged me to stand. I slipped off the stool to look at his artwork. It was Ziggy Stardust meets Jessica Rabbit. David Bowie would totally approve. "This is something else. Would body glitter make it too much?"

"I knew there was a reason I liked you." Tyrese sauntered around the store looking for some body powder. The world was his runway, and while I doubted drag would come as a shock to Malcolm, I wouldn't out my best friend.

He came back with a shallow jar filled with shimmering powder. His smile dazzled, but the sadness was back in his eyes.

"Are you all right?" I asked.

"I'm not ready to talk about it yet."

"You have my number when you are ready." My phone buzzed. The text from Jade made my heart skip a beat, even though it was a mere seven characters long: "cu later." Not exactly a declaration of love, but I would take it.

Tyrese rested his hand on my arm. I jumped. "Jesus."

This time his smile met his eyes. "You better go in back and change. Glitter is forever, and I don't want to mess up your favorite black jeans."

My jeans were at half-mast when the music stopped. "You're not going to leave me half-naked in the dark are you?" I shouted, a bit too loud for cavernous space. My voice echoed off the high ceilings. Any further protests were drowned out by old school salsa music. Elvis Crespo's "Suavemente" was blasting loud enough that I could do nothing more than dance as I extricated myself from my skinny jeans and shimmed into the dress. The volume meant the store was closed for the night. I shoved my discarded clothes and sneakers into my bag. The sneakers couldn't do harm to my casual clothes, so I didn't bother with caution.

I padded back into the showroom barefoot. The agony of heels would wait for my dismount. Tyrese was dancing with Vanessa. He let her lead of course. Vanessa was taller than Tyrese and smooth as silk, though she preferred latex and leather over the finer fabrics. The scent of Black Beauty Latex Polish was heavy in the air. The floor-to-ceiling windows had no curtains, which meant Vanessa hadn't bothered with modesty and changed in full view of the street.

Tyrese was too busy dancing with the *nena morena* to help me with the finishing touches on my outfit. I was cautious with the shimmer powder; the last time I used it I got overzealous, and my black blouse looked like I had scarfed a box of powdered donuts. The next song up was a duet between La India and Marc Anthony. "Vivir lo Nuestro" was much more romantic than "Suavemente." I was so caught up in the lyrics that I didn't hear Vanessa approach.

"Can I help you with those?"

I dropped the heels out of arousal rather than fright. Since I couldn't think of a thing to say, Vanessa took action. She lifted and set me back on the makeup stool, then she knelt before me. I shivered as her fingers touched my skin and suppressed a gasp as she fit the slim silver tongue into the small buckle at each ankle. Tyrese was mysteriously absent. Once the shoes were on, Vanessa gracefully stood in a way that would have made me teeter if I had attempted it.

"You look lovely."

The compliment was welcome, but Vanessa was the real beauty. Her skin the color of dark honey. Her high cheekbones and angular jaw would have been severe on another woman, but Vanessa's full lips and luscious eyelashes softened her appearance. Her undivided attention was disconcerting in the most delicious way. Her latex jumpsuit was zipped low enough to showcase the natural fullness of her breasts. I felt a mild stir in my loins. I had a thing for punk rock girls, but lacked the balls to trust my body to this particular mistress. I wondered if I'd packed more than one pair of panties. "Thank you," I said in a voice that squeaked. Oh yeah, that was sexy. Not.

She cupped my cheek as she stepped into my personal space. "One day, when you are ready for me, I will come and *take* you."

I blinked. My mouth opened and closed, but I couldn't form a thought, never mind a sentence.

"Vanessa, stop teasing the animals."

Vanessa's chuckle was deep, throaty, and so damned sexy. I wanted to kiss her, and I didn't care if she ruined my makeup. It would be worth it. Tyrese appeared by my side before I could do anything foolish. The look he gave me made me worry that damning thought bubbles were appearing above my head.

"When she removes her baby dyke training wheels, you can have at her." Tyrese was firm but not harsh. He was right. I was so not ready for anything Vanessa had to offer.

"I told her as much." Vanessa smiled at me; her lips were a velvety red. "I have to go to work now."

"Work" was her job as lead mistress at Pandora's Box, a dungeon so exclusive it would take me months to afford a small segment of her time. She was out the door before I could say a word.

Tyrese closed my mouth for me. "Time for your lashes. Yours are full and long enough on their own, but I think you could pull off these." He showed me a set of thick lashes with alternating long and short strands. The tips of the longer strands were frosted with droplets of red glitter.

"Might as well go full-on femme drag." I closed my eyes so he could apply them. Whenever I tried to apply lashes, I always ended up gluing my fingers together. Tyrese helped me to stand and walked me over to the full-length mirror. I loved it all: the makeup, my vampy dress, my platform shoes. But those shoes would never be the same again. Whenever I touched the buckles, I would think of Vanessa. "You did an amazing job, Tyrese. Those drags are going to try to snatch my wig!"

Tyrese playfully tugged a spike. "Just stay away from the hunks and twinks and you'll be fine."

"Phew, then I am in the clear. They have a little too much going on down there for me to be interested."

I had the butterflies I always got when I knew I was going to a queer space. Just getting ready set me off balance in a pleasant way. Escuelita was a mixed bar in the garment district, a stone's throw from Times Square. They had a nightly drag show, which usually meant there were more boys and drags than lesbians, but Friday night's show was different. They catered to lesbians and had mostly female go-go dancers to draw in a crowd. Watching Jade's performance while she danced was the only acceptable time for me to stare at her. The other go-go dancers were my friends, so they didn't mind my fascination with their considerable charms.

Tyrese cleared up his station, and I followed him as he set the alarm and locked the tall wooden doors to the shop. "Are you really going to walk all the way uptown dressed like that? Even I would draw the line at walking over thirty blocks in heels."

I shrugged. I only had enough money to take the PATH home, so the subway wasn't an option and a taxi was out of the question. "Yes. Even if I could afford another way up, I'm going to be early. The walk takes long enough for me to get there after the doors open."

"You know Rob would let you in early, and Rose likes having you around as she sets up." Tyrese removed the monstrous chain from his bike and swapped the chain with the seat he had stowed in his backpack. People stole bikes all the time, but a seatless chained bike was less attractive to thieves. Who wants to take a New York pothole on a bike without a seat? "Angel Sheridan likes you enough to let you into her inner sanctum as she puts on her face."

Angel Sheridan was the star and drag show master of ceremonies. I loved her to death but always felt like I was imposing. Escuelita was too important to me to overstay my welcome. Besides, Jade was my backstage pass for the night.

She offered to put me on her guest list, but I demurred. There was another way around the price of admission. I handed out flyers for Escuelita outside bars and clubs. I either froze or sweated my ass off, depending on the season. Flyering didn't pay much, but it did get me out of paying the cover charge. With my limited resources, ten or fifteen dollars would mean the difference between going out or having to stay at home. "Are you going to meet me there?"

Tyrese smirked. "Not tonight, dollface. I have a date with tall, dark, and handsome." His smile was as beautiful as his smooth, dark skin. All he had to do was tend to his eyebrows and apply lip balm to look runway worthy. I didn't hate him for it. It wasn't his fault I needed all the bells and whistles he could apply to my face to tempt...someone like Vanessa.

I gave him a big hug. "Thanks for the free makeup, again."

"No worries. I welcome any break from the retail madness. If I get another lily-white Bridge and Tunnel girl asking for the natural look, in MAC of all places, I will scream." He was gentle as he held my chin. "You're a sparkling diamond. I love femming you up."

"I'd kiss you, but that would mess up your hard work." I gave him a bear hug and let him loose. "See you at brunch on Sunday?"

"My treat?" he teased.

"One day, I'll treat you. I promise."

"Go on ahead with your broke-ass self. Have fun." He gave me a girly finger wave then launched off toward the Lower East Side where his boyfriend lived.

I only walked well-lit streets at this time of night. The mostly empty sidewalks still held danger. I kept my gait brisk and purposeful so no one would mistake me for a tourist. The hodgepodge of nonsensical streets that made up Greenwich Village gave way to the orderly grid pattern of Chelsea as it blended into the Garment District near FIT and Madison Square Garden. The closer I got to Times Square, the safer I felt. Crowds were a good thing.

Even though I took my time, I was so early that there was no line to get into Escuelita. The music wafted upwards as I took the dark black staircase down into the club. The boy behind the register waved me on past the thick black curtains into the empty club. The walls were black. A few strategically placed neon lights cut the gloom.

Employees outnumbered customers. Jade wouldn't show up until midnight, so I had some time to kill. Rose was my first stop. She was cutting lemons and limes for garnishes. A modest ponytail kept her brown hair out of her eyes as she stocked the ice chests with beer.

She looked up at the sound of my heels and gave me her genuine smile, the one reserved for friends. "You need me to hold onto that for you?" Rose nodded at my messenger bag. I gave her a grateful smile, even though it stung that I couldn't tip her for her kindness. I didn't bother extricating my wallet. One, there was no place to put it on this dress. Two, I wouldn't be buying drinks. If I got thirsty, the bathroom faucet would have to do.

I knelt on the bar stool so I could lean over the bar and give Rose a quick hug and a kiss on the cheek without getting fruit juice on my dress. "Love you."

"The feeling is mutual. Have a seat. She won't be here until later." She glanced meaningfully at my platform heels. "You might as well be comfortable."

I blushed and said nothing. My crush on Jade wasn't exactly a secret. Waiting was making me jittery, so I decided to burn off the nervous energy on the dance floor. I closed my eyes so I could really listen to and follow the throbbing beat. The cool air was warming up, and the mingled scents of perfume, musk, and cologne mixed with the vanilla emanating from the smoke machine. Each new track drew me in farther. I let go of my inhibitions and immersed myself in the passion of the bass.

Someone wrapped their arms around me and held me close. "There you are."

I sucked in a breath. My eyes were still closed, but I recognized Jade's perfume.

"Come on, I need you to help me get into my corset."

"Sure," was all I could manage to say. My arousal left me lightheaded. I turned in the circle of her arms and saw something I had never seen before, *desire*.

Author's Note: I named this piece "Remix" because I drew from my personal memories of my baby dyke years in the '90s and early '00s. There are real people mixed with fictional ones, as well as places that no longer exist. That MAC store has been gone a very long time, and Escuelita closed their doors in 2016. One of the things that made me sob and left me inconsolable was how much Pulse Nightclub was like Escuelita. If the massacre happened at Escuelita, I would have known the people murdered that night. I could have been one of the dead. I dedicate this story to those whose lives were taken at Pulse Nightclub. We may not have met, but I love you and will never forget you.

This story is for those we have lost and for the places that keep on disappearing. Lesbian and gay bookstores, bars, and clubs eased my coming out and gave me a home. A place to feel safe, special, and loved. Here is a list of some of the places in New York City that have closed over the years: A Different Light Bookshop, Oscar Wilde Bookshop, The Clit Club, Meow Mix, Crazy Nanny's, HerShe Bar, and SheScape. My one touchstone and solace is that Henrietta Hudson is still open. They celebrated twenty-five years in business in 2016 and remain the longest standing lesbian bar in New York City.

Black & White Strobe Lights

by Rebekah Weatherspoon

KC and I laugh over cheap drinks
And argue over just how far you should
Put your hand up another person's body.
It's my first time. I'm the only woman in this men's bar,
But I have black lady cred so they white boys
Welcome me.

KC leaves for the bathroom.
I eat more onion rings
And watch the guys playing pool.
One of them joins me.
He comments on how he wishes
There weren't so many Mexicans in there tonight.

I go home with that sour feeling in my stomach.
This is not a space for me.
I'll try again.

We leave work late,
But we're still early.
There's somewhere H wants to take me.
In between nondescript doors
In South Central. I'd never know how to find it.
Brown women just like me, wall to wall.

We dance all night.
Cheap drinks and a show.
Perfect music and girls so cute
I'm too afraid to approach.
I don't know who's with who.
I can't wait to go back.

But next time, it's closed.
For good.

I'll try again.

I'm not excited about this party.
The article has already come out.
There's too many straight women
Taking their bachelorette and birthday candles to this bar.
I go anyway. I'm their queer passport.
I try to dance.

That doesn't work out.
The white boy who finds me
Is on something stronger than I'd ever consider.
When he grabs my breast and yanks,
I'm done dancing for the night.
I sit. I wait. I wait some more.

Feeling pissed and violated.
I'm done with this shit. For now.
I know, I'll try again.

"How many of us are there?" J asks.
She's smiling at me.
We've just left the Tim Burton Exhibit.
It's been almost 12 years since
The summer we spent singing
Blue Swede to each other behind the circulation desk.

It's me, you and L for sure, I say.
3 out of 5 from our pre-k play group.
Queer as hell.
I glance over at her.
I don't know that I've seen her this excited before.
She's going to tell her parents finally.

We dance all night surrounded by girls like us.
J moves away. Next time she's in love
And we all eat wings.
And the next she's engaged and there's music in the park.
The next she's married.
Our family grows.

There's distance between us. GirlBar is closed,
But J&T will always be there for me
When I'm ready to try again.

F^2, S and I find the connect.
They travel miles and miles so we can do this
At least once a year, but GirlBar^2 is closed now too.
We hit the boys' bar. Get a good spot.
Dance until there's more groping by white boy hands
And a glass is spiked off my knee.

We head out into the night.
Food is a must. The dancing is done.
I won't try again until I see them again.

I finally find something permanent.
People who don't need plane tickets
And hotel rooms to see me.
We are ourselves. They get my non aesthetic
And need for very specific good times
And free parking.

We try again.
The DJ is terrible, but the dance floor is huge.
The DJ is fucking terrible.
I make it most of the night with men keeping
Their hands to themselves, but even in this
Safe space they can't manage it.

My big blackness is too much to pass up.
I look so grabbable. I look so jolly.
I look like so much fun.
Too much to leave alone.
I go home with a sore arm
And a scowl on my face.

We'll find another place
Another space.
A much better DJ.

We'll do it together.
We'll try again.

A NIGHT BEYOND THE CITY LIMITS

S. Renée Bess

"Where the heck are we going?" I asked Marie.

I'd been hesitant to take this trek, but my friend kept harping on my need to escape the funk I'd been in about Terez.

"You need to get out and enjoy yourself," Marie said.

It seemed like we'd been in Marie's car for hours. We'd driven down busy four-lane roads and passed by shopping strips and a large mall, a movie theater complex, and at least two entrances to the interstate. Acres of brightly lit commercial spaces yielded to ribbons of residential areas. Houses, some large, but mostly medium sized, with deep porches that suggested early evening beers shared with neighbors eager to trade gossip, lined our trail to a destination I'd only heard of, but never visited.

"Tell me again why we're heading so far away from the city to buy a drink and gawk at women we don't know," I said. "Are there any women of color out here?"

I knew the absence of black women wouldn't bother Marie. Two of her former girlfriends were white. A third was Asian.

Marie squinted at the road ahead of us. "Hold on. I don't want to miss the turn. It's around here somewhere."

She tightened her grip on the steering wheel as she lifted her foot off the gas pedal. "Here it is," she said. "Now, just three-quarters of a mile to go."

I gritted my teeth and looked at the darkness surrounding us. A setting like this one used to awaken my curiosity. Now, post Sandra Bland, the isolation reminded me to be on the lookout for police cars with flashing red lights. My belief in the existence of places where people just accepted each other peacefully had been dashed by cameras that bore witness to the anger bubbling from fear that was generations old.

"Marie, you've driven us to the middle of who knows

where. There aren't even street lights out here."

Marie laughed. "Don't worry, Jaie. I guarantee you'll have a good time."

"How many times have you been out here to this bar?"

"Two."

I shook my head. "Why did I let you talk me into this?"

"Probably because you're tired of sitting at home alone on a Saturday night."

"Not really," I answered. "And if I were, I could always go to Señora's or The Spot."

"The Spot?" Marie was indignant. "Now that we've vowed to never spend another dime in that place because the owner is a racist? You can go back there if you want to, sister, but I won't."

I'd forgotten about that crap and about the protests. Everything that had happened between Terez and me had given me temporary amnesia.

"I'll go to Señora's because it's the only women's bar left in town, but I won't step inside The Spot." Marie's voice slapped a stamp of finality on her pronouncement.

We approached a sharp Y in the road, and Marie steered to the right. Fifty yards or so beyond, she turned the car onto an unpaved expanse of property. A one-story building stood at the far end of the rut-filled area.

"We're here." Marie aligned her car with other ones.

I looked through the windshield at the unadorned building that faced us. "I'm not impressed."

Although the bright floodlights jutting from the eaves at either end of the building showed us the way, the structure's painted white bricks, steep cinder-block-edged steps, and decrepit Lodge No. 42 sign posted above the entrance were jarring, not welcoming.

"You have to admit parking here is better than driving to the rooftop of that vomit- and urine-infested indoor lot down the street from Señora's."

We got out of the car. Just thinking about the smells that lined both sides of the alley leading to Señora's made me hold my breath for a second longer than necessary. I exhaled and saw a thin trail of my breath rise past my nose. When I inhaled again, winter's sharp cold air stung my nostrils. I hugged the front of my peacoat and pulled it closer to my body. Carefully, I picked my way over and around the hard-edged mini-craters of soil and pebbles scattered throughout the parking area.

"This lot must be a muddy mess when it rains," I said.

"Probably," Marie said. "But breathe in this country air. No bad odors."

And no homeless people hunched against the city parking lot's street-level walls. No anonymous figures walking toward us silently as we hastened our pace to the bar's entrance. No reason to mentally run through the best way to escape a pickpocket, or worse, in case the stranger turned against us at the last second. No tug-of-war between the pangs of guilt and the feelings of self-preservation as we admitted to ourselves that we'd racially profiled one of our own.

"So how did you learn about this place?" I asked.

"A friend of a friend told me about it last summer. I was curious, so I came out here with Karen." Marie paused. "That was before Karen and I stopped seeing each other, of course."

"Of course."

"Anyway, everyone seemed friendly, especially after a couple of beers."

"How's the music?"

"The first time I was here, the Country & Western was on heavy rotation. But the second time, there was a black deejay. She mixed a lot of house music and older R&B. I picked up the deejays' schedule, so I know she's here tonight."

"Good evening, ladies."

Marie and I looked toward the top of the steps and saw a woman supervising our approach.

She held a beer bottle in one hand. Her other hand was jammed in the pocket of her unbuttoned jacket.

"Hi." Marie spoke for both of us.

The woman nodded. I figured she was the bouncer.

Short and solid, with a no-nonsense bearing, she had the physique and temperament for it. When she reached to open the door for us, the canister of Mace hooked to one side of her belt came into view. Static from a walkie-talkie on alert under the other side of her jacket buzzed through the air.

"It's Oldies Saturday. We have a two-drink minimum and, like always, no drugs and no smoking on the premises. Go on in and enjoy yourselves."

"Thanks," I said. Suddenly, I remembered I didn't know exactly where I was, or whom I might meet inside this bar.

"Do you ever need to use that Mace?" I asked her.

The woman's lips formed a half-smile. "Once in a while we get some teenagers doing a drive-by. They like to shout things, you know?" The bouncer took a swig of her beer. "They're basically harmless."

"Okay," I said and held the door open for Marie.

"If I didn't think they were harmless, I'd have my gun on my hip instead of this here can of pepper spray."

I found the woman's words as reassuring as the bar's façade was warm and welcoming. That is, not at all.

We entered a large room. The rectangular bar filled one-third of the space. Two women filling drink orders were stationed at opposite ends of the bar. The deejay's booth was really a small platform tucked into a corner. Mirrors of all shapes and sizes covered most of the wall space, and the retro sounds of an ancient Marvin Gaye mid-tempo tune bounced off those walls.

I spied an empty table with two chairs and signaled Marie that we should set up camp there.

"Go get that table and I'll get us drinks. What would you like?" Marie asked.

"I'll start with a Coke."

Marvin Gaye morphed into Diana Ross as I walked past several small groups of women. Some were young, most were older, but all the same ethnicity, and it wasn't mine and Marie's. After I sat down, I tried my best to make eye contact with the women seated closest to me. One woman answered my attempts with a smile, so I nodded and smiled back at her.

"Here you are, my dear." Marie handed me a glass of soda as she pulled out her chair and sat down. She held up her hand and gestured toward the room. "What do you think so far?"

"It's not Señora's," I answered.

"Yeah. The lighting's completely different. And the women aren't glammed up."

"And there's only three of us women of color here. You, me, and the deejay." I turned to bring this third person into clearer view.

A woman younger than we were, dressed in jeans and a

plaid flannel shirt, captained the deejay's platform. She wore her hair in long dreads tamed by a ribbon at her neckline and descending like narrow ropes down her back. She was a study in constant motion, dividing her attention between a knot of women waiting to talk with her and the twin turntables all set for her to cue Prince's "Kiss." She seemed to know the women who awaited her attention, and she acknowledged their song requests with a self-confident smile and a quick nod.

Marie moved her head and rapped on the table in time with the music. "Wanna dance?" she asked.

I touched my chest and feigned surprise. "Me? No thanks. I dance better in my head than I do with my feet."

Marie laughed.

A woman sitting at an adjoining table must have read our lips, because she came right over and extended her hand to Marie, who jumped up and glided her way to the dance floor.

I watched my friend move fluidly with her dance partner, and I began to relax. We might have been in a place that was new to me and semi-new to Marie, but it really was familiar territory. It was a place that offered us the freedom to drink, dance, laugh, fall in or out of love or lust with a woman, and not be judged for any of that. It offered us space to simply be.

David Bowie, Janet Jackson, and Drake all had their turns coaxing the dancers onto the floor before Marie came back to the table and took a long swig from her bottle of beer.

"I'm getting too old for this," she said.

"Nonsense. It looked like you were keeping up with your dance partner."

"That's because the deejay plays a lot of old stuff that I used to dance to."

The lights dimmed slightly and Bonnie Raitt's voice drew a contingent of dancers to the floor.

Marie looked at me. "So, do you miss having Terez in your life?"

I focused on a pair of dancers who held each other tightly. "I'm really not in the mood to talk about her."

Marie nodded. "I'm getting another beer. Are you ready for something stronger than Coke?"

The intimate dancers reminded me of that evening so long ago when I first saw Terez standing in the rear room of the women's bar in Allerton, where we both lived at the time.

"Yes, please." I reached in my pocket for my wallet and withdrew some money. "Could you get me a scotch, neat?"

Marie took the bills. "You got it."

Rick James's reedy voice covered Bonnie Raitt's final notes as Marie walked toward the bar.

Just then, a high-pitched female voice split the air. "Stop playing all that nigger music!"

Marie must have heard the ear-piercing command as clearly as I had. She stood stock-still for a second and then turned around and began walking back toward me.

The deejay stared at the space above the women who were closest to her small raised platform, her eyes expressionless. I imagined her lungs were depleted of air.

I stood and put on my jacket. I gathered Marie's from her chair and handed it to her as soon as she was close enough to reach for it. Without saying a word to each other, we walked toward the bar's door.

Outside it seemed twice as cold as it had been when we arrived an hour earlier.

"Leaving so soon?" the bouncer asked.

Before we could answer, we heard the squeal of tires as an old truck sped by the parking lot.

A young man's sneering face filled the space where the truck's passenger window should have been.

"Faggots! Fucking faggots!" he yelled.

"See what I mean?" the bouncer said. "They don't even know this is a women's bar. They're stupid, but harmless."

"Yup," I said. Then I gestured to the road where the truck had been seconds ago. "Why bother with those teenagers when the real harm is inside the club?"

"What? What do you mean?" the bouncer asked.

Marie and I began our trek to her car. I never stopped to explain what I meant. I just kept walking with total disregard for the parking lot's shards of broken macadam and rocks that tried to disrupt my progress.

In the days and months that followed, I did talk to Marie about that night and about that bar. I mentioned the young dread-locked deejay, and we asked each other if we should have invited her to leave the bar with us. Marie called to find out if she'd returned to her place in front of the turntables after that night. She hadn't.

I still go to Señora's now and then, because from time to time I need to hear loud throbbing music, drink overpriced scotch, and feel that particular kind of energy that only exists in lesbian-filled places. I have to admit though, whenever a deejay is in the middle of an R&B set, I still hear that bigoted woman's hard-edged voice spitting out her hateful command, and I feel a little less safe in a space that used to offer me shelter.

The Not So Good Old Days

by Penny Mickelbury

Catastrophic events—the horrible, unspeakable, mind-blowing kind—often bring people together in a strange way, especially if those events involve horrible, unspeakable, mind-blowing death. Such was the case of the terrorist hate crime perpetrated on...at...the Pulse nightclub in Orlando, Florida, on June 12, 2016. People across the nation and around the world shared a range of emotions, from shock and disbelief to pain and sadness to anger and rage.

Then came the fury: How dare this perverted son of a bitch bring his violent hatred into OUR space, the place where we enjoy ourselves and each other free from the critical judgment of the outside world! Not since Stonewall, perhaps, has such a universal sense of violation been felt. The police were the invading force that New York night—also in June—and the one word, *Stonewall*, carries a universal sense and meaning as does, and will, the word *Pulse*.

Following the initial outpouring of feelings and emotions came a second wave: Stories of fond memories of life and love in the gay clubs, the places where we "could be ourselves." I don't have many of those. My coming of age happened well in advance of the big dance club venues like Pulse. In my case it was Tracks in Washington, DC, and by the time it opened, I was well into the pursuit of a career that left me very little time or energy for dancing the night away.

During my party-till-you-drop-days, however, the bars and clubs that catered to gays generally adhered to the established and accepted social codes of the time. There were women's bars and there were men's bars, and most of them didn't welcome Blacks. In most cities, we had our own bars, but because being queer was a dangerous proposition in those days, many of those bars were located in dangerous parts of town. Fortunately for me, my coming-of-age years took place in Washington, DC, the home of the house party! We didn't need no stinking bars. The memories that warm me are of a couple dozen women dancing the night away, singing with Al Green, "Let's Stay Together," which, of course we didn't do because, after all we were twenty-something; and singing with Marvin Gaye, "Let's Get It On," which, of course we did do with great regularity because, after all, we were twenty-something.

The house party life extended up to Philadelphia, and those lasted all weekend—from after work on Friday until time to go to work on Monday. Seriously. I'm from Atlanta, born and raised, and I fled to DC right out of college, but I had never experienced anything like a Philly house party. Several residences were involved, and the party moved from house to house over the course of the weekend. There was as much eating as drinking and dancing. They did this twice a year, the Philadelphians. Even now, after the passage of more years than I'm willing to admit to, those remain some of my best memories. The warmth, the sister-and-brotherhood, the camaraderie—the absolute joy of the bodies and voices engaged in the total and complete pursuit of a good time—all took place in a house party, not in a bar or a nightclub. But people couldn't be expected to host parties in their homes every weekend, and if we wanted to enjoy ourselves in the company of others like us, the bars and clubs were the only options.

Fortunately, it didn't take long for the rapidly changing times to give birth to more and better clubs, though it would still be years before the arrival of the big dance party clubs like Pulse. I specifically recall several Capitol Hill locations— a women's bar among them—which were convenient for me because I lived in the area, within walking distance of a couple of them. We were admitted, but we weren't welcomed, and that drained all the pleasure out of the experience.

Men often experienced more blatant hostility, being required to present two or more forms of "valid" ID for admission. In the days before Homeland Security, few people had more than one form of ID (the driver's license) unless one included the work ID, which nobody would show to enter a gay bar.

Passing time brought more "progress." The larger, more-popular venues instituted special nights when specific populations would be welcome—Black nights, women's nights, and in New York in those early days, Latin nights. I found it interesting, albeit startling, that the Pulse massacre occurred on Latin night, a regular Saturday night occurrence there. I'd like to think—and I certainly hope—that Latin night at the Pulse was a nod to the significant Spanish-speaking population of Orlando rather than something more sinister, as was the case in the early days of gay club life when special admission nights were designed to control "undesirable" populations.

Many Blacks, myself included, simply stopped frequenting venues with such policies; it was embarrassing and demoralizing. We worked hard all week, too, many of us at jobs that we would have been fired from had our employers known of our homosexuality, and like everyone else, we wanted to let our hair down on the weekend, to be with each other in a place where everyone was like us.

We had a code among my women friends if we discussed planned activities on the telephone at work. The question we asked was whether we planned to attend sorority meeting on the night designated for us. "Are you going to sorority meeting" meant are you going to the bar? Eventually, however, many of us just stopped going. Though I have frequently over the intervening years shared warm, happy, did-we-really-do-that? memories with friends, I didn't, until now, wonder why those wonderful people opened their homes to us. Now I know. It was so we would have a safe place to fully enjoy being our true selves.

By the time the famed Tracks opened in DC in 1984, I wasn't much interested in club life, though the Tracks experience truly was unique. The place was so large it boasted three or four different dance areas, a video room, an outdoor volleyball court (you read that correctly), and an outdoor bar/lounge, which was my destination of choice in hot weather, of which DC had plenty.

One of the things I found most moving about the information that became public following the events at Pulse was the range of people who had gathered there that Saturday night in June. Women, men, homosexuals, bisexuals, transgendered people, and the mother of a young gay man who was there because she enjoyed hanging out and dancing with her son and his friends. Truly things have changed. But sadly, not enough.

My first mystery novel, *Keeping Secrets*, introduced investigative newspaper reporter Mimi Patterson and her lover, Police Lieutenant Gianna Maglione, head of the Hate Crimes Unit. When I created these characters, I also created the Hate Crimes Unit—the DC Police Department didn't have such a thing at the time. Of course, that changed and police departments across the country instituted some form of hate crimes investigation as governments—city, state and Federal—passed hate crimes legislation. All that notwithstanding, I fully expected that, by now, I'd no longer be able to sustain the Mimi/Gianna novels and the characters because I fully expected that we'd have moved past hatred of each other based on race, gender, sexual preference, and religion. We have not. The person who massacred forty-nine people in the Pulse nightclub on June sixteenth did so because he hated them, and he hated them because of who they loved. But what's every bit as dangerous and frightening as his hatred is his belief that he had the right to express it with violence. What's equally as dangerous and frightening is that he's not alone.

Because hatred is alive and well, I won't have to retire Mimi and Gianna after all. They'll soon appear in a new adventure. I suppose, in some perverse way, I should be pleased.

Drinking 7-Up on Bourbon Street

by Johnny Townsend

The first gay bar I ever heard of was the Upstairs Lounge. I was eleven at the time, and the images on the front page of the *Times-Picayune* seared themselves into my memory. A man looking up in horror as his friends burned to death. The right shoe and lower right leg of a man trying to back out of a window, the only parts of the poor soul not charred black. And the most horrific—the head, arms, and upper torso of a dead pastor jutting through another window where he'd died trying to escape the inferno started by an arsonist.

The article accompanying the photographs described the patrons singing around a piano when the fire started. "United we stand, divided we fall." Bodies of three of the patrons were found huddled underneath the piano.

It would be another fifteen years before I ever set foot in a gay bar myself, after my two years as seminary class president and another two years in Rome serving as a Mormon missionary. Jerry, my home teaching assignment from church, confided in me during one of my visits that he was gay. After pumping him for information for a couple of months, while never revealing my own orientation, I finally ended up spending the night. At that point, I think he figured it out. It still took me another year emerging from a homophobic religion in the homophobic South to fully come out. French Quarter gay bars helped make it possible.

Jerry and his new boyfriend took me to the Mississippi River Bottom, where they had rum and Coke and I had a 7-Up. Afterwards, we walked a few blocks toward the river and ate beignets together at the Café du Monde.

Being gay wasn't as degenerate as I thought. Maybe I should look into this some more.

I befriended a guy in my Faulkner seminar who I suspected was gay.

Dirk and I started to dance together at the Parade. The dance bar was on the second floor over another bar called the

Pub. I had flashbacks to the Upstairs Lounge photos, making sure I knew of multiple ways to escape the building. While dancing there one night, images from a porn movie flickered against the wall. I looked away, still afraid the warnings of addiction my church taught me were true. Dirk, however, happily watched as we danced along to "Brand New Lover." I never did become addicted to porn, not even after working in a porn shop, though the fact that I published porn myself and posed nude for professional photographs wouldn't have convinced my Mormon friends much.

The New Orleans gay bar scene at the time was concentrated in the Quarter, with a few other bars downriver in nearby Marigny and Bywater. Guys would buy a beer, served in a plastic go-cup, and walk from bar to bar to bar. We'd start at the Pub and then walk to Café Lafitte in Exile, back to the Pub, over to Good Friends and then Rawhide, maybe over to the Roundup, and back again. Maybe we'd venture farther to the Corner Pocket if the weather was good, but probably only if we wanted to see the male dancers on display that evening.

The lower French Quarter was a haven for gay men in the late 1980s. Rents were still affordable, and I saw the inside of many a historic building. Walking down the street one day, I heard someone call out to a female friend, "Mary!" But four gay guys turned around instead.

One Mardi Gras, when I walked along with my boyfriend Don, a man with a thick rural accent commented in astonishment to his friend, "Oh my gawd! Th'ar holding hands!" The Quarter was a place of refuge—in fact, I met another ex-Mormon at a gay piano bar, The Refuge, on Royal Street—but it was also a place where we could take a stand, even offer teaching moments to the tourists. Whenever an exhausted mule pulled a carriage down Bourbon Street for a tour, I'd grab Don and kiss him on the lips.

One time, we heard the tour guide pointing to Café Lafitte. "This is where gays go to get AIDS," he said. And then, pointing to a tiny storefront across the street where the NO/AIDS Task Force was just starting, he added, "And that's where they go to die."

The AIDS era was frightening. We watched friend after friend sicken and die, hoping against hope we'd escape.

But we were happy nonetheless, dancing to George Michael's "Faith," Madonna's "Vogue," and When in Rome's "The Promise."

The biker-looking leathermen at Jewel's chatted about Bach and Beethoven. Over at the Phoenix, another Levi/leather crowd, there might be a drag show.

During the talent portion of the Miss Upper Schwegmann Heights contest, one contestant body-slammed pizza dough. After rehearsing at St. Mark's for a show at Margaritaville, several of us from the Gay Men's Chorus would go over to the Monster for a drink before heading home.

At Big Daddy, I might speak Italian with a friend of mine who lived in the neighborhood.

Gay cast members of the "Pirates of Penzance" performing at Le Petit Theater just off Jackson Square changed one of the lines on closing night. Instead of singing, "to the ship, to the ship, to the ship," they sang "to the Mint, to the Mint, to the Mint." The Mint was a bar on the very edge of the Quarter, across the street from the old New Orleans mint that used to produce coins along with four other mints across the country.

I watched Ricky Graham perform there week after week. The day after Lucille Ball died, he did one of his impersonations. "Ethel! Ethel! Help me! I've stolen John Wayne's wings!"

Life mostly centered around the bars. Deep into the Bywater, on Louisa Street, was the Country Club. A bar with a pool and hot tub out back and plenty of space for sunbathing. The place was clothing-optional and was rented for sex parties as well. During normal operations, volleyball tournaments took place out back in the swimming pool. The jukebox played Louis Armstrong's "What a Wonderful World" and Fats Domino's "Walking to New Orleans."

The Country Club closed at midnight, and one evening, Judy, the straight bartender, went back to her apartment a few blocks away, where she was badly burned in a house fire that suffocated her kittens and boiled her goldfish. I remember visiting her in the hospital a few days later and being shocked to see that the tips of her ears were black and crispy. Judy had to wear tight elastic clothing to help reduce her scars, but she also faced the monumental task of rebuilding her life from scratch, so the bar held a fundraiser and accepted donations of furniture and household goods to help get her settled in a new place. And as soon as she was able to work again, her job was there waiting for her.

There was a warmth and camaraderie at the gay bars in New Orleans. Part of it was due to the era of advancing gay rights mixed with the horrors of AIDS. But another part of it was a result of the genuine friendliness of Southerners.

When I relocated to Seattle after Hurricane Katrina, I never found the bars there to be as welcoming. Part of that may have to do with the fact that I'm much older now and less marketable, but part of it was unquestionably cultural. New Orleans had its share of vicious queens like anywhere else, but overall, it was a friendly place to meet people for a drink or for a game of darts.

And as an ex-Mormon, I never did consume any alcohol, sticking with 7-Up every time I went to a bar, which was a lot. Bar culture may have contributed to alcoholism among some gay men, but it didn't have to.

I'm not sure what "the kids" are doing these days, but I suspect a lot of people are meeting online, and that bars are not the focal point of our lives as they once were. While I feel a certain nostalgia for those great old days in New Orleans, I think it's better that we're no longer as dependent on bars, that we're so much more accepted now that we can meet someone at a Star Trek club or a quilting bee, a political protest or a book club. We've come a long way from the time of the Upstairs Lounge, when gay men were so afraid of being fired that they couldn't even tell anyone at work they'd just lost their entire circle of friends.

We will always need bars in our lives. Even fully acculturated straight people need bars, so we certainly will, too. I only hope other people can find the comfort and affirmation today that I found in those great iconic bars of my gay youth.

THE TRUE TALE OF THE TONGUESTON TRIO—1959

by Merril Mushroom

Gay men and lesbians were friendly with each other in Florida back then. Besides having our separate social spaces, we also hung out together at times, and there were some real friendships as well as cross-dating for appearances.

The Onyx was mainly a faggot bar, a classy place with entertainment that also drew some tourist trade. There was a lesbian dance bar in an adjoining space, and we girls would often spill over from there into the Onyx to catch the show.

There usually were drag shows and some excellent comedy, and every Monday night was talent competition—open to the public—when the local queens displayed their talent (or lack of such) onstage to vie for prizes and glory, especially the glory.

Whether bad, good, or outstanding, the performances were always outrageous. The makeup of the queens was divine and their costumes spectacular, but the performers were always faggots. There never was, nor had there been, a woman in any of the shows. Penny, Connie, and I complained to one another about this. We told each other we needed a little representation on stage. After all, we bought their liquor, didn't we? We decided that what the Monday night show needed was a drag butch number, a male impersonation to balance all this drag queen stuff; and who could possibly do this better than the three of us butch numbers ourselves? No one, of course. Thus, the Tongueston Trio was born.

We really got into doing this. We discussed and rejected various performance schemes, finally settling on a heavy rock 'n' roll set that we would pantomime. We talked about costumes and decided to fancy up our usual duck's ass hairdos with pompadours and to dress alike in black pants, white shirts, black neckties, white socks, black loafers, and sunglasses. We would be fabulous! We set a date to rehearse that week at Connie's apartment then left each other to go home and learn our lyrics.

Once home, I sat down to ponder my own predicament. This little caper was going to present some problems for me. I was underage, like many of my friends, and had phony identification to get into the bars. I also lived with my parents and had a strict curfew, especially on weeknights. I was going to have to do some scheming, lying, and sneaking, and I was sure to get into trouble in the end, as usual. But I knew this would be worth it.

I escaped to Connie's apartment for rehearsal by saying I was going out to do homework and listen to records with a girlfriend. I wasn't out as a lesbian to my family at the time. I took my schoolbooks and records and, hidden in my book bag, my brother's loafers, borrowed with his consent, which I would leave at Connie's so I could wear them for the show the following Monday.

At Connie's apartment, we rehearsed and re-rehearsed our numbers, pantomiming in front of each other and before a mirror, working out our routine to perfection. We fell naturally into our parts: Connie, who was short, dark, and heavyset, did the lead; Penny, who was short, blonde and heavyset, did the low parts; and I, tall, brunette, and heavyset, did the high parts. We were swinging. We were entertaining. We were funny. And we were great! We got totally into our numbers, moving in unison, doing the synchronized stepping that was part of performing rock 'n' roll onstage. As planned, I left the loafers and records at Connie's, careful to get home on time.

Monday night finally arrived. I packed up my schoolbooks, gave the same story about girlfriends, homework, and records, and left the house. I really wanted to say, "I'll be late tonight. I'm competing in the drag show at the Onyx. Wish me luck," but I didn't dare. I was wearing a typically teen outfit—black jeans and an old white shirt of my father's, shirttail hanging out. Hidden away in my pocket were my phony I.D., my sunglasses, and Dad's thin black necktie, which I had secretly swiped that afternoon.

Safe at Connie's, I changed my sneakers for my brother's black loafers, tucked in my shirttail, and borrowed a thin black belt from Connie. I switched my spectacles for sunglasses and slicked my hair back "greaser" style, with pompadour, wingsides, and duck's ass perfectly creased down the middle. When we all had finished the dressing and doing our hair ritual, we admired one another for a while. Then we ran through our numbers one last time and, swallowing our nerves into lumps in our bellies, set out for the club, clutching the records and trying to hang onto our cools.

Word had gotten around that we were going to perform, and every lesbian in town must have showed up to cheer us on. The club was jammed. As we stumbled through the crowd on our way backstage, men and women clapped us on our backs and shoulders, wished us luck, sent us on with good feelings and a growing excitement.

The straight man who worked as lighting technician stepped in front of us. "Good for you girls. I promise I'll give you light effects that will be remembered."

We managed to push our way to the backstage door and stumbled through into stares of disbelief from the three drag queens who were waiting to compete. We barely had time to check our records in with the sound technician when we heard the emcee announce that it was "Show Time At The Onyx"; the roar of voices from the room outside faded away.

Penny, Connie, and I paced and fidgeted and tried to keep quiet, while the drag queens in turn went through their numbers. Then they were done, and it was our spot. We were on! "And now," the emcee announced, "the Onyx Room is proud to present a brand-new act—The Tongueston Trio!"

The curtains parted, and hot red-and-blue lights moved over us as we trotted onstage in perfect step, waving and smiling. Then three separate spotlights came up, one on each of us, and merged into one big spot. All the girls in the room screamed, and the faggots screamed, too, and Penny, Connie, and I bunched together, ready to start. The lights went down, all throats hushed, and out over the speakers came the opening instrumental notes of our first number, "Bad Boy" by the Jive Bombers.

Almost before we knew it, the set was over, but not the glory. We came back onstage with the three queens, while the emcee held his hand over our heads each in turn, inviting the audience to indicate by their noise which was the favorite, who would win the competition. When he came to us, faggots and lesbians screamed their throats raw and applauded until it seemed as though the club would burst at the walls from the noise. We were declared the winners.

We came off the stage and into the barroom, and people hugged us, mobbed us, bought us drinks. "You were wonderful!" they all said, and of course, we were. I pushed my way through the crowd, because toward the back I had seen Geraldine watching me with very big eyes. I liked Geraldine a lot, and I suspected that this would be a good time to ask her for a date. I smiled, keeping the excitement that was filling my belly in a careful place of its own.

Geraldine put her hand on my sleeve. "You were really great."

I moved closer to her and put one arm around her waist. "Yeah," I said, all tough butch now, "so why don't you buy me a drink to celebrate?"

"Sure." Geraldine moved slowly toward the bar, keeping within the possessive circle of my arm.

The hell with my curfew, I thought happily. This is worth being grounded for a month.

"What'll you have, star?" the bartender called. "This first one's on me."

Merril Mushroom: I am an old-timey dyke who performed at the Onyx room in 1959.

Gay Bars: A Sanctuary for All?

by Brian Heyburn

In the wake of the horrific shooting at Pulse Nightclub, and the accompanying flurry of social media posts in response, I found myself needing to retreat and to process my own emotions and reactions. In our era of sound-bite news and social media, I often find it difficult to keep pace with the speed at which news is presented to us while also taking the time and space I need to process my own emotions. A day or so later that I was finally able to get a handle on what had happened and my response to it.

A part of my processing involved a reckoning with my own experiences in gay bars and bars generally. As I continued to delve into my emotions, I realized something was keeping me from experiencing the well of sadness that I saw other LGBT people expressing in the wake of this event. Perhaps the reason I was having a hard time making a deeper connection with this event, aside from the distress I was feeling from witnessing the massacre of forty-nine fellow humans, had to do with the fact that gay bars have not always felt like a place of refuge for me as a gay disabled man.

As responses to the attack increased, much was made about gay bars as places of refuge and sanctuary for queer communities, which is true for many queer people. Gay bars serve as a space to escape the heteronormative societies and world that we inhabit, and that's important. However, I think if we are to hold ourselves accountable to all members of the LGBT community, it's critical that we consider the perspectives of those who, even within our own oppressed community, continue to live on the margins and for whom gay bars are inaccessible at best, or places of hostility towards them at worst.

For me, gay bars have rarely felt like places of refuge or sanctuary. When I show up with my cerebral palsied body, speech pattern, and movements, I'm often greeted with patronizing comments, a mocking of my movements, or outright denial of entry because the bouncer thinks I'm already drunk. In my experience, though, I have a certain level of privilege in being able to pass as nondisabled in certain circumstances because my outward appearance and the way I present myself to the world have conventional elements to them.

Because I walk this fine line between passing as nondisabled, but also exhibiting certain outwardly apparent characteristics of cerebral palsy, I present a conundrum to others who are unable to make sense of the person in front of them. The most readily available explanation is I'm intoxicated. This assumption, in which someone reads my natural embodiment as being a result of intoxication, is deeply invalidating. Lack of control due to intoxication is a state at which to hurl ridicule, or at which to gawk in disbelief, and when those responses are directed towards someone for whom those characteristics are a natural part of their being, meaning is created about others' estimation of that person and the esteem in which they are held.

For that person at whom others' reactions are directed, significant implications are made apparent about that person's place in our social order—that of something at which to gawk, less than human, or an object for others' entertainment. Indeed, it's important for disabled people to discredit these views and to refuse to let them become definitive indicators about their place in the world. However, it cannot be ignored that these perspectives exist and have an impact on disabled people in social spaces.

I'm discussing only one particular kind of prejudice towards disabled people based on my experience of bars and social settings, but there are numerous others specific to other kinds of disabilities. The difference in my speech pattern also presents difficulty when loud music, dark lighting, and commotion are present. My speech differences produce reactions in strangers in many areas of my life, but the barriers to communication are heightened in bar settings, in which it is difficult to make myself understood, on top of trying to make people take my embodiment seriously. For these reasons, gay bars haven't been the first places to which I've gone in order to seek refuge or sanctuary, due to the pervasiveness of these social conditions. It often feels like too much to deal with, and the experience is fraught with potential micro aggressions.

A feeling of disconnectedness to queer community sometimes arises because bars are relatively inaccessible for me. Certainly, there are other outlets, but as gay bars have been a prominent mainstay of queer community, it's difficult not to feel separate.

I've also had some positive and fun times in bars, gay and not. However, I think there are larger social forces at play that are creating exclusion within our community. These are in desperate need of our attention and are illuminated by the experiences of marginalized members of our community. We have a responsibility to listen to, amplify, and internalize the knowledge produced through these experiences to be sure that we offer space for the breadth of diversity that our community represents.

I've been able to access spaces that many other disabled people with different disabilities than my own can't, which points to the need for more work to be done in improving accessibility and broadening our concepts of who is to inhabit these environments. The voices and experiences of those living at marginalized intersections must be amplified and the knowledge generated from their experiences must be regarded as valuable in our efforts to create lasting change.

At A Bar
In the Morning

by Lee Lynch

Sun rays fell like cobwebs through the dusty bar window. The small room held several round Formica-topped tables between the short counter and the window. On one side of the door to the back room stood a shining new jukebox whose flashing lights made it look like a visitor from the future. On the other side of the door, garishly painted women in bathing suits posed on an old pinball machine with an Out-of-Order sign.

Sally, the bartender, skinny as a bar rail and tall, with a cap of short blonde hair, leaned over the bar on her elbows to stare past the Café Femmes window sign. She smiled to see Gabby's short, bobbing figure beyond it.

"Hah!" breathed Gabby as she pushed through the door, sounding the cowbells that hung there to warn Sally of customers.

"Hah, yourself, Junior."

Gabby protested indignantly, fists on her broad hips. "What's the matter with you that you call me Junior every morning now, Sal? I'm pushing forty like you." She took off her plaid wool jacket and climbed onto a stool, shaking her sweatshirt away from her body and her worn work pants. "Got hot out there. I'm sweating like a pig."

Sally smiled at her. "You looked like a Junior, coming past that window. Like a little kid coming home."

"After my night on the town?"

"Where'd you end up last night, Gab?"

"Here." Gabby sighed, looking bored. "Liz said it was your night off."

"What'd you do?"

"What I'd like to do more of right now, Sal."

"Ten a.m. fix coming up. By the time your unemployment runs out, you're going to be a real lush."

"Why the hell not?" Gabby downed the shot and picked

up her beer. "Hair of the dog, like they say."

Sally ran her rag over the top of the bar, picking up the circle of moisture left by Gabby's beer.

"Nobody in yet?" Gabby asked.

"You're first, as usual."

"Come on, Sal. Meg's usually here before me."

Sally stretched her long body and yawned.

"You working all day, Sal?"

"Somebody's got to keep you high."

"Thank goodness for that. Couldn't stand it otherwise."

"Can't you get into some unemployment program?"

"And do what, clean the streets? I'm not ready for that, no matter what the politicians think."

"It'd keep you away from the sauce a few hours a day."

Gabby's face closed. "Lay off me about that. This is my life."

"Sure, sure. You know I don't want you to end up like Meg. She used to be so sharp and funny. She'd come in here Fridays after work in her business suit and have a mixed drink or two."

"You know I'll get back on my feet, Sal. I'll get a job. I'll find a girl. I'll get a decent place to live. Right now, I need a vacation."

"From everything?"

"Don't you ever feel so damn tired you can't lift your head off the pillow in the morning? The only reason I get up is because there's a Café Femmes to come to. I'll get my energy back, Sal. Haven't I always before? I'm tired of falling in love, then breaking up. Finding a job, then getting canned. Making an apartment nice, then losing it along with my girl or my job. You can talk—you've got this place here."

"Which Liz and I worked damn hard for."

"At least you had the wherewithal to get what you wanted. Not everybody can own a gay business." Gabby set her glass down hard. "Let me have another setup."

As she poured, Sally said, "Liz told me Meg cadged more drinks than usual last night. She shut Meg off, but we can't do anything about people who keep buying her more."

"What could happen to an old rummy like that?"

"What happens to all the other old rummies on the street? You think she can't get sick or hurt just because she's a dyke?"

"No. Maybe. She's getting like the guys on the Bowery, isn't she?"

"One step away, Gab, that's all."

"I can't believe that."

They fell silent. The mailwoman, Jenny, pushed through the door and jangled the cowbells again. "Sounds like I'm down on the farm when I come in here. How are you today, Sally? Gab? Where's Meg?"

"I don't know," Sally said. "We were just talking about her. You see her around, tell her to drop in, okay? Want a shot?"

"Love it, honey, but that's all I need to do—get caught smelling of it. I'll take another raincheck?"

"Sure, sure, anytime." Sally sorted through her mail. "We'll see you later, right?"

"Could be—it's Thursday!" The door slammed behind Jenny, rattling the bell. Thursdays, Sally and Liz extended happy hour.

Gabby rose, took her beer, and wandered to the pinball machine. "Friday's a lousy day to look for a job, too, you know."

"Any day's bad for you from what I see."

"Really, Sal. Friday, the bosses are looking to sail their boats, not   start someone new. Especially not someone who looks like me."

"How you look doesn't matter with the kind of jobs you're after."

"It shouldn't." Gabby pushed aside the Out-of-Order sign and put a quarter in the machine. "You haven't fixed this yet?"

"The repairman's supposed to come today."

"One stinking ball for a quarter."

"Keeps you on your toes. You need to do really well on one quarter. Here, take some replacements." She spilled some coins onto the bar.

"No. Never mind. I'm not in the mood. Too much work."

She watched Gabby walk to the window.

Gabby spoke toward the empty street. "You know how many damn girls I thought I'd be with forever? Five. Five damn girls. Maybe it's me. When it comes to making it work, I don't have what it takes. Falling in love is fine. I have that down pat. But when love starts to be an uphill battle, all I seem to be able to do is take off. Unless they leave me first. If only I could keep a job. Or if we could adopt kids—that would make us work to stay together. Even if we had families who'd get upset about us splitting, it would help. We come down here, and what is there? A bunch of chicks looking to make it with somebody, no matter who or who it'll hurt. And like a damn fool I, can't resist them. It's so easy to cheat on your girl. Plus, when you're high? You don't give a rip. Until she finds out. So why try settling down? What's the sense?"

Sally was dusting the bottles behind the bar. "Love has its good points." She thought of Liz coming home that morning and slipping naked into bed with her.

"And jobs. I'm not smart. I'm not good looking. I can't get a job in an office because I look too much like a dyke to fit in. I can't get a job in a factory for anything but minimum wage because I'm too small, too much a woman to do men's work. I used to give my all to get ahead in a job, but I never had what it took. Going at top speed on piecework earns me enough for a few more beers and a sore back. I tried everywhere. And I know I'll get something eventually, some crappy job at the end of a subway line. But who wants it?"

"So, you drink."

"Why the hell not," Gabby said again, returning to her stool. "How about I go across the street and get us burgers? Might as well make myself useful somewhere."

"Sounds good to me."

"No sign of Meg out there."

"Why don't you stop at her place on your way to lunch?"

"Where's she live?"

"Around the corner. One-thirty-six. Top floor."

"That flea trap?"

"At this point, she's lucky to have that. One of her old lovers helps with the rent."

Gabby shook her head. "Wow. I didn't know she was that broke. Just give me a beer this time. Then I'll take off. Maybe she'll show up while I drink it. How high is this top floor?"

"Only five."

"Shit. That's a long haul."

They sat watching the bright street outside the window. The sun had moved overhead, and its light no longer reached them. Passersby would see two figures inside, shadowy and still. Only the bottles shone in the mirror behind them.

"Sally!" cried Jenny the mailwoman as she flung open the door. The cowbells thudded only once and tonelessly.

"Is it Meg?" Sally asked, knowing in her gut that it was.

"Is it ever. They found her early this morning. She fell down the stairs."

"All the way from the top?" Gabby asked, her voice filled with horror.

"She must have stumbled into the bannister. It collapsed and she fell to the fourth floor."

Sally was hustling out from behind the bar. "Is she—"

"She's not dead. Weak as she is, the neighbor said she was alive when the ambulance took her." Jenny's laugh came out bitter. "You can keep us down, shut us up, make us hide all our lives, but we're damn tough to get rid of. She was asking for a drink when they put her on the gurney."

"A drink," Sally said. "Sometimes I hate this business."

"I better go visit her." Gabby headed for the door. "See if there's anything she needs."

"Could need a lot," Jenny said.

Sally grunted. "Don't we all."

"She's at St. Vinny's," Jenny said. "I'll go over when I finish at work. You want to go with me, Sal?"

"Definitely. How about that hamburger, Junior? Before you run out on me."

Gabby stopped as if Sally had yanked on a harness. "Sorry, Sal. You're stuck in here. I'll bring it right back."

Jenny stared after her. "I haven't seen Gabby move that fast in months."

Smiling, Sally said, "It's sure nice to see her all lit up about something. It's the wakeup call she needs."

Jenny gathered up her mailbag. "I'll come by for you, Sal."

"About four?"

Several minutes later, Gabby rushed in and slid the burger along the bar's polished top to Sally. "See ya!"

Sally ate in short-lived peace and quiet. Why did the kids continue to buy Meg drinks? It was cruel.

Once more the cowbells made their jaunty, raucous sound, as four women and a large pizza crowded through the doorway.

"Hi, ladies!" Sally set up glasses for four beers.

"Want some pizza, Sal?"

"Thanks, no." She accepted their money. "Gabby brought me a burger."

"Yeah," another woman said as she fought to control a string of mozzarella. "I was looking for her. Where's Meg?"

"Well," Sally answered slowly, smiling. "Meg's had a fall. But Gabby's on her way now."

This story originally appeared in Common Lives/Lesbian Lives *and in a collection of my stories entitled* Old Dyke Tales *from Naiad Press.*

The Bathroom Line

by Joan Nestle

Dedicated to the lesbians of the fifties

We had rituals, too, back in the old days, rituals born out of our lesbian time and place, the geography of the fifties. The Sea Colony, a working-class lesbian bar in New York City's Greenwich Village whose world I was a part of from the late fifties until the mid-sixties, was a world of ritual display—deep dances of lesbian want, lesbian adventuring, lesbian bonding. We who lived there knew the steps. It was over forty years ago, but I can still peer into the smoke-filled room, feel the pressure of bodies, look for the wanted face to float up out of the haze into the circle of light, sense the tumult of recognition.

"I wondered how long it would take you to come here." The teacher welcomes her adoring student and then retreats into the woman-made mist.

Because we lived in the underworld of the Sea Colony, we were surrounded by the nets of the society that hated us and yet wanted our money. Mafia nets, clean-up New York nets, vice-squad nets. We needed the lesbian air of the Sea Colony to breathe the life we couldn't breathe anywhere else, those of us who wanted to see women dance, make love, wear shirts and pants.

Here, and in other bars like this one, we found each other and the space to be a sexually powerful butch-femme community. We entered their nets with rage, with need, and with strength. The physical nets were visible, and we knew how to sidestep them, to slip by, just as we knew, holding hands in the street, clearly butch-femme couples, which groups of straights to stay away from, which cars flashed danger as they slowed down at the curb.

We knew how to move quickly. We had the images of smashed faces clear in our memories: our lovers, our friends who had not moved quickly enough. It was the other nets, the nets of the righteous people, the ones that reached into our minds, that most threatened our breathing. These nets carried twisted in their invisible windings the words *hate yourself because you are a freak, hate yourself because you use your tongue, hate yourself because you look butch and femme, hate yourself because you are sexual.*

The powers of the mainland controlled our world in some obvious ways. The cops would come in to check their nets, get their payoffs, joke with the men who stood by the door. They would poke their heads into the back room to make sure we weren't dancing together, a crime for which we could be arrested. Of course, the manager had flashed the red light ten minutes before the cops arrived to warn us to play our parts. We did, sitting quietly at the square tables as the cops looked us over. But if they had looked closer, they would have seen hands clenched under the tables, femmes holding on to the belts of their butches, saying through the touch of their fingers: *Don't let their power, their swagger, their leer, goad you into battle. We will lose, and they will take pleasure in our pain, in our blood.*

But the most searing reminder of our colonized world was the bathroom line. Now I know it stands for all the pain and glory of my time, and I carry that line and the women who endured it deep within me. Because we were labeled deviants, our bathroom habits had to be watched. Only one woman at a time was allowed into the toilet because we couldn't be trusted. Thus the toilet line was born, a twisting horizon of lesbian women waiting for permission to urinate, to shit.

The line flowed past the far wall, the bar, the front-room tables, and reached into the back room. Guarding the entrance to the toilet was a short, square, handsome butch woman, the same one every night, whose job it was to twist around her hand our allotted amount of toilet paper. She was one of us, an obscenity, doing the man's tricks so we could breathe.

The line awaited all of us every night, and we developed a line act. We joked, we cruised, we commented on the length of time one of us took, we made special pleas to allow hot-and-heavy lovers in together, knowing full well that our lady wouldn't permit it. I stood, a femme, loving the women on either side of me, loving my comrades for their style, the power of their stance, the hair hitting the collar, the thrown-out hip, the hand encircling the beer can. Our eyes played the line, subtle touches, gentle shyness woven under the blaring jokes, the music, the surveillance. We lived on that line; restricted and judged, we took deep breaths and played.

But buried deep in our endurance was our fury. That line was practice and theory seared into one. We wove our freedoms, our culture, around their obstacles of hatred, but we also paid our price. Every time I took the fistful of toilet paper, I swore eventual liberation. It would be, however, liberation with a memory.

Serendipity

by Ian Cassidy

For a whole lot of reasons, my first time probably doesn't count. To begin with, I didn't even make it inside, only getting as far as a table on the beach-side balcony. Next, it was more a restaurant than a bar and what disqualifies it most of all from being a real virginity-taking experience is the fact that I was with my dad and my little sister.

On that early Friday afternoon, the beach at La Jolla was pre-weekend packed, and it seemed everyone had finished work early that day. My sister, Daisy, and I were playing in the surf, struggling with a boogie board Dad bought us soon after we landed at San Diego International.

Dad was close by on the hot sand, looking out for the notorious rip tide, but probably more worried by the unexpected responsibility of looking after us without the help of a more reliable adult. He made the occasional foray into the water, checked on us, and returned to his beach towel. He was a very poor instructor, but he had an excuse. He is English and the chances to learn to surf are few and far between on that side of the pond. Uncle Fred was the surfer, but he was at work. The university apparently couldn't spare him even though we could only manage to spend a week in Mom's old country.

Mom was out shopping with Aunt Mary, but they weren't shopping for anything frivolous and wildly expensive in the high-end boutiques of San Diego or LA. Aunt Mary had taken her sister bargain hunting at the Vons on the edge of town. Always a "blue light special" obsessive, she planned a weekend of trawling for cut-price tat. She had lived in California for twenty years, but she spent less time browsing the bling on Rodeo Drive than my Mom, who had lived in England for almost the same amount of time

Back on the beach, Dad waded waist deep into the surf. "I'm going to that restaurant to get us some Cokes," he bellowed as the waves splashed over him. "Don't stay out here too long or your drinks will get warm."

He strode out of the water and headed up the beach, damp Speedos clinging. He wore Speedos even when his beer belly should have told him to send them to the thrift shop. He always contrived to have just a little too much cock on display.

He strode across the bar's porch with the seawater still glistening through the hair on his chest and his still wet Speedos hintingly transparent.

On into the bar itself he advanced only to discover a packed room completely untroubled by females. His grand swashbuckling entrance caused quite a stir; who was this milky-coloured, hairy-chested exhibitionist?

He quickly realised he had picked the wrong venue for a Coke with the kids, but his progress was too far advanced to allow him to do an abrupt about-face. He was too polite and too English to walk out so obviously. His confident stride vanished away and slowly he made it to the bar where he uncomfortably ordered a beer and two Cokes, whilst trying hard not to catch anybody's eye. Drinks in hand, he sidled out to a table on the balcony where he sat on the edge of his seat, looking out to sea.

His relief when Daisy and I arrived five minutes later, covered in sand, complaining of sunburn, and braying for Cokes, was palpable. He drew us to him in a quite uncharacteristic public show of affection. The guys at the next table smiled and one of them asked, "On holiday?"

"Yes, staying with the wife's family, in Del Mar, up in the canyon."

"I know it, lovely spot."

"You're from across the pond."

"That's right, but my wife's American, from way upstate, Fortuna."

"How'd she meet an Englishman?"

That was it, Dad was away. He had another beer, bought a round for the guys, and soon he was holding court, flirting outrageously with the lithe young men, who once they had noted our presence and accepted on what side his bread was buttered, were happy to laugh and joke with a brash, generous Englishman.

My second time was a mistake also, but a happy mistake.

Serendipity, you might even call it.

We were trawling Soho, celebrating the end of our exams, three ingenues at sea in the capital, blinded by the bright lights, suckered by the prospect of sin. Well, the other two were. I oscillated between apprehension and downright terror. I was dreading winding up at a strip show, but most of all, I didn't want my companions to know I was dreading it.

We had a drink or two in some of London's less salubrious establishments, and then with the drink making its way south to their loins, my friends could resist the call of the "Live Sex" signs no longer. We were too naïve to realise that the "sex" on offer was nothing of the sort. These dingy clip joints offered nothing. My friends picked one and plunged through the door. I held back, but I couldn't think of an excuse, so slowly I followed, praying that something would save me: maybe the doormen would turn us away, or the police would pick now to raid the place.

I was in luck; my friends bumped into me as they made a hasty exit. I didn't have to thank a belligerent bouncer or the Metropolitan Police for my salvation, just the good old avarice of Soho's club owners; the prices were simply too rich for our blood.

"Let's have a drink next door."

We didn't know we were entering one of Soho's most famous gay bars.

And what a night to do it!

The underground bar was staging the after-screening party following the English premiere of *Last Exit to Brooklyn,* quite a coup for a Soho pub. We stumbled upon the aftermath; the complimentary booze was gone and only a few curling sandwiches remained. A scattering of the cast still mingled. Production assistants handed out sepia stills of Jennifer Jason Leigh, and Alexis Arquette stood by the bar.

We hovered on the edge of the party, looking at stills and the publicity packs. A production assistant in the shortest skirt and the sheerest black tights started chatting to my friends. I looked on. I only had eyes for her legs. I wasn't going straight; I wanted to look like she did.

I noticed what sort of bar it was; I relaxed and got tense at the same time. I was excited, a bit drunk, a bit sweaty, and a bit naïve.

I was shyly chatting to a nice publicity co-ordinator from Fresno when one of my friends poked me in the back; "Drink up, we're leaving."

"Why? What's up?"

"It's a fucking gay bar."

"So what?"

"I want a piss and I'm not going here."

"Oh grow up. Go and have a pee and we'll move on."

Grumbling, he left in the direction of the lavatories.

A minute later, the other one rushed up; "Hold hands with me."

"What."

"I've just told the big bloke at the bar that we're an item so he'd leave me alone."

"Oh, please." I apologised to the guy from Fresno and held my friend's sweaty hand as we walked up the stairs to the street.

Two nights later I went back, alone. And so it began.

Masquerade

by Angela Garrigan

In a narrow, dimly lit street in the heart of Liverpool, there once stood a small, dimly lit club. I first walked through its doors in 1981 and entered a world that I'd been looking for all my life. This club became the centre of my universe, and I loved it.

I was impressed by its location. There it was in the city centre, hidden in plain sight. It would be entirely accurate to say that some unfortunate souls have spent the best part of an evening searching for the front door, not all of them searching from the outside.

After I located it, I had to find a way to gain admission. I stared at the scuffed black paint until I spotted a small black bell. A man trying very hard to look comfortable in a tuxedo opened the door, signed me in, relieved me of my fifty pence admission, and tipped his head toward a flight of stone steps. In the dim light it looked like the threadbare carpet running down the centre was probably once red. The double doors at the bottom swung open.

Welcome to the Masquerade.

More or less square, the room had a few pillars supporting the ceiling and the occasional drunk. Tables were scattered around the pillars and the perimeter of the dance floor, which was impossibly small. A glistening disco ball fought hard to overcome the muted lighting.

I settled myself on one of the two bar stools and ordered a drink from Steve, a beautiful gay man who wore sparkling spandex and stunning make-up. It wasn't yet ten thirty, and we had the place to ourselves. I nipped into the toilets and ran a comb through my short but unruly hair and checked myself in the mirror. Faded jeans, white shirt, black jacket. Not bad. This could be my lucky night; you never know. I think I have the look; all I need now is the nerve.

Back on my bar stool, I sipped my beer and tried to appear cool. I hoped that the beer would drown the butterflies churning around in my stomach. I watched as the rest of the hopefuls, and a few of the hopeless, ambled in. I nodded to one or two women that looked my way. They didn't nod back so I sipped my beer instead.

Once the pubs closed, the place filled up fast. The DJ turned up the music, and a few of the men took to the floor, shirts off. The dykes weren't far behind as they took their partners, or someone else's, for a dance. They kept their shirts on, although one or two looked tempted.

It was a mixed crowd. A group of butch women eyed up a few femmes. The S&M dykes looked mean and moody, and a group of feminists tried to keep their eye rolling to a minimum. As I turned back to my drink, I noticed a newcomer saunter over to the bar. She ordered a pint and turned to face the crowd. She looked and waited and so did I.

She drained her second pint and looked my way. She raised her eyebrows and nodded toward the dance floor. I returned the non-verbal communication with a frown and a shake of my head. She got the message and ordered another drink. I might have said yes, if she'd asked, but a nod and a wink?

She finished her third pint and made her move. I couldn't believe my eyes. She swaggered across the club, and it looked like she was asking one of the butches to dance. A ripple of disbelief seemed to run through the group. She got turned down. She moved to the next woman. A shake of the head. She went through the whole bunch. No one accepted her invitation. She returned to the bar completely unaware of the stir that she'd created. She downed another pint and headed toward the rest of the crowd. I lost track of her, but I bet she was hitting on every woman in the place. I caught sight of her leaving with a tall woman wearing beads. Maybe I should have danced with her. Oh well.

A couple of straight women sat huddled together, sniggering. Everyone knows who they are and what they want. Word got around. They want a dyke to make a pass at them just so they can cause a scene. No one went near them, and as the night went, on they struggled to hide their disappointment.

The club got hot and smoky. Harry, he's the owner, glided around the tables as if he was on wheels, a tray of curled-up sandwiches held high. Big Bertha was in her corner selling her wares. She's pretty good at the sleight of hand, but everyone knew what she was passing.

My bar stool provided me with a great vantage point, and I continued to survey the crowd. There was Shazza, swaying at the other end of the bar. She'd been carrying a torch for a woman for nearly two years. Unfortunately, the woman of her dreams thinks that Shazza is a nightmare, so she drinks. She picked up a pint in each hand and headed back to her table.

She tripped and landed face down, arms outstretched, and the pints of beer only lost their froth. She got to her feet and shot me a triumphant grin. I raised my glass and smiled back. I couldn't help it.

One woman thinks she's Elvis. That's one helluva quiff. She has a very unusual way of trying to impress women. Only last week she was barred from a pub for biting a piece out of a pint glass. Maybe the bar snacks were lousy.

The small woman walking through the door is the local Robin Hood. She's a shoplifter who specialises in children's wear. Don't ask me why. She said she hardly ever gets caught because they don't see her behind the rails. One of the advantages of being four foot eight.

I noticed a couple sitting near the dance floor, holding hands, staring into each other's eyes. They got up together and headed into the toilets. I realised that I needed to go too. I crossed the club and went in. From my cubicle, I heard the unmistakable sounds of sex. I smiled to myself and wished it was me in there, before I realised that they probably have no place to go to be with each other. I sighed as I washed my hands and left.

As I ordered another drink, a fight broke out on the dance floor. The gay boys scattered and the dykes whaled on each other. Within seconds the bouncers broke it up and ejected the combatants. I sipped my beer and wondered why it always seemed to be the dykes that started fights.

It looked like I'd be heading home alone again. Maybe I should put a bit of effort into this, instead of sitting there like a wallflower. If I'm honest with myself, I kind of admired the tenacity of that woman who asked everyone to dance. Next time, I promised, next time.

I sipped my beer, and as I put the glass on the bar, the

DJ played one of my favourite songs. This is it, I'm going in. I headed toward the dance floor and threw myself into the music. I danced at the Masquerade on my own but surrounded by my kind. It's crowded, everyone's bumping into everyone else. Someone behind snaked her arms around my waist and squeezed just a little. I couldn't turn to see who it was. She was gone. The song ended and I drifted back to my seat.

I looked around the club once more. That was when I saw her. She was leaning against one of the pillars staring straight at me. I stared back. She was tall; well, taller than me. Her short, black hair framed a face that looked like it enjoyed its fair share of mischief. She walked slowly toward me. I liked the way she moved. She stood right in front of me. She had a twinkle in her eye. I seemed to have lost the ability to speak. She kept staring at me. She held out her hand and I took it. We left the club.

Many clubs and bars have come and gone in my life since then, but it is the Masquerade that I carry in my heart. There, I found safety and adventure. There, I found myself.

Club Music Taught Me

by Mercedes Lewis

Like Sylvester, "I Who Have Nothing" will stand proud.
Like LaBelle, I am a Nightbird, free to fly in the moonlight.
Like Donna, I am "Hot Stuff."
"I Love Music."
It's okay to "Le Freak" here, because I am not the only one.
These are "Good Times," subject to leave me with a "Love
Hangover."
You can "Ring My Bell" as we bask in "The Glow of Love."
Take me to "Funkytown" "That's Where the Happy People
Go" and
"Keep On Dancing."
"Don't Stop Til You Get Enough," there is no "Shame."

Harvey Milk, "Don't Leave Me This Way," we cried.
You did say these were "Risky Changes" but let your
"Young Hearts Run Free," you were a "Hot Shot,"
they wanted "Romeo and Juliet" Acts 1 & 2
it gave them "Vertigo," but "You Make Me Feel, Mighty Real."
They hired the "Devil's Gun."
You were "The Boss," and because of you
"I Will Survive."

I Caught One

by Nahshon Anderson Fuentes

This is my journey through thunderstorms and tears of joy, over the rainbow from the West Coast to the East Coast, and a few of the characters I met along my transition.

In the mid-90s, my older brother, Lee, was beaming with joy. You would have thought he'd won the lottery as he proudly displayed unflattering photographs of his girlfriend, Damonica, to our family. Months later, my grandmother received a phone call from Damonica, who was barking, foaming at the mouth, and probably needed a dozen rabies shots. She dished out all of hers and my brother's grime. She excavated the dirt as if she were in a landfill and included the fact that she was born with testicles and not ovaries.

Lee claimed he didn't know Damonica's birth gender.

I'm sure when Grandma Betty received the phone call, her blood pressure shot through the roof. I never heard her curse, but when speaking of Damonica, she referred to her as the "bitch."

Luckily, my family wasn't vengeful or ignorant. No one cared about Damonica's rant. However, she did become the source of a fabulous family giggle.

At the same time, my teenaged hormones were erupting like a volcano. I was obsessed with cruising and trolling malls, parks, bathrooms, gay clubs like Nardis and Encounters in Pasadena, X-rated theaters, and alleys in Los Angeles. My goal was to have anonymous trysts with men. On one occasion, when I was in West Hollywood at Circus of Books, I met Aaron, an older male who befriended me and introduced me to the shady, razor-sharp, dramatic, Black gay club scene.

While I was in high school and just sixteen years old, I assumed the legal privileges that any twenty-one-year-old would have. My brother, Lee, allowed me to use his California-state-issued ID. He would always say, "Just 'cause you gay, don't ever let no man beat on you."

I began frequenting hole-in-the-wall bars with Aaron, like The Study on Hollywood's Western Avenue. It was usually full of older black men playing pool, sizing each other up, and blowing smoke up each other's asses. I found my tribe and became friends with Rick, who loved to snap his fingers, and Alberto, both from Pasadena. They were very fashionable gay guys, both older than me, but not yet twenty-one. We could often be found in Rick's black Jetta, gossiping on our way to shopping and club hopping at venues like the Catch One disco.

The Catch One, owned by a lesbian named Jewel Thais-Williams, was in Los Angeles on Pico Boulevard and Crenshaw in Korea Town. A clandestine club with blacked-out windows, dark doors more appropriate for a castle, and grand stairs fit for a queen, it was the oldest Black gay club in Los Angeles and in the area where I resided with my Afro-Latin family members, the Fuentes.

There was a time when the Catch's top floor mysteriously turned into a furnace. Jewel pointed the finger of blame at business people who were gentrifying the area, although an official cause was never determined. Forced to close for two years to rebuild, Jewel was defiant in the face of those who, according to her, wanted her out.

The Catch One was like a carnival for me, and I became a regular patron during mid-spring of 1995. On Fridays and Saturdays, I spritzed my body with Giorgio Armani's Aqua Di Giorno cologne. I knew to don my best boyish outfits and be prepared to stand in a line that sometimes wrapped around the block, as I waited to be frisked by the security guards, 14k and Deborah, for weapons. Inside, I was shell-shocked to view black masculine and muscular men who were searching for love from each other. While liquor flowed freely and elbows often hit my rib cage, our bodies gyrated under strobe lights and a lone disco ball at the center of two of its seven rooms. If they were lucky, the patrons may have been dancing next to Madonna, Janet, or Sharon Stone, as they were often guests.

We knew it was the last call for alcohol when house music like, "Walk for Me," "Turn Me Out," "100% Pure Love," "Up and Down and Inside Out," pumped through the speakers and made our eardrums beat faster than our hearts. With the change in beats, the dance floor often parted like the Red Sea. The masculine men, aka trade, hated it! With the extra room, the queens commenced to show their colors like peacocks. They sashayed with hands on their hips, and their arms and legs flailed as if they were experiencing a million seizures accompanied by unintelligible sounds like animals in the jungle. They called it *vogueing*. The floor became their catwalk as they glided by dressed in their imaginary million-dollar couture gowns and posed as if the paparazzi were taking photographs and screaming, "Ru, Naomi, Tyra, Iman, Beverley!"

On Sundays, I lounged in Griffith Park as the latest Hip Hop and R&B music wafted through the air from Black and Latin gay men showing off their cars and sharply sculpted physiques. As bottles were secretly passed around, chatter ensued and people became excited at the sight of R&B singer Tevin Campbell cruising around in his silver Land Cruiser.

Near sundown, I made my rounds at The Study, and in the evening I attended the Catch One, where I was entertained by the roaring, evocative, Panamanian Drag Queen, Diva Extraordinaire, Ebony Lane. She reminded me of Li'l Richard when she hosted her Leading Ladies Review with performers Rene Deveraux, Ms. Tyra Bell Principal, Fila Masters, Fontasia Lamour, and the legendary Mother Rose. Ebony could often be heard shouting, "Go in, catch it, you're a late lady." She commanded the stage in opulent floor-length gowns, a veritable Miss Universe, with her hand out waiting for dollars. Often she ended up on the floor, flailing like a drunken person drowning.

Once glass began shattering, the wise ones knew to exit early, unless they were interested in watching, and possibly becoming a part of, a wrestling match as the last tunes played and wigs hit the ceiling. By the end of the night, someone was always offended and would don boxing gloves and emerge with a face full of Vaseline.

As the evening closed, some patrons were making wedding plans, drenched in euphoria and sweat. Others left wearing handcuffs and black eyes. Some naïve *clubbers* would have to sprint like track stars to their cars, and a few often had an uninvited guest follow them home and rob them. Still restless, large groups of us would head east to Beverly

Hills to Larry Parker's restaurant. We would gossip and *Kiki* about the night's events till just about sunrise.

When entering the club and purchasing liquor (which was rare), I was bewildered why no one ever questioned my real age. I didn't look any older than eighteen. Had a club employee zoomed in on the ID in my possession, surely they would have known I was not the male in the photo. Some club patrons weren't fooled. In dealing with men, my confidence usually soared through the roof and my aggressiveness turned some off. One night while cruising around the club, I noticed an older male. I don't recall how I introduced myself, but he shot me down rather quickly, when he barked, "You're searching for a daddy and I'm not him!" I felt like running from him, dissolving in a puddle of tears, and sitting alone in a corner.

In early summer, temperatures rose, and folks began riding around with their convertible tops down. The Black gay community was preparing to celebrate the upcoming weekend, ATB on the beach in Malibu at Point Dume. The week turned somber during the Fourth of July. We were mourning the loss of our lesbian sister and R&B legend, Ms. Phyllis Hyman. She committed suicide by overdosing on pentobarbital and secobarbital in the bedroom of her New York City apartment.

She left a note which stated, "I'm tired. I'm tired. Those of you that I love know who you are. May God bless you." Instead of celebrating her forty-sixth birthday the following week, she was memorialized. I was too young to know how legendary Ms. Hyman was. I could tell she was loved by how highly people spoke of her.

With HIV/AIDS still a taboo subject in the Black community, we suffered tremendously. That weekend, Jamaica Carter hosted a benefit for HIV/AIDS causes and Cee Cee Bloom performed as Ms. Hyman. It also seemed like every weekend there was a new benefit, fundraiser, funeral, or scam (as some children claimed) for an individual with HIV/AIDS.

After I received my high school diploma, my school friends urged me to apply to California State University, Los Angeles. My application was accepted by the university along with that of my high school classmate, Jay. We resided in the same apartment on campus. While I was busy neglecting my studies and enjoying the gay club scene, I often had friends over. That rattled Jay's and our roommate's nerves. At the time, I didn't realize that my friends enjoyed visiting frequently in order to gawk at my roommates in their boxers.

After attending class for two semesters in 1997, I put my higher education on hold to pursue a career in entertainment. That summer, I discovered Buena Vista Television would soon be producing a new TV show with the comedian Keenen Ivory Wayans. I conducted research and sent in my resume to the production office. Within months, I was a production assistant on *The Keenen Ivory Wayans* late night talk show.

When I was nineteen, in 1998, I rented my first apartment in Studio City, California. It was five minutes from The Lodge, a gay club on Lankershim that I would frequent on Thursday nights. The Lodge was rare. No one ever fought. Its patrons were mainly white men and a few Blacks and Latinos.

After residing in Studio City for nine months, I was evicted. To my rescue came Mr. Baker, an older, snappy queen, who worked in entertainment, and published a shoddy Black gay magazine, *SBC*. He opened up his home to me and hired me as his full-time assistant. I often watched him guzzle brandy like air as he ranted about his failed acting career. Mr. Baker resided conveniently near Crenshaw and Pico, which meant that I could crawl to the Catch One disco. It was nice to return there now that the cancerous gray clouds had finally disappeared. California had banned smoking in public places.

I often frequented the clubs with my best friend, Tory, who was a makeup artist. Even though we had the same taste in men, it didn't prevent our friendship from blossoming. We usually swapped stories about who were potential mates and which ones we should avoid like the plague. When not clubbing, Tory would often dust my face, transforming me into a beauty queen, and unleashing the shy woman inside me. Tory also encouraged me to crash an audition with him. I found myself cast as a principal in a Nintendo TV commercial and thanked him a million times.

After six months at Mr. Baker's, I relocated. In the Spring of 1999, I began living in a studio at 740 S. Detroit Street, which was in the mid-Wilshire area known for the La Brea

Tar Pits. I was pursuing a career in acting and modeling, and at Mr. Baker's urging, joined the Screen Actors Guild. An older gay male lived in the house to my left. To my right was the sexy smooth talker, Ivan Daniels, who, with his lover Ron, promoted a club called First Fridays. In my apartment building, I had a neighbor Lori, who was Caucasian, lesbian, and a massage therapist. She always greeted me with a smile while she had her massage table in tow.

About this time, I met my first transgender friend, Jody Ray. She was from Berkeley, California, and had relocated to Los Angeles in the mid-80s. Jody's exotic looks often caused people to stop, gasp, stare, and photograph her. She relished that. She survived in the artistic circuit of fame seekers by performing in numerous plays and reading her poetry to an enthralled audience at Green Circle Theatre on Fairfax Avenue. However, in spite of her many talents, Hollywood never auditioned her. We used to converse for hours on the phone, till sunrise. Jody provided me with giggles and gossip for a lifetime. She also taught me how to seduce men. Under her robust influence, I began cross-dressing and slowly weened myself from gay clubs.

In April, thanks to Mr. Baker, I popped champagne bottles on my twenty-first birthday. I then became proud to use my own ID at the clubs, as I no longer had to walk on egg shells when entering. On Friday nights, I sashayed west five minutes on Wilshire Avenue to the El Rey Club, where the Boy Trade Girl Trade was hosted. I often saw dancers, actors, models, and choreographers like Frank Gaston, director Billie Woodruff, celebrity makeup artist Eric Foreman, Eric Farell, and others I knew who worked in entertainment or who were trying to steal the spotlight.

When I returned, I could always count on seeing familiar smiles from my past at the Catch, like my older cousin Rita, a lesbian, and in 2000, Jermaine, my former high school and college roommate who reminded me of Olive Oyl. Although I always suspected he was gay, he was comfortable in the dark where hangers resided. It didn't matter to me at the time, as he had always been very supportive. We hadn't spoken in a few years, and he invited me to his graduation. I watched Jermaine in his cap and gown, surrounded by his family and friends who were overwhelmed with jubilation. While he was receiving his degree, my heart smiled and turned to stone and acid at the same time, because I wasn't gracing the stage. However, that wasn't anything the Catch couldn't temporarily cure.

I was drawn back to the carnival where I heard, "The next performer, Ms. Damonica." I almost squeezed my beer bottle transforming it into a mosaic. Damonica was the transgender individual who had once phoned my grandma regarding my brother, Lee, with whom she had a relationship. Realizing I was finally going to see the person who had been whispered about for years amongst my family made me feel like I was at a Michael Jackson concert. That's how thrilled I was. I had always heard about Damonica, but I wasn't sure what to look for. She slowly made her way to the stage and attempted to dance as she lip-synched. Her neck was in a brace. That didn't surprise me as I was sure there were plenty of folks who attempted to break it due to her legendary theatrics. After the curtains closed and the entire drag show ended, I made sure to wait around to introduce myself to her with the hopes of getting the scoop on her and my brother's tumultuous relationship.

When Damonica exited the performer's room, she was dressed in jeans and T-shirt, an outfit far from the semi glamour she had just presented onstage. Her ratted wig or weave should have been retired years prior. As her body shook and wobbled, I approached her like a fan and said, "Hi, I'm Nahshon. Years ago you used to date my brother, Lee."

She popped her lips and quickly placed her hands on her hips and replied, "Oh, you a girl!" At first I wasn't sure how to respond. Then I quickly realized she was being catty because I was feminine. She quizzed, "That's your brother?" She then started rummaging through her bag. I backed up hoping she wasn't going to slash me. She pulled out a photo album as we stood under the dim light and began to show me flicks of her and my brother from years prior. Of course I had a dozen questions. When I attempted to turn the pages, she slammed the album shut and left silently as I gnashed my teeth and knew Grandma Betty was right. Damonica was a bitch!

I left speechless and was more convinced than ever that my brother knew Damonica's birth gender. In my eyes, she wasn't passable, no matter how much tape she tucked with.

However, the judgment lies in the eyes of the beholder.

Jamaica Carter told me that Damonica wore the neck brace because one night in 1993, after Catch One closed for the evening, Damonica wanted to entertain the local residents. So she continued her performance on Pico Boulevard as the cars kept zipping by. In search of her stage, she climbed on top of a compact car's hood in high heels without breaking a nail. Terry, who had been drinking, was behind the wheel, and the car slowly started moving. Damonica blew kisses and waved at folks on the sidewalk. They cheered her on like she was a beauty queen wearing a million-dollar tiara as she rode in a parade.

For reasons unknown, Terry sped up. Damonica flew off the hood and tumbled. She landed with a twisted neck in the middle of the street. Terry fled the scene. Jamaica consoled her while she lay motionless. She was taken to Cedars Sinai Hospital and arrived there with no ID. Damonica was in a coma for five months, and after that, her life was never the same. She had slurred speech due to a medically necessary tracheotomy.

During a Saturday night in the Spring of 2001, I went fishing at the carnival as usual. Within an hour or two of making my usual rounds of licking my lips and scanning the regulars at the Catch, I noticed an older male dressed in a brown suit and a fancy hat. Black gay men from Los Angeles weren't usually dressed like him, so I knew he was from out of town. He was tall, dark, thick, and mature. I made my way near him and flirted, and his eyes lit up.

The next morning, Dan and I woke up in my bed and he had to prepare for a flight back to Brooklyn. After tons of long phone conversations, I knew I finally *caught one* and desired to visit him.

As the seasons changed, my joy turned desolate. In August of 2001, when the world was mourning the loss of the beautiful, angelic, R&B Diva Aaliyah, in a Bahamas plane crash, the Los Angeles Black and Latino gay community was mourning the loss of three of her crew members: hair stylist Eric Foreman, wardrobe stylist Anthony Dodd, and makeup artist Chris Maldonado. They had just finished filming a video for "Rock Da Boat," from Aaliyah's hit album. I knew them from my TV production career and had often danced with them at clubs. Eric Foreman's funeral was held at First AME church. I attended the funeral, and that was the first time I glimpsed so many members of the LGBT community come together outside of the Catch One to celebrate the life of one our members.

The weeping continued on the morning of the terror attack in New York on September 11, 2001. I was biting my nails and praying to Yahweh that Dan wasn't injured. I knew his office was located in Manhattan, but I wasn't sure where. All was well when I heard his soothing voice, and he reassured me that his office wasn't near the affected area.

Weeks after 9/11, I flew to New York just in time for Halloween. Dan and I attended the Halloween parade and club Octagon. After a taste of New York, I knew I had to have more of the Big Apple and Dan. Even before I left, I gave my thirty-day notice to relocate to New York.

Very reserved, quiet, and stable financially and emotionally, Dan was a professional of Caribbean descent. My first friendship with an older, discreet male blossomed, and he began spoiling me. He was a breath of fresh air, as most men I'd been meeting in Black gay clubs were very anti-fem as well as catty, cruel, and relentlessly competitive. They always came for me, and I rarely sent for them. Dan didn't attempt to control my behavior or gender expressions. He was also very comforting and encouraging, as well as a great listener whenever I poured my bleeding heart out to him regarding unrequited love. I felt safe with him.

In February of 2002, I relocated to Brooklyn, New York, near the old Navy Yard. I slept on Dan's couch. He treated me with a lot of affection and attention, unlike any other man had. He gave me a tour of Brooklyn and schooled me on the seedy things that took place in Fort Green Park after sundown, explaining why so many used condoms were strewn around. He also walked me through Prospect Park. We were lucky to make it out. Some didn't and were often found stabbed to death, waiting to be identified in the morgue.

Dan introduced me to the Two Potato club and Chi Chi's in the Village where he played pool. On Thursdays, in Brooklyn, I made sure to have enough money for cocktails and strippers at Langston's. I would cruise for twenty min-utes from Dan's home to gawk at black men in G-strings sweating as if in a sauna, with baby oil dripping to the ground and swinging around the club.

I loved and lived to be entertained by male strippers. I often ventured to Stella's, a gay male hustler strip club, located in a low-ceiling basement on West 47th Street. You could go there to enjoy sexy go-go dancers, have a drink, and feel a little scandalous (and if you tipped enough, maybe feel a little skin, too). It shut down due to the redevelopment of the Times Square district. I then realized that I couldn't cope in New York due to my social anxiety and complications from post-traumatic stress disorder, so I bid my farewells to Dan, and returned to Hollywood.

After bouncing around Southern California, in 2006 I settled in West Hollywood, aka Boys Town. On Monday and Friday nights, I religiously trekked to Club 7969 aka Peanuts. I could strut five minutes to the club, this time in heels, skirts, and my face beat for the gods! There I made my foray into the transgender community.

Transgender friends, like the performer Ms. Kiwi, taught me how to shave when we were booked to dance for Sheryl Crow while she sang "There Goes The Neighborhood" on the 1999 American Music Awards show. Muffin, who has since passed, Jaguar, and Jazzmun would always greet me with open arms and dish me the scoop on which men to avoid.

You could often find me pinching my nose due to the excessive perfume T-girls bathed in and fanning myself due to hot flashes. With the abundance of sexy men inside the club and those parked outside waiting to spoil us, I never had to walk home.

The music stopped playing in November, just for a night, when we mourned our fallen transgender brothers and sisters at the annual Transgender Day of Remembrance event. I attended my first one in West Hollywood.

After cross-dressing for years and fighting the urge to further feminize myself, I began conducting more research as well as speaking with other transwomen regarding transitioning. I believed I wanted to live full time as a woman. So, in 2007, I slowly began undergoing laser hair removal. I traveled hundreds of miles via Greyhound Bus to Tijuana, Mexico, to have Dr. Molina inject black market silicone into my buttocks. I took intramuscular female_hormones that left my skin red, swollen, itchy, and tender and forced me to spend hours sitting in the sauna and steam room.

The further I transitioned from male to female, the more members of the transgender community I met, which meant there was always a new narrative to hear and "T" for me to spill and dish. I was unprepared for the challenges I would have to deal with regarding my new gender identity. I took solace in knowing that I wasn't the only transgender in my family. The real reason Grandma Betty was so pissed off at Damonica was that she may have brought back memories of my Grandfather, Private Milton Lee Ratcliff, who had white male lovers and enjoyed entertaining dressed as a woman.

Always in search of entertainment over the years, I longed to get another glimpse of Damonica's act and to see her at Peanuts. I was stunned when I heard her performance career had ended. Damonica, aka Bling-Bling, had passed away from unknown causes. Her family misgendered her in life, and when she died, they buried her as Ricky. Damonica's demise meant I would never know the full extent of her relationship with my brother. To this day, Lee professes to be heterosexual, as do so many men that date, hate, fall in love with us, and take our breath and life away.

Lesbian Bars in Los Angeles in the 1960s-70s

by Ardy Tibby

I want to memorialize the lesbian bars that I knew and went to during the 1960s and into the 1970s in the southwestern area of Los Angeles, because they were the foundations of lesbian life and culture then.

A lot of drinking (mercifully I got sober along the way) and dancing and socializing went on. That period featured softball teams and pool teams and camping trips and shows, usually fundraisers for someone who had to move, been fired or injured, or who was in strife. Even though most activities were at the weekends, you could go there at any time and find companionship, even if only from the barmaid. The bars offered beer and passion. They offered sanctuary. We found belonging.

You could ask any taxi driver in any medium or large city to take you to a lesbian bar and they would, sometimes asking if you wanted them to come back at closing time to pick you up. Immediately upon meeting a woman you suspected might be lesbian, mutual questions about cities lived in/visited, followed by the names of bars/lounges frequented there would establish a connection.

I loved that time and those places. I love myself at that time. But it's so far back in time it's almost folk tale or a myth. But it was real. And I was there.

In 1963/4 I was twenty-two years old. I had just figured out I was a lesbian and was taken out dancing by a lesbian couple I'd met, to The Starlight Room on Vermont in south LA. I started going there often, made friends (still too shy to try sex with anyone), went to other bars with them, and started getting acquainted with gay life.

Here are some generalizations about those bars then. All had beer, twenty-five cents a glass, one dollar a pitcher; some had wine, but I never saw anyone drinking it; some had booze. A pool table was a constant feature. The bars were usually located in out-of-the-way places like industrial, isolated, or remote areas or not-too-well-off neighborhoods, or easy-to-miss facades. All were dimly lit and smelled stale and exciting. Some of the smaller ones were owned by lesbians, but most by straight investors/landlords/shady characters. All the bars were bastions and upholders of butch/femme traditions.

The Starlight had a female bouncer at the door who looked you over (refusing you if you had on jeans, which were considered work clothes), took an entrance fee, and made sure bar patrons behaved themselves inside. A male bouncer in the parking lot kept women safe when they went back to their cars.

Inside, a longish bar had ten or twelve stools along it, usually with men and straight couples sitting there. A large archway led into the "big room" on the right with a dangly, clacky, beaded curtain, and only women could go in there. Most women wore slacks of some sort (zipper front or side were code for butch or femme), some wore dresses or skirts. Other codes were white socks for butches and pinky rings for all.

Through the beaded curtain there was a big dance floor with tables and chairs around the edges and a huge, brightly lit juke box. And there you were in lesbian heaven. Waitresses brought drinks to the tables so you didn't have to go to the bar. Lighting was very dim. Everyone put quarters in the juke box, and it might take hours for your song to come up. Women sat at the tables or stood at the edges, and an important butch might lean against the juke box. A pool table stood in the far back.

The Candle Room was so small it didn't even have a pool table. It had absolutely nothing to recommend it, except it was where lesbians went. A lesbian who frequented that place sang beautifully to the jukebox. Her specialty was Dinah Washington. We all went quiet when she sang, many of us cried, and she was bought more beers than any human being could possibly drink.

The Club on Western Avenue in Gardena had a burned-out neon sign and sat between a laundromat and a lumberyard. It became my home bar. A straight couple who lived upstairs with their kids owned it. Eventually the woman came out with one of our most attractive butches.

Men weren't allowed to approach the women unless the women invited them, which usually only happened when friendly gay boys or men in drag would come in. When a straight couple—"tourists"— would come in, we "gay gals" would pick one of us to ask the woman to dance, and if she did, the couple was allowed to stay. Often the women would return on their own.

I met my first great love, Cecilia, at The Club. She came on a week night dressed in red slacks, white shirt, and red V-neck pullover. She approached me saying, "What is this song on the juke box?" I said, "It's 'People' by Barbra Streisand. It became our song. It was 1963 and we stayed together until I broke us up in 1971.

The Merry-Go-Round was a very large bar with a medium-size dance floor, a huge number of tables and chairs around the outside, and two pool tables off to the side. While most of the bars I went to were usually white and working class, there were equal numbers of Latina and black women at the "Go-Round." Every Saturday night was like New Year's Eve. Sounds of music, laughing, singing, talking, shouting, arguing, dancing, snapping of fingers rolled around inside and out the door.

Bev's in the Valley was owned by Beverly, who'd been a drummer in the women's bands, especially Ina Rae Hutton's, which was famous from the mid 1930s into the 1950s. Her band was even on TV in the early days and featured lots of lesbians. Bev's was considered a "classy" place.

Scotty's was on the Beach Walk in Venice and was grotty, steamy, murky, and gritty with damp beach sand. It was pretty mixed, but mostly lesbian. Cops frequented it looking for drugs, but really wanted sex with gay men.

The Venetian Room and The Que Sera were both in Long Beach. The Venetian Room was the only bar that was raided while I was in it. A magnificent butch shoved me out the back door in time not to get caught because she knew I was a school teacher.

The Que Sera often had small bands or singers, most notably a very young and wild Melissa Etheridge. Several of the bars had live music at the weekends, usually a duo or trio of lesbians often wearing satin long-sleeve or fluffy tuxedo shirts. We adored them. We followed them from bar to bar, and when the bars closed, we'd converge on somebody's house and close the door to party and dance till dawn.

Some other places were located in Pasadena and in Orange County, but I've forgotten the names, as well as a few others dotted about. These were the ones we went to frequently enough to be known and to know others. Often they were small drag bars.

In the early 1970s, The Blue Fox opened on Artesia Boulevard in Redondo. It was large, with ninety-five percent lesbians, and featured disco music. Dee was my best friend then, and we practiced dancing together so we could strut our stuff and make a good impression. Later, in San Pedro, there was the Diamond Horseshoe that had Thursday dyke night to which they'd allow men in drag, but not butchy women.

The Palms in West Hollywood was a kind of dress-up bar and outlasted most of the rest.

In the early 1970s the bars I went to were more the disco bars, and by 1975, the community I identified with became the newly emerging political one. I moved quickly—within a year—from being a closeted, bar dyke, school teacher to becoming a radical, lesbian activist. My life changed focus, and I rarely went to the bars. It didn't feel like home anymore.

What became home for me were the places of community, cultural, political activism like the Gay Community Services Center, the Alcoholism Center for Women, and the Women's Building with all the dances, marches, demos, meetings, ideas, ideals, and exuberance. So, in my mid 30s, my life moved from being centered in dark secret places into a world we were making our own, out in the open.

But I do not forget the dear faces in those places of my first lesbian belonging.

The Long Walk Home

by Katharine E. K. Duckett

The Carousel II, Knoxville, Tennessee, 2004

I go to a gay club for the first time on my eighteenth birthday. My mom drops my friends and me off in her minivan outside the Carousel II, the reincarnation of a club she herself used to dance at in the '80s. We sneak some peach schnapps in the bushes outside and then enter the grimy, glorious playground that is the Carousel, with its sweaty dancing pit and its smokers crowding the roof and the sticky floors of its perpetually filthy bathrooms.

In East Tennessee in the mid-'00s, it was a revelation to see so many queer people together, out and open. The diversity in age and color and background of the people around us spoke to the fact that there weren't many other places to go. This was a haven for all of us, even if we might not want to see what the place looked like with the lights on. The only other sanctuary my friends and I had was the Tennessee Valley Unitarian Church, which hosted a gay youth group once a month. My friends and I ran around the church building after hours, making out, setting bras on fire in the parking lot (less as a political protest than as a form of bored mischief), and feeling secure in our weirdness and our queerness in a way we never did in school or at the mall or anywhere else in our conservative Southern city.

A few years after my friends and I went to college, a man from my hometown walked into that church on a Sunday during a youth theater performance and pumped shells from a 12-gauge shotgun into the crowd, killing two people. After his arrest, he told officers he wanted to kill all liberals, especially gays. He knew where to find us: in the spaces where we felt safest.

Diva's, Northampton, Massachusetts, 2006

It's my first year of college, and I'm at Diva's, the gay nightclub where KJ Morris, a victim of the Orlando massacre, used to perform drag as "Daddy K." I'm with a group of girls from my hall in the dorms. We're the "Queer Hall," one of the specialty housing options we could select on our college housing forms. I grew up in the South, and the campus of Hampshire College and the streets of Northampton seem like a wonderland to me.

Western Massachusetts is filled with queer people, with lesbian couples holding hands, with transgender people and non-binary people and people who are defying what mainstream America tells them they should be in a million big and little ways. At Diva's, I sing Spice Girls karaoke with the girls from my hall, and I return throughout the years for drag shows and drunken nights, for some light lesbian drama and hardcore dance-offs with my friends. I'm disabled—a genetic joint condition gives me a limp and awkward, stilted   movements—but the darkness, the flashing lights, give me a confidence I don't always feel in less chaotic environments. Here, a stumble can be disguised as a stylish swerve; here, the thumping bass often beats the throb of my deep-down bone pain, distracting me long enough to throw myself into the crowd without worrying about the next time I'll have to withdraw to sit down.

The thing about Diva's, though, is that it's on the edge of town, not on the relatively welcoming main drag in Noho. We always took a car from campus to the club, so I never thought much about the isolation, but over the years, I heard about people getting harassed on their way back to their cars and apartments. It didn't surprise me. The radius around every queer nightclub I've known is a danger zone, an unprotected area where people can prey on us when we're drunk, when it's late, when they know where we'll be. That's always been the most perilous part of going out to a gay club—the long walk home.

Or at least that's what I used to think. Call it naïve, but in all that time at Diva's, dancing among my friends, I never thought about someone who wanted to hurt us just coming in the door.

Real, Almaty, Kazakhstan, 2011

Our friend Sasha takes us down an alley to an unmarked door. Gay clubs in Almaty open and then shut down all the time, and the key to their survival is usually staying under the radar. The bouncer lets us into the warehouse-like space, and I enter along with my friends, a group of queer Peace Corps volunteers who have remained in varying degrees of in-the-closet during our time in Kazakhstan.

I'm nearing the end of my two years in the country, and I'm not officially out to anyone in my village, though I think some of them are beginning to suspect my "boyfriend," is a myth. I made him up so that the teachers at my school will stop trying to get me to marry their sons. Before I broke up with my long-distance girlfriend, I had to pretend she was a cousin, a friend, a sister, when someone came up behind me unexpectedly when I was Skyping with her. I had to use public Internet cafés for my first year in the country, which it turns out is not the best way to keep your lesbian relationship under wraps.

This club, so like the other clubs I've known from New York to Northampton, is thrilling. Onstage, a drag queen dressed as Shakira, flanked by two young Uzbek men in vests, is scaling scaffolding to perform a lofty dance routine. On the floor, people of all the many ethnicities of Central Asia are dancing, drinking, laughing under the strobe lights, downing vodka, and making out. Two lesbians start a traditional Kazakh dance, complete with hand flourishes, as the music of gay pop idols thrums through the club.

We dance, we drink, we laugh, and for the first time since I left the U.S. two years ago, I feel like I can finally be myself in a public space. In a majority-Muslim country, in a largely conservative culture, my friends and I have found our people, and it turns out gay clubs across the globe share the same language.

Shakira is joined by Cher, and Tina Turner, and many others, until all the drag queens form a kick line above the flaming sparklers and the waving rainbow flags on the stage. I'm ecstatic, as is everyone around me. Outside, on the streets, all of us would be in danger if we kissed. If we held hands. If we blurred the lines of gender. But here, inside our club, we are free. The pulse echoes from here to cities across the world, through basements and dive bars and multi-level discotheques, and we all dance, sweaty and sure, to variations on the same sweet beat.

In the Cards

by Rachel E. Bailey

One Night

"Hmmm."

Camela put down the next card and I held my breath. But only after demanding, "Hmmm? What does *that* mean?"

Biting her lip and making the scrunched-up annoyed-face she always made, at least since *I've* known her—since we were four, and she'd punched me in the arm for stealing her Ken doll and forcing him to marry my He-Man action figure— Camela didn't even glance at me while shushing me with a wave of her elegant, be-ringed hand.

"If you give me a hot second, I'll be able to tell you what *hmmm* means, love." She waved her hand over the cards already laid out in what she called a Celtic Cross and blew her blonde, rainbow-streaked bangs out of her eyes. "Okay...the Lovers card, in conjunction with the Devil card *here*"—she pointed to the two aforementioned cards—"indicates that you will meet and fall in love with a handsome stranger—"

"Who happens to be Satan?"

Now, Camela glanced up at me, annoyed. "No. Not Satan, dunce. You don't even believe in Satan. Or the Goddess. Or anything else, for that matter. In fact—" She paused in the middle of placing another card in the spread. "Remind me why I'm giving you, of all people, a reading in the first place."

I crossed my arms over my chest and pulled a lofty sort of face. "Because I'm curious."

"You mean desperate?"

I squared my shoulders and stared her down for long moments. Of course, she won. She always won our stare-downs, to say nothing of our arguments. "I mean curious. You do readings for all our friends, but never for me, and curiosity finally got the better of me."

Camela's eyebrows shot up under her bangs. "Love, I do readings for you all the time, you're just never there when I do them. And curiosity, I can work with. Curiosity is the first step to enlightenment."

"And enlightenment is the first step to bullshit." I rolled my eyes but smiled at the same time she did. A moment later, she laid down the next card. It was a crazy-looking thing, on which coins seemed to be a theme.

"That's interesting."

"Dare I ask why? Will Satan and I be moving in together? Adopting ShihTzus, perhaps?"

Camela rolled her eyes again. "For your edu-tainment, smart-ass, Nine of Pentacles—in conjunction with two Major Arcana cards, The Lovers and The Devil—means that you're going to meet this dark, handsome, wealthy—"

"Now he's wealthy, too? Satan's got it goin' on!"

"—stranger and he'll sweep you off your feet. Literally."

"Literally? Like, Rhett Butler and Scarlett O'Hara-style, sweeping me up into his arms and carrying me up the mile-long staircase—"

"Okay, maybe not *literally*. But, yeah, kind of literally."

"You keep using that word. I don't think it means what you think it means," I muttered, and Camela smacked the side of my head.

"Ow!"

"You deserved that, douche. Okay, so yeah. Dark, handsome, wealthy. Very into you."

"Would that be literally, too? Because I wouldn't be averse to some dark, handsome guy getting very into me sometime very soon," I said, aiming for lascivious, but ending up sounding pathetic instead. Camela and I shared a look of total commiseration.

It'd been a while for us both.

"Well, according to the cards, it's going to happen for you, at least. And pretty soon. Within the next week, I'd say. Maybe sooner." Camela frowned, and she placed down another card. Her eyes lit up and she squealed, tapping the picture thereon—a brightly rendered star took up most of the card—with one long, black-lacquered nail.

"The Star," she said happily. She licked her lips and blew a bubble with her purple gum. I rolled my eyes.

"Meaning he'll be famous?"

"Nope. Meaning that he—Mr. Dark, Handsome, and

Wealthy—will help guide you to where you need to be."
Camela sat back proudly and stared at her spread like a
mother gazing down at an extraordinary child.

She snatched up her glass of Sangria and took a gigantic
slurp. "Yep. The cards have spoken. You're for it, love. Mr.
Right is coming your way, and fast."

I made a face and wished I could believe her, but I
remembered that I didn't believe in...well, anything, really.

"Hopefully he'll be coming along slowly enough that I can
lose five pounds before he knocks on my door. Or fifty-five." I
sighed and ran my hands over the mini-keg that I had in place
of a six pack. The less said about the rest of me, the better.
"Do another reading," I commanded, and Camela's eyebrows
shot up again. "Tell me the odds of me looking halfway
attractive sometime in the near future."

Camela made *that* face. The one that meant she was
about to cover my hand with her own and actually call me by
my first name—something she almost never did. It was
always "love" or "babe" or "honey." Or—more often as we'd
gotten older and less careful of each other's jaded feelings—
"douche."

"Damien, honey." She sighed, and her hand was cool and
gentle on my own. "You *are* attractive. And more than just
halfway. You're a total hottie."

I snorted and pulled my hand away. The last thing I wanted
was pity, even if it was nattied up as compassion. The fact was,
Camela had always been gorgeous. She'd never had an awkward
stage, let alone one that'd lasted from twelve, till...well, whenever
mine decided to end. "Maybe on opposite day. On another planet.
That's in another dimension. Where geeky, big-boned guys who
are *not* software moguls are considered a catch."

Camela bit her lip again, her big blue eyes round and
stricken, sympathetic. "The cards," she began to say brightly.
But I grabbed my Sangria and stood up, not at all steadily and
not meeting her kindly gaze. It was unbearable to be pitied by
one's lifelong bestie.

"Let's forget about the cards for tonight, huh? It's Friday
night, and I don't have to be back at that viper-pit I call a job
for another two-and-a-half days. I want to party!"

Camela sighed. "You? Party? Is there a *Firefly* marathon
on that I don't know about?"

"No." I drew my dignity up around me like a cloak and flopped on the couch. "First off, the marathon isn't till Sunday afternoon. Read *TV Guide* and learn yourself some knowledge. Second, I mean I want to *go out* to party. To a club, or a place where people drink overpriced alcoholic beverages and shake their asses to shitty house music."

"That sounds like a club, alright," Camela said tentatively, looking confused, now. "But you hate clubs. Whenever I want to go to one, you whine for, like, ever about having to come with me as my pseudo-date."

"That's because you pick skeevy clubs to go to."

"No, I pick clubs that will let us in," Camela said primly, and I opened my mouth to contradict her...only to close it.

"You make a good point." I took another healthy sip of my Sangria as she sat daintily next to me. "Okay, so what's the least skeevy club you know of that we can actually get into?"

"Gay or mixed?"

"Does it matter?"

"If *I* want to maybe meet *my* Mr. Right, too, it does."

I glanced at her, surprised when I realized she wasn't joking. "You really think I'm going to meet this dark, handsome, wealthy, non-Satan guy, don't you?"

"Possibly even as soon as tonight." She glanced back at me and smiled. "Honey, it's practically fated."

"I don't believe in fate," I said automatically, but I shivered when I said it, like Donald Duck watusied over my grave.

"Doesn't matter. Fate believes in *you*, love." Camela winked. I shivered again and gulped my Sangria.

Later That Night...

I sat in a corner booth of Lenape Landing's most mainstream gay and lesbian club, nursed a tequila shooter, and played with the light fob on my TARDIS keychain—a rollicking game of *How Many Times Can I Shine This Directly Into My Eye Before I Go Blind?*—for about forty minutes. My head ached, I was bored, and the table—the entire booth—was sticky. I was certain when I stood up to leave I'd find the soles of my shoes stuck to the floor.

Not to mention that I'd have to get my clothes dry-cleaned before I was satisfied they were wearable again.

Whose damn idea was this clubbing thing, anyway? I asked myself miserably.

I looked up at the dance floor. When the crowd shifted a little, I got glimpses of Camela's frantically flinging body and wild, rainbow hair as she danced with whoever would dance with her, guy or girl. She looked kinetic and sexy, and I knew I wasn't the only one staring enviously, if not lustfully. Not that I wanted to be Camela, but if I had been a guy version of Camela—or at least a hotter version of myself—that would've been pretty neat.

I rubbed my eyes. The damned contacts, which I never wore, were starting to irritate them, and my vision was all wonky, anyway, because of the flashing lights and fake smoke. Why on Earth had I wanted to go clubbing? I hated clubs, gay or otherwise. They weren't for chubby, pathetic, geeky, non-white guys like me.

They never had been.

"This place blows," I told my keychain as I flicked the light on and off. On and off. On and—

"Tell me about it," a voice said. Startled, I found myself looking up and up...and up a little more.

A tall, insanely good-looking guy in a brown leather jacket that was worth more than I made in a month, was leaning over the top of the booth seat from the other side. He was grinning the most gorgeous grin I'd ever seen. The kind that only years of braces and dental appointments could possibly produce. He had slicked-back dark hair, eyes the color of melting milk chocolate, and a jawline like Scott "Cyclops" Summers, as illustrated by the late, great Jack Kirby...it was that fucking perfect a jawline. The rest of his face was a photographer's dream: aquiline nose; full, sensual mouth; cheekbones so high that 747s must have crashed into them on a daily basis.

Holy moly, but this guy was staring at my keychain. More specifically, at the TARDIS light fob on it.

"Wow," he said, his milk-chocolate eyes lighting up as they met mine, twinkling like brown dwarf stars...or maybe The Star. "Is that a miniature Time and Relative Dimension in Space replica?"

I blinked and my jaw dropped—literally—to my collarbone.

"Yes, yes it is," I said. The guy's grin widened, and he stepped around the booth. (The rest of his outfit was easily worth more than the leather jacket, if I was any judge. And I wasn't, not really, but even I could spot expensive duds when I saw them.)

Then I was holding out my warm, sweaty hand for shaking, and it got engulfed in the guy's big hand, which was warm, but not overly so, like mine. And it was dry, too. Big hands equals big feet, and big feet equals big other stuff, too! Not that I even have a chance *of finding out what else is big on him, but still, I can dream, can*'t I?

"I don't mean to be forward, but just based on that keychain, you're the most interesting person in this place," the guy said. He held my hand a bit longer than was necessary while I blinked up at him again, like some village's missing idiot. "And I wanted to introduce myself before someone else came along and monopolized your time."

"Me? Time? Monopolize? Someone else?" I stammered then stopped myself before I repeated his entire sentence back at him completely out of order. I tried on a nonchalant laugh that merely sounded fake and creepy. "I mean...yeah, 'cuz...that was happening, just a little while ago. Just, uh, nonstop, with the monopolizing of my time. It was like, 'No, guys, back off...just go away...you're monopolizing me.'" I laughed again. And to my absolute horror, I hiccupped in the middle of it.

The guy's eyebrows quirked just a bit, but he didn't stop grinning. Nor did he let go of my hand.

"The name's Jason. Jason Cambion."

I tried to grin and was glad when I didn't hiccup, this time. Damned Sangria. "And I'm Damien Camb—I mean Foster! Damien Foster." By that time, I was vermillion, but thankfully, blushes didn't show up on my complexion. Much.

"May I join you?" Jason slid into the booth, still holding my hand. My eyes felt like saucers. Like ball bearings about to fall out of their...ball bearing-holder.

"Yeah, sure, um." I looked out at the dance floor but couldn't see Camela anymore. Ah, well. Turning back to Jason, I tried on another smile. This one felt more natural.

I've been told my smile is quite nice, so I turned it on full force. "I could do with some company."

Jason returned my smile and my hand, but only reluctantly for the latter, and it wouldn't stop tingling.

And I couldn't stop staring at it till Jason cleared his throat and laughed. But it wasn't a mean laugh. It seemed like he was laughing with me rather than at me, even though I wasn't actually laughing.

Though, after a few seconds, I did wind up chuckling.

"You're awfully cute to be sitting in a place like this alone," he said, under the beat and boom of the shitty house music, and I blushed again. "I mean, I noticed you before, with that girl with the rainbow hair, and I thought you were a nice couple."

There was a question in that last statement, and I shook my head fervently. "No. She and I are friends and roomies. Nothing more. I, uh, like g-guys," I stuttered, trying not to put too fine a point on it. Jason grinned and leaned closer.

"What a coincidence," he murmured. His hand covered mine on the sticky, gross table. His eyes were almost hypnotic, the way they held my gaze. "So do I."

I was so red, complexion be damned, he had to see it. "Okay, I'm not really good at reading people, but...are you f-flirting with me, Mr. Cambion?"

"Shamelessly."

I was blinking and gaping again. "Uh...why?"

Now, Jason was the one to blink, as if no one had ever asked him that before, and I, for one, was quite mortified that I had. But it just slipped out. "Why? Why am I *flirting* with you?"

"Well, yeah..." It was too late to take it back; may as well own it. "Why me?"

Jason sighed, but he was still smiling a bit. "So, I see an adorable guy, by himself, playing with a TARDIS keychain, in a club that's got a surprising dearth of personality and I say to myself, 'Jason'—I call myself Jason—'Jason,' I say, 'grow a pair and go over. Introduce yourself. See if he really likes *Doctor Who*, or if that keychain was a gift from some well-meaning friend.' And so, I nonchalantly ambled over."

Jason shook his head a bit wryly and glanced up at the flashing, twirling lights in the rafters. "Heard you making the

TARDIS sound and whistling the *Doctor Who* theme song and thought: 'Okay, Jason, talk to him before the so-called ambience of this place scares him off. *Allons-y.*'"

Melted-chocolate eyes met my own once more. "Was I right to nonchalantly amble over, or should I have kept nursing my Sapporo and eating my heart out?"

I couldn't quite believe that he was interested in me, of all people, but I found myself smiling for real again. I couldn't not smile, looking at him. He was easily the most beautiful man I'd ever seen, and he was a big geek!

He was seemingly perfect. And he was interested in me. Which made me wonder...what was wrong with him?

It could be anything, I thought with almost detached fascination. He could just be neurotic and annoying, or he could have bodies buried in his mother's backyard. He could run the gamut from mild crazy to full-on Ted Bundy psychopathy, for all I knew.

But whatever it was, no sane guy who was this hot could want anything to do with me, right? I mean, as fucked in the head as that kind of thinking was, it made a certain kind of sense.

Why would a perfect ten settle for a five, at best?

I wasn't sure it was in my best interest to find out. And I opened my mouth to say just that, ready to slide out of the booth, grab Camela, and make tracks.

What came out of my mouth was, "What other sci-fi do you like?"

Jason's returning smile was slow and warm, like heated honey.

"I'm probably dating myself when I say *Babylon 5* is one of my favorite shows of all time." And he looked down, laughing a little. But I found myself turning my hand under his so that I was grasping his hand, and he looked up at me questioningly.

"Will you marry me?" I asked, and he laughed again, squeezing my hand, little knowing that, in that moment, I was serious.

In that moment, he could've killed six orphans with a rusty metal spork right in front of me and I would've turned a blind eye.

A Few Hours After That...

"...then Ronny pointed and said, 'Shit, Abilene is five hundred miles that-a-way.' And he started running."

Jason finished his story with a flourish, laughing, and I joined him. I took a sip of my hot cocoa and blushed as he watched me with those melty-chocolate eyes. Then he glanced down at his cappuccino. Around us, the mostly empty café was silent, but for the melancholy strains of some Chopin nocturne or other.

"Okay, I've told you my life story," he said. "Now you tell me something about yourself, Damien Foster. Are you originally from Lenape Landing?"

He turned my hand over, palm up, and continued stroking the underside of my wrist, where my pulse beat.

"Yep. Born and raised. I'm distantly related on my father's side to the duBarres—you know, *the* duBarres— *and* the original Lenape tribe, like so many mutts in the Landing." I snorted. "But my mom was from Pittsburgh."

Jason's face was solemn when I chanced a look at it. "Was?"

"She passed away when I was nineteen."

"I'm so sorry." Jason squeezed my hand, and I smiled, though it felt a bit wooden.

"She was sick. By the time she passed on, I think she was glad to go." And I was glad, she went, glad her pain was over. Even though her death nearly killed me, it was for the best. "Anyway, abrupt change of subject. I want to hear more about you, Mr. Cambion. I'm boring," I added when Jason began to protest. "Tell me what brings you to Lenape Landing. Business or pleasure?"

"Business, of a sort," Jason said a bit evasively. "Personal business. Something I've been putting off for a long time." With a distinctly charming smile, he squeezed my hand again. "Another abrupt subject change—are you seeing anyone, Damien Foster of Lenape Landing?"

Filing away the evasiveness for later consideration, I found myself blushing yet again. I could only imagine the blood was getting sick of rushing to my face. "Me? Seeing someone? Uh, no."

Jason eyed me curiously. "You say that like it's a foregone

conclusion that you wouldn't be."

"It kind of is."

"I don't see how it could be. I can't imagine you don't have guys pounding down your door," Jason said simply, sincerely, and I shook my head, bemused.

"Are you for real, Jason Cambion?" He looked so confused, I laughed a little uncomfortably. "Never mind. No, I'm not seeing anyone."

Jason looked down and swallowed visibly, as if nervous for some reason. Then he looked back up at me. "Would you like to be seeing someone?"

I blinked and gaped. "Wha...?"

Now Jason was blushing. "Listen, I've done my share of dating around and sport-fucking, and it's left me hollow and hungry. I'm ready to settle down and find Mr. Right. A keeper. And I know I've only known you for a few hours, but I'm starting to think that I have."

I felt like I was dizzy and going crazy. This whole night had been dizzy and crazy. "Okay, coming from me, this is going to sound ridiculous, but are you saying all of this to get in my pants? Because if so, let me tell ya, kid, you're working too hard. You had me at Time and Relative Dimension in Space."

Jason pulled my hand up to his face. He kissed the palm lightly and stood, pulling me up with him and into his arms. I'd be lying if I said being held by him didn't feel amazing.

"Let's get out of here," he murmured softly and I shivered.

"But I haven't finished my cocoa, and your cappuccino is still foamy," I protested lamely.

Jason leaned in to kiss me, so teasing and quick it only registered as a tingling of my lips after the fact. "You're adorable, Damien."

"My place isn't far," I whispered.

Half an Hour Later...

"This is me. Come on in." I flicked the light switch as I waved Jason in, hoping my bedroom wasn't too much of a disaster area.

It was, but Jason didn't seem to notice. He glanced

around, and his eyes lingered on the many, many paintings and drawings—all sci-fi and fantasy art and graphic novel layout pages, signed—before returning to me.

"Please excuse the mess," I said meaning the clothing, books, and papers everywhere, and not just in my bedroom. "My roommate and I aren't exactly neat-frea—"

But Jason was pulling me into his arms and kissing me for the second time, and I just melted in his arms. My legs went wobbly, as if they couldn't hold me upright anymore. I felt tingly and weak and hot-cold all over.

In moments, it seemed, we were on my bed, still kissing, and tugging at each other's clothing. Jason's hands were, respectively, cupping my face gently and squeezing my ass not at all gently. My hands were sweeping up and down his back which, even through his shirt, was quite hot. Like he'd been lying face-down in the sun for hours.

Or like he was running a fever.

"Are you okay?" I broke the kiss to whisper, and Jason stole another kiss and hitched my body closer against his. He was hard in all the right places, and I moaned desperately.

"I don't think I've ever been better," he murmured, his melting-chocolate eyes smiling into my own. Then we were wrestling with his shirt—popping off buttons in our haste—until it went sailing across the room to land on my R2-D2 replica wastepaper basket. Jason kissed his way down my neck, and I was just feeling him up—his muscles, his skin, the solidity of his bones—with my head turned to the side, watching our shadow-selves as they writhed on the canvas of my bedroom wall. My pudgy, unflattering shadow gasped as Jason's buff, beautiful shadow rolled on top of it and straddled it.

Fuck, I thought with chagrin and more than a little envy. *Even his shadow's hot. That's so not fair. Sheesh, I think I can even make out his six-pack. And his delts. And glutes, for sure. And those biceps...and those wings...and horns...*

Wait a minute— *Wings? Horns?*

I whipped my head back to look at Jason, who loomed above me, as handsome as ever, no wings or horns evident. Confused, and uncertain of what I'd seen, I glanced quickly back at the wall. Six pack, delts, glutes, biceps...and wings and horns.

This time, when I looked back at Jason, his smile was gone, replaced by an expression as serious as a churchyard on Sunday morning. His melty brown eyes slowly but surely turned a different color: a deep crimson, the exact shade of arterial blood. And his complexion darkened from a café-au-lait color, about twelve shades lighter than my own, to a crimson that matched his eyes. And an alarming heat radiated from him.

"Please," he said softly, his voice gone hoarse and rough, and I looked at his shadow again. The wings had spread out, like a hang-glider, but then they began to enclose his shadow...and my own. "I need this, Damien. I need *you*."

Jason turned my face to his own, leaned down till our mouths were millimeters apart, and inhaled sharply as I exhaled shakily. I felt my breath drawn swiftly out of me along with something else I couldn't define or describe. Some intangible that, with its departure, left me feeling suddenly weak and lethargic. Rudderless.

Above me, Jason began to glow red, and I began to struggle listlessly. But it was too late, I realized. Far too late.

The Morning After

I stared into my cup of coffee, perfectly made, and poked at my eggs, cooked just the way I liked them, runny-side up, and tried to remember just what in Hell had happened last night. Camela came yawning out of her bedroom, dressed in an oversized Mickey Mouse T-shirt and clearly nothing else. I was wearing its mate, the oversized Minnie Mouse T-shirt—which wasn't as oversized on me as I'd have liked—and my boxers.

"I smell a breakfast with all the fixin's," Camela said sleepily, stretching her arms up and out. Her spine made little pops and cracks. "What's the special occasion, hon? One of us finally get laid again after nearly a ye—eeee!"

She let out a little screech when she saw Jason, who was checking the flapjacks he'd made from scratch for signs of char before placing two on my plate. At Camela's screech, he looked up and smiled. A ray of sunshine happened to slant across his handsome face, and Camela's mouth dropped open, just like mine had and still did every time something drove home just how beautiful Jason Cambion was. How totally out of my league.

And yet, here he was, making me breakfast the morning after...

After the night I couldn't quite remember.

"Hullo," Jason said warmly. He placed the pan back on the burner and stepped toward Camela. He was six-foot-two, two hundred pounds of perfection, dressed only in black silk boxer briefs that accentuated abs like *WHOA*—plus a package UPS would be proud to deliver—and that gorgeous smile. He held out his hand, and Camela scurried back as if he'd offered to undress her.

"Oh, no, I couldn't." She looked like a deer caught in the headlights of a truck. "I haven't even put my face on yet."

Jason glanced at me questioningly. I shrugged, put my fork and coffee down, stood up, and drifted toward him slowly, almost as if half-asleep. Everything felt like a dream and had since early this morning. I'd woken up in bed, not alone, and been suddenly afraid my bedmate would disappear in a flash of dawn light. I forced myself to stay awake while he slept on soundly, occasionally touching him to make sure he was real.

"What she means is, 'Good morning, handsome-stranger-in-our-kitchen.'"

"Ah," Jason said, smiling again and nodding to Camela, who nodded back once. She looked stricken and mesmerized. I knew the feeling. "And good morning to you, too, lovely-lady-whose-kitchen-I've-wrecked. For which I'm sorry, by the way."

"Uh..." Camela looked around at the kitchen, which was actually cleaner and neater than we'd left it yesterday. Jason had cleaned it when breakfast was cooking. While I'd ogled his perfect body and tried to remember more of last night than just a blurry, but powerful, orgasm and Jason's dark eyes above my own—the only stable point in a shifting, amorphous sur-reality. "Wrecked?"

Jason held out his hand to me and, when I was close enough, took mine and pulled me close for a kiss. A long and minty one, since we'd both used my toothbrush not an hour ago. And even if we'd both still had morning breath, that kiss? Would've been so worth it. When it ended, my knees were so weak, I had to hold onto Jason to stay upright. His kisses, and even his touch, had a way of leaving me feeling weak and almost lost. Dazed and hazy.

"Yeah, I got a little enthusiastic about breakfast." Jason glanced at Camela for a moment before looking back at me. He reached up and caressed my cheek so, *so* tenderly. "But I promise I'll clean up when I'm done."

And the staring went on until Camela cleared her throat and said, "Damien. Babe. Love. Explanation, please?"

"He followed me home, Cam," I said dreamily, blinking when I thought I saw a flash of crimson in Jason's melty-chocolate eyes. But it was gone before I could be sure, and I glanced over at Camela, whose gaze darted between Jason and me, before looking back at Jason once more. I couldn't help myself. He was so beautiful. "Can I keep him?"

Another maybe-flash of crimson in those melty-chocolate eyes. "Cambion! Cambion! Cambion!" a voice in my head gibbered warningly, almost fearfully, sounding not like my own, but that of the deadbeat father who'd disappeared on my mother and me when I was seven—and Jason grinned at me. And kept on grinning.

Cambion: The mythical half-demon offspring of a succubus and an incubus.

One Side of a Cell Conversation

by Darryl Denning

Hello.

No, this is not Martin.
I just answered his phone.

No, you can't talk to him.
He's slumped over the counter.
I think he's dead.

The bartender called 911.

Oh, you're his boyfriend.
I thought he looked gay.

No, this is not a gay place.
The decor in here is terrible.
Maybe that's what killed him.

Sorry, I know this is no time for jokes.

Well, I'm glad you appreciate my humor.

Yes, I'm gay.

You sound interesting too.

I guess I'm about the same age as Martin,
6 feet, 170 lbs., sort of Scandinavian looking.
How about you?

Nice.

Martin? Oh, they've taken his body away now.

Sure, I'd love to meet for a drink,
But not here. Some gay bar.
This place is really tacky.

Monday Morning Masks

by Lisa Carlson

Rainbow jello shots, sexy sailor boys, and drag queen devils set the tone for a Halloween weekend soirée at "The number one gay bar" in New Jersey. The diversity of race, religion, economic status, and sexual orientation here in Asbury Park is as vast as the grains of sand that grace the shores of this up-and-coming seaside town.

While the gay community is often credited with helping bring this town back to life, there is still division. There's a place for the rich, a place for the poor, a place for the blacks, a place for the Jewish and the non-Jewish, and a place for the gays. Far from the glistening, hipster block where one can buy a million dollar condo, sits Georgie's. This gay bar is literally steps from the train tracks. It is the wrong side of town.

Despite the locale, we are surprised to discover we can't find a spot to park. Georgie's is packed. All three of the people in my party can count on one hand the times we have been in gay bars. We are not gay. Two of us are women and one is a man. I have the most experience. I'm reminded of an uncomfortable label from my college days. Apparently, I am a fag hag.

My two comrades for the night discuss their strategy before they will go in with me. They agree that they will not go into the bathroom.

"Laughable," I say.

I pay the cover for the three of us, and the woman and man I am with proceed to engage in the protective behavior of being overtly heterosexual in an effort to ward off any advances. Immediately, I realized this left me free to roam.

As I make my way to the bar, I introduce myself to my bar mate. When he offers to move over so I can be next to my friends, I tell him thanks but no thanks. We quickly engage in the "Why are you here?" conversation as he assumes I am not gay. He claims he is straight, married, and curious. We agree that we both like it here because it is a no-judgment zone. Yes we are straight, yes we are married, and yes we are comfortable here. What does that say about us? Why are we comfortable here? Minutes turn into hours and eventually my bar mate leaves with the sexy sailor boy. I don't judge. I don't ask the questions that go through my head. Does his wife know he is here? Is it ok with her? I am curious.

In many ways, my life has come full circle. Something pulls me back to people and places that accept me for who I am. I seek places free of pretense. I want peace. I want freedom. Something pulls me back to this place, this community. Leaving the Halloween party, I ask my friends if we can do this again next year. A tentative "maybe" comes from both of them. They wonder if I've got it out of my system. I don't think I have. I don't think I ever will.

A Message for Steve

by Katherine V. Forrest

Maybe you remember me. We met in one of Detroit's gay bars in May of the year the twentieth century turned sixty, a month after I turned twenty-one. I saw you perhaps half a dozen times during that late spring.

The particular night I met you I was with a group of friends at a small bar on Gratiot Avenue, a bar whose name I've forgotten, but maybe you'll remember. Later that year it ended its brief tenure as a haven for queers and became a "black and tan" bar—slang in that highly segregated city for a place that welcomed blacks. I remember the city in those days as being glamorously grungy and vital, but safe, not the violent, dangerous place it was soon to become. But I also understand that I felt safe because I was young—and that some confidence of youth is taken away by the years. How I hope that yours remains undimmed.

That night in the bar I was with three other lesbians: Joan and Ann with their short, dark hair and men's pants and white shirts, visibly butch; and Carole, with her slumberous, blue eyes and simply cut dark hair, a young woman I knew from General Motors where I worked and whom I was nuts about (and would shortly lose to Joan—not that I exactly had her to lose). Carole was also butch but conventionally very pretty, as butch woman often are, and she was playing femme for Joan—role switching that made better sense to me later on when I had more knowledge and some perspective on lesbian fluidity.

We had come to the bar from a crowded coffee shop on Woodward Avenue where, over coffee, I had been immersed in the company of my lesbian companions, especially Carole. What happened afterward still reverberated in me as I sat in the Gratiot Avenue bar, because I couldn't, wouldn't discuss my feelings with my companions. I didn't know what to say, and for all I knew, I was the only one troubled by what occurred.

We'd gotten up to leave the coffee shop and were single-filing our way through tables to the door when it began. My entire body seemed to burn in the rising cacophony of whistles, laughter, catcalls, taunts. While I had been obliviously drinking my coffee, everyone else in the place had identified us as lesbians—probably due to Ann's and Joan's butch drag—and they were now indulging in a litany of ridicule: "Come back, come back, we can save you"; "It's your last chance, girls," called individual male voices accompanied by explosions of female giggles. "Don't go out that door"; "Turn back, it's not too late"; "You, the one on the end, there's still hope..." Carole was the one on the end. I can still see her sheepish expression as I looked back at her, her shoulders lifting and rounding as if warding off rain.

I had been singled out before, stared at during the one month in which I had become a regular in the bars. The bars were the only place I knew to be, and I was still acclimating myself, trying to figure out where and how I fit in, with very few signposts for deciphering such behavior as the cult of butch and femme. Likening this radical culture to heterosexuality was to compare palm trees to teaspoons. I seemed too tall and awkward in my skin to be femme, yet I couldn't envision myself adopting the clothing or the attitudes of a butch woman. So I was puzzling through the rules of the bar culture, its sexual signals and permissions.

I had been brought to these very bars one month earlier, on my birthday, by heterosexual friends whose idea of formal introduction to adulthood was that I should look at the seamy side of life, that I should go look at queers. But what I had seen, with a lightning strike of unwilling recognition, was the truth about my life: these were my people, and this was where I belonged. I returned alone the following night, electrified with apprehension but pulled there as the tides are pulled by the moon. So now I was one of the queers on exhibit, to be gaped at by slumming heterosexuals who came to sit in our dark, smoky bars and watch us slow-dance to wailing Connie Francis songs or twist to writhing Chubby Checker tunes.

But being stared at in a shadowy bar where I was an indigenous inhabitant was different from being singled out in the public world of heterosexuals. And so I sat in that bar on Gratiot Avenue with my insides thrumming with the aftershocks of the gauntlet I had walked through in the coffee shop.

When you strolled up to our table.

I don't know how Joan knew you, how the two of you fit into each other's lives, but you greeted each other with jocular familiarity. Those were the days before separatism and other hostilities, before the women's movement led us to a place in ourselves where we found such a depth of fury and rebellion that many of us lined up every male in the world in its focus. But back then wars and enemies were a far simpler matter, and so you sat down at that table with us, leaned back, crossed an ankle over a knee, and entered my life.

This isn't enough to have you even recognize yourself, much less remember me, so let me describe you.

You wore your straight, blond hair in close-cut neatness except for a cowlick at the crown of your head that you couldn't tame no matter how much you patted or wet-combed it. You had a fine broad forehead, wide apart powder blue eyes, pale blond eyebrows, a good nose; but there was a boniness in the shape of it, that endearing element of rawness young men sometimes have. The sprinkling of acne scars across your cheeks only added to your attractiveness.

You weren't a student but you dressed collegiate in the fashion of those days: open-throat white shirts and what were called continental pants—a style using a two- or three-inch flap of fabric as self-belting—that looked pleasing on your trim body and long legs. In the chilly spring evenings like that one, you added a crewneck sweater, usually navy blue, and I loved its rough wool and masculinity. Your pants were conservative dark colors, but once you wore baggy trousers in a snappy-looking houndstooth, and that first night your pants were tweed, in a small checkered pattern. You were never expensively dressed but always immaculately (though not meticulously) neat, and you smelled of a clean scent of aftershave lotion. You were always smart looking in the casual chic way that young people today or any day would kill to achieve.

I immediately loved your look and I still do. I still love it when any gay man (or better yet a butch woman) dresses even somewhat the way you did. I envied your style. You exuded a charming combination of boyishness and maturity. You were a field of dreams...you still are.

I don't remember what any of us talked about in the bar that night, but it didn't matter. In that small, dark, intimate place your talk was light, free, and confident, and your words were like music to me.

We went out into the brightly lit street. Your bearing and slenderness added to an impression of height, and most beautiful of all was the ease in the way you moved. You seemed to contain in your body the freedom of a dancer who dances for himself and then for others.

"I took this guy home last night," you said, talking to Joan. "He was a doll, a real doll, really sweet." But then somehow your words—your welling laughter—became directed at me. "Let me tell you, I wasn't what he expected. We were in bed and I was making him very happy. I just turned myself around, and was he ever surprised at what he had in his mouth." And you flung your head back and laughed so joyously, and you strode so buoyantly at my side along the street, and your strides were so long and confident and cocky. "So he found out all about sixty-nine. He was such a doll."

I laughed with you in my own sheer delight, not at the story you told me in such intimate, audacious detail, but because for the first time I could take unalloyed pleasure in the company of a man without any fear of complications.

Much more than that. Your joy in your life and your confidence in your sexuality were balm on those burns from the coffee shop.

The image of you striding along that Detroit street, your naturalness with the profound mysteries of sexuality, unfolds as easily and as vividly in my mind as if on film. At the time, I didn't know anything else about why this image of you was so vital to me, why I clutched it so close inside myself, how much it meant to me.

Joan and Carole—and you—soon disappeared from my landscape, which is another story, and the following year I fled to California, carrying all the despair and confusion of my profound homophobia with me. A very long process followed, of struggle and anger and healing, of support from good people in aiding my growth and evolution, before I could find the ease within my own skin that you showed me on that Detroit street, before I could dance for myself and then dance for others.

You gave me the first of the building blocks on which I learned to shape my lesbian pride and self-esteem; you were part of the genesis from which the affirmative images of lesbian life and love eventually came into being in all my books.

In the many years since that May night, friendship and camaraderie with gay men have taken their rich place in my life. Our two communities needed that time apart in the seventies to explore our own identities and culture, and then the devastation of AIDS brought us all together. You were the first gay man I ever knew. You were the first to show me the promise of what we have since brought into each other's LGBT lives.

I don't know your last name; I don't know what you did for a living. I don't know the name of the bar where we met; I don't know what happened to you.

I only know that on the lonely streets of that city all those years ago, you were light, you were hope, you were possibility.

Today all gay men are my brothers. But you, Steve, you were my first.

From *Sister and Brother*
Lesbians & Gay Men Write About Their Lives Together
Edited by Joan Nestle and John Preston
Harper San Francisco, 1994

Gateway to Heaven

by Jen Silver

London, 1968

She peered around the street corner. According to the directions, this was the right place. Her heart pounded wildly. The pep talk she'd given herself on the journey from her aunt and uncle's house in Camden seeped away as quickly as the Dutch courage gained from drinking the bottle of her uncle's Pale Ale, taken from the pantry three days ago and hidden along with the clothes she was now wearing.

They thought she was meeting up with an old school friend to go to a play in the West End, happy that she was starting to come out of her shell. In the three weeks since arriving in London from Plymouth to take up a clerical position with an accounting firm, she hadn't ventured out in the evenings at all.

Now here she was, embarking on an adventure she spent years dreaming about. She was in the big city, walking the same streets as people she had idolised from afar. The other day on Oxford Street, during her lunch break, she was sure she had seen Mick Jagger and Marianne Faithful. And tonight, to reach her destination, she walked down the King's Road, fashion centre for London and the universe.

From her vantage point, lurking in a shop doorway, she watched as two women came up the street. They were laughing about something. One of them looked like she modelled herself on Dusty Springfield with the full beehive hairstyle. Both were wearing tight-fitting tops and miniskirts leaving nothing to the imagination. They walked confidently up to the green door and disappeared inside.

She licked her lips and then rested her head on the wall. Could she really go through with this? Maybe she should have gone to see the play instead.

The clothes she'd bought on her Saturday excursion to Carnaby Street were a loose fit. She hadn't been able to try them on, telling the salesman they were for her brother. At least she knew how to knot her tie; it was her old school one, but no one here would recognise it. The tie was in her jacket pocket. Tom, the hairdresser who told her about this place, told her to wait until she was inside the club to put it on.

Her aunt hadn't been pleased when she spent her first week's wages on a short haircut, unimpressed that it was the look favoured by Twiggy, now a famous model.

"You don't want to look like that stick insect. Oh, your beautiful hair. You must let it grow back before your mother sees you."

She had no intention of letting it grow too long again. With it slicked back, she hoped it gave her the image she was trying to achieve. All the doubts that assailed her during the week attacked at once, keeping her rooted to the spot. Would she be able to talk to anyone, ask anyone to dance? These city women wouldn't be interested in a country hick like her. Did she look the part? What if they didn't let her in? Did she look gay enough?

Giving herself a mental shake, she stood up straight. She was here now. All the preparation shouldn't go to waste. She crossed the street, repeating the name she had chosen in her head. It had taken her many hours on the journeys to and from work over the last two weeks to decide on the right one. She wanted to seem dashing and mysterious. Eventually, having gone through the list of usual names, she hit on one that was obvious, considering the place of her birth.

She approached the green door and opened it cautiously. A steep flight of steps led down. Two very large, tough-looking women stood near the top of the stairs. They gave her a quick glance and then nodded. She pulled the tie out of her pocket and draped it around her shirt collar as she walked down. She gave the woman at the desk at the bottom a tentative smile, hoping the thumping of her heart wasn't loud enough to be heard. This was the bar's owner. Tom told her that Gina ran a tight ship and wouldn't tolerate any troublemakers.

"Do I look like a fighter?" she had asked him as another lock of her hair fell to the floor.

"Not at all, sweetie. But if you make the moves on someone else's girl, you could find yourself in a brawl."

She couldn't imagine having the courage to "make the moves" on anyone. Her plan for the evening was to stand by a wall and observe.

Gina looked her up and down before saying, "Sign here." Relieved that she passed muster, she signed her new name carefully in the book.

Entering the smoky atmosphere of the bar, she glanced around and decided she didn't look too out of place. She knotted her tie while waiting at the bar to order a pint of bitter. Glass in hand, she retreated to a corner of the room to watch the action. The tables were all occupied, so she leant against the wall. Breathing in a lungful of smoke, she wished she'd thought to buy a pack of cigs before coming. She wasn't a smoker, but holding an unlit cigarette could have emboldened her to ask someone for a light, start up a conversation at least.

Slowly she felt herself relaxing. She'd made it. The women were enjoying themselves, chatting, laughing, couples holding onto each other. It was beyond anything she had imagined. All were dressed as they wanted to present themselves: femmes in pretty dresses and skirts, with makeup and teased hair. Butches, like herself, wearing either shirts and ties or doing James Dean impersonations attired in tight muscle shirts and jeans.

Humming along to the song currently playing on the jukebox, Bobby Vee singing "Take Good Care of My Baby," she slowly became aware of someone who had stopped in front of her.

"Hi. Haven't seen you here before. What's your name?"

It was the Dusty impersonator she had seen on the street earlier.

"Um, Devon." She gave a nonchalant shrug. "Friends call me Dev."

"Pleased to meet you, Dev. I'm Sandy."

Dev put her glass down on the nearby table. "Would you...um?" She gestured towards the middle of the room where others were moving to the music.

"Gladly."

Just as they reached the edge of the dance area, the song changed to a slow tune, another one she recognized: "Release Me." The dance floor filled up rapidly, and

Dev wasn't sure how to proceed.

Sandy pulled her close and whispered in her ear, "Move with me."

****

Running for the bus, she caught up with it when it stopped at the lights and swung herself lightly onto the platform and continued up the stairs. The evening was everything she dreamed about and more. With the prospect of repeating the experience the following Saturday night, she knew the week at work would pass slowly, like the lead up to Christmas as a young child. But she would be able to get through the long days, uncomfortable in the clothes, wearing the requisite uniform of frilly blouse and knee-length skirt with stockings, putting up with the leering old men in pin-striped suits—all this would pass. Now she knew there was a place for her, a place where she could feel at home in herself, no longer the outsider, no longer alone.

When the conductor stopped by her seat to collect her fare, calling her "sir," she just handed him her money and took the ticket without comment, but inside she was celebrating. She passed. And that made the evening feel even more wonderful.

****

She adjusted her skirt, made sure the zip was at the back, and clutched her balled-up stockings in one hand as she entered the house.

"Fiona, dear," her aunt called out from the sitting room. "How was the play?"

She popped her head around the door. "It was...good."

She had told them she was going to see the musical version of the Canterbury Tales at the Phoenix Theatre, and they were satisfied, apparently thinking it sounded educational. She had read parts of the book at school, which meant she would be able to sound knowledgeable if quizzed about the performance.

"Well, you look like you enjoyed it. There's some milk left if you want a hot chocolate before you go to bed."

"Thanks. I'm a bit bushed. I'll just go straight up."

She couldn't wait to get under the covers and relive the evening over again. Her body trembled with the memory of holding Sandy close while they danced, drinking in the heady scent of her perfume, and imagining what it would be like to kiss her full lips. During their last dance of the evening to the appropriately named "Sweet Dreams," with the hypnotic voice of Patsy Cline reverberating around the small room, Dev could hardly contain the euphoric sensation that swept through her—the on-top-of-the-world feeling that had given her the courage to ask Gina for a membership form before she left.

Sleep enfolded her eventually as her body was liberated by the knowledge there would be other nights like this at the Gateways Club—her gateway to heaven.

Chances

by Shelley Thrasher

"Great wall," I said to the bartender, glancing over my shoulder through the archway that led outside to a large open area.

"Yeah. It's a natural limestone outcropping. Makes a perfect exterior wall for our patio," she said. "It's the only one of its kind you'll find in an Austin bar."

"How tall is it?" I'd propped myself against the edge of the wooden bar that thousands of hands had worn smooth, and now I gripped it as if I might fall flat on my face without it. Had any of those hands been as clammy as mine?

"Oh, it's fourteen, fifteen feet high, I suppose." She stared at the nearly deserted area beyond it then fastened serene blue eyes on me. "You new in town or just visiting?"

"Visiting. I lived here once. Back in the sixties."

"Yeah? Sixth Street looks a lot different now, doesn't it?"

"Sure does. I mostly remember a bunch of discount stores, pawnshops, and boarded-up, run-down, old Victorian buildings on it back then. Kind of a skid-row atmosphere. Now it's wall-to-wall shops and bars that seem to be doing really well."

She shrugged. "Things change. Why'd you leave Austin?"

I studied the limestone wall outside again. It probably hadn't changed at all in the past twenty years, except maybe for a few more weeds or saplings growing out of the many cracks in it. When I lived here, I'd most likely walked or bicycled right past this little cinderblock building on Red River a million times without even noticing it or the impressive stone formation it backed up to.

I picked up the vodka sour I'd ordered earlier and took a drink. It had exactly the right combination of sugar syrup and lemon juice. "We moved away because my husband got a teaching job near Beaumont. Too bad, though. Austin was really a happening place back then, with Hippie Hollow and all that political stuff going on." I sighed. "We loved to spend time in the parks, watch foreign movies in a little theater near the UT campus, and raft down the rivers around here with a group of hippies." I sighed again, remembering those idyllic student days. "We were the token straight couple—in both senses of the word. The others in the group always chose us to calm the local farmers who got mad when we ignored the barbed-wire fences they'd stretched across whatever river we were rafting on. Everyone else in the group smelled too much like pot to have a decent conversation with 'em."

The bartender gave a knowing laugh. "Exactly when did you live here?"

"A year after the UT Tower shooting and during the time Martin Luther King was killed. From fall '67 through summer '68, I think it was." I scratched my head. "And we moved back the next year just for the summer. We were here when they landed on the moon for the first time. 'One giant step for mankind.'"

The bartender suddenly looked sad. "I remember those years and those events. Funny how the violent ones stay with us so long," she said then shook her head. I guessed she was thinking about last month, when the *Challenger* exploded and all those astronauts were killed. She said, "Austin hasn't changed that much, if you know where to look. It's bigger now, with more traffic, but it has the same liberal attitude." She looked directly at me. "You still live near Beaumont, I suppose."

A couple of women walked through the front door and, with a wave to the bartender, strolled outside through the large archway and turned to the right.

I took another sip of my drink, and its sweet bite soothed my dry throat. "Yes. I got a teaching job, which I love, so I'm probably there to stay. It's next to impossible to find work here."

"Depends on what you're willing to do, but it is hard to find, mainly because a lot of the thousands of students who graduate from all the universities and colleges in the area want to keep on living here. But you already know that."

"Yeah. I hated to leave, though the Gulf Coast does have a few advantages, such as the beach nearby, a nice, cool breeze, and lots of rain. But the mosquitos and the refinery emissions and the high humidity aren't much fun." I grimaced then drew in a deep breath. The air seemed fresh in spite of the lingering odors of cigarette smoke. "I'd forgotten how early it warms up inland like this. Smells like spring already."

She nodded. "Excuse me a minute." She pulled a draft beer into a frosty mug, poured a glass full of white wine, and carried them outside on a tray.

I took another sip. Maybe the alcohol would loosen the tightness in my throat. Heck. In my whole body. I put down my glass, held out my hands, and stared at them. At least they weren't trembling quite as badly as when I first got here. In fact, I'd been afraid my jangling nerves would make me run out of the local women's bookstore on Sixth Street before I finally worked up enough courage to ask for directions to this place.

The bartender took her time coming back. Meanwhile, I studied the dartboard hanging on one scarred wall and the two flashing red Xs of a Dos Equis sign behind the otherwise dark bar. I'd almost finished my vodka sour by the time she reappeared.

"Good. You're still here," she said.

"Did you think I'd run away?" Was I that obvious?

She took her place behind the bar, seeming as steady as the limestone formation outside. "The thought did cross my mind."

I let my tight shoulders drop a fraction of an inch. "Why'd you think that?"

"Not many women wear a frilly, off-the-shoulder dress when they show up here." She raised an eyebrow. "Let's just say you look like someone who'd feel more at home at a small-town family picnic than in a bar."

I couldn't stop my grin. "Busted. What else do you see?"

"Hmm. For starters, I *don't* see a ring, so I'm making a wild-ass guess that either you took it off for some reason before you came in here or it's off for good."

I noticed more than just her unflappable blue eyes this time. Tall and wiry, she appeared to be an athlete, or at least in top physical condition. I pushed my empty glass toward her. "How about another drink?"

"Always glad to oblige a lady," she said, her accent momentarily slipping into the honeyed tones of the Deep South.

She moved with the grace of a ballerina as she turned to grab a bottle of Smirnov from the clean, orderly rows behind the bar.

"So which is it?" she asked as she pushed my drink, complete with a cherry, toward me ever so gently.

"Which is what?" I couldn't keep my eyes away from her long, slender fingers.

"The ring—or lack thereof."

"Oh. That." I studied my tanned ring finger. "It's off for good. But I imagine you'd already guessed that."

"How long?"

Her simple question rocked me, but suddenly I felt uncharacteristically brave. Listening to the keynote speaker at the conference I'd been attending must have affected me more than I realized. "It's been several years now. In fact, I've taken off two rings during the time I've lived there."

"Busy lady, eh? Learned your lesson and finally scoping out the alternative?"

I nodded. I'd been doing exactly that for the past several years, but this was the first time I'd consciously admitted to myself that's what I had in mind.

"First time in a lesbian bar?" Her tone was gentle.

So much blood rushed to my face, I was afraid the rest of my body would dry up without it. "How'd you know?" I was truly puzzled, not to mention mortified, thrilled, and petrified.

"If you stand behind a bar long enough, you learn to see a lot." Her wavy blonde hair caught a random ray of the setting sun as it beamed through the large opening from outside. She seemed as steady and as timeless as the natural limestone wall I kept feeling pulled toward.

"And just how long have you been standing behind a bar?" The knots in my legs and stomach were beginning to loosen, so I slid onto a tall stool next to where I'd been standing all this time.

"This one—about ten years. And before that, several others here and there in town."

"But you didn't grow up in Texas, did you?"

This time she looked almost as surprised as I'd felt earlier. She straightened the already tidy rows of bottles. Now that I was quizzing her, her movements seemed suddenly more erratic, jerkier. She finally spoke. "Where do you guess I'm from?"

"Somewhere in Mississippi, I'm thinking."

She glanced at me then quickly focused on a questionable spot on a wineglass and rubbed it so hard I was afraid she'd break it. "Damn. How'd you know?"

I smiled, feeling more at home now. "I'm a linguist. That's why I'm in town—on the UT campus, to be exact, at a conference for women scholars. Dozens of us running around trying to show off how smart we are."

The bartender chuckled. "Brains as well as beauty. Hmm. I like that combo. If you're a professional, I guess my birthplace isn't all that obvious to the simple folks I usually associate with here, eh?" She set down the supposedly dirty glass and rested her elbows on the bar.

"What's wrong with being from Mississippi? After all, Faulkner and Welty were born there. Can't be all bad." Why in the world would she want to hide such a trivial fact?

"Maybe I'm a serial killer on the lam or I've kidnapped my own children and been hiding out in the Lone Star State from an abusive ex all this time."

The bartender's attempt to appear menacing failed. In fact, her grin completely belied her teasing scenarios about being a killer or a kidnapper and her earlier sarcasm about associating with "simple folks."

I let my second drink sit idle, fueled more by this woman than by the alcohol for a change. "And maybe I actually *do* have a loving husband at home and am just out looking for a good time to amuse myself while I'm in town."

Her loud laugh seemed to come from deep inside her. "Okay, Ms. Linguist from near Beaumont. How about we start over? I'm Diana. I was born and raised in Clarksdale, Mississippi, and hauled ass out of there as soon as I could manage." She stuck out her hand.

I took it, and its soft warmth filled me with a welcome sensation. "Glad to meet you, Diana, goddess of wild animals and the hunt. I'm Eve, and I feel like I was just created, since this is the very first time I've been in a lesbian bar."

Diana waved offhandedly as a woman walked in and headed right on out to the patio. Then she fixed me with those amazing blue eyes. "Welcome to Chances," she said. "And by the way. That couple who came in awhile ago?"

"Yes." I leaned back in my surprisingly comfortable barstool.

"They asked me to give you a message."

"What? I've never seen them in my life."

"I know. But they noticed you. They told me if you don't plan to meet someone else here, to please join them, if you're in the mood. They're sitting at the very back of the patio."

I took a deep breath, then another, feeling like a soldier who'd just survived her first battle in a foreign country. Finally at ease in this strange, new territory, I picked up my glass and held it toward her.

"Thanks, Diana. I owe you." I finished my drink and set the empty glass on the bar.

"Can you find them?" She chuckled. "Or do you want me to show you the way?"

I looked at the limestone wall outside one more time and slid from my stool. "I think you've done just that. Thanks again." I held out my hand, which no longer shook, and she took it.

The last rays of the setting sun lit up her hair and her smile as she squeezed it firmly and said, once again, "Welcome to Chances."

On the way out

by Kitty Kat

Walk on by, walk on by
Keep your distance, pretend you don't see
It's nearly time, but not yet
Courage escapes me, just for now
One day I'll be ready, make the leap
'Til then I'm too scared, just on the way out.

Music blaring, lights and people
Coming and going, confidently striding
Already accepting, happy and part of
Could I just do it? Be me and open
Nearly, just nearly , crossing on over
The doorway it beckons, on the way out.

Into the darkness, sounds and sensations
Fear overtakes me, but a smile from the corner
Beckons me into a welcoming haven
At last a home waits for and wraps me up tight
I've found what I needed, waited so long
A place for all of us, on the way out.

Girls Just Want to Have Fun

by Cheryl A. Head

Out for the evening, but not OUT. Our first trip to a lesbian club.

This is Detroit. Circa 1985. Our small circle of women friends, like us, are closeted and don't venture to the clubs, but someone has told us about this place on the outskirts of town. Far enough away, we think, from the professional lives we occupy.

We open the door. Not like trail-dusty cowboys brashly pushing through a saloon's swinging portals, but meekly, like Presbyterians entering an AME church. A wedge of outside light splits the dark interior, and my stomach tingles. We are entering the world of a secret kinship.

"Good evening," says the female Adonis in black cargo pants and T-shirt, her hair shaved to a buzz cut. She peers down at us from her celestial height, gives us a discerning once-over, and after a couple of moments, allows that we know where we've come. Jan and I have been advised of the practice of providing ID and have our driver's licenses at the ready. "Thanks," she says and returns our cards. I hold out a twenty-dollar bill for our entry, but our greeter-slash-bouncer waves it off. "There's no cover until 10 p.m."

The club is called The Crossing. Over the bar, a wood plaque affixed with two railroad ties forming an X is the only decor supporting the theme. The place is cavernous. A paint-speckled, bar countertop takes up much of the left side of the room, and a smattering of populated tables nest in the shadowy recesses on the right. In between, an expansive cement floor is sprinkled with stars projected from the ceiling. I survey the room and see only three other African-American women. One sits alone at the bar; the others mingle with friends.

We walk what seems a thousand steps, through stars, to a ledge that hugs the wall across from the door. I imagine the eyes of curious women following our trek, and I'm suddenly concerned my jeans are dowdy—certainly not sexy.

A petite, blonde server, with a tray under her arm and a half-apron pulled snugly across a white T-shirt, ambles toward us. My spine stiffens. I know nothing of club etiquette.

"Hi. Can I get you anything to drink?" She smiles, revealing a tiny chip in her front tooth, tugs a napkin and pen from her apron pocket, and flips the tray to make a writing surface. She's no older than twenty-five.

I exhale, audibly, and return her smile. "I'll have a Piña Colada," I say, remembering the sweet concoction of pineapple and coconut I've tried a few times at sit-down restaurants.

"We don't have that." She's still smiling.

Three women leaning on the ledge not far from us are talking and smoking cigarettes. They hold long-necked, amber bottles. But I don't like beer, so I try to remember the drinks served at the home gatherings we attend.

"Oh, okay then. I'll have a rum and Coke."

The girl nods, makes a squiggle on the napkin, and turns to Jan.

"Uh, what kind of wine do you have?"

"A house white and a house red."

The bar server is still pleasant, but her terseness begs Jan not to push for more options. I feel my anxiety returning.

"I'll take the house red," Jan says obediently.

"Okay, be right back."

I peek at our neighbors to see if they've noticed our faux pas, but they are deep in conversation. Occasionally they tilt back their heads, lips meeting those of their raised bottles. Their shirts are rolled up over muscled arms, and they fill tight, western-style jeans. They wear thick belts, with large buckles, and boots. I look down at my loafers.

"What do you think?" I ask Jan.

"I think we should have worn something different."

I'm wearing a collared shirt, a black blazer, and jeans that graze my ankles. Jan's pressed khakis and tan vest complement her brown, shoulder-length hair. We're basically dressed for casual Friday at the office. Sadly, we also carry purses.

"I'm glad it's dim in here," I say.

The server returns quickly with our drinks. She watches me dig into my clutch, and I believe I see amusement behind her patient countenance. I pull out a ten and a five-dollar bill. "Keep the change," I announce with swagger.

She gives the best smile yet. "Thank you. Enjoy, ladies."

Her next transaction is with the beer drinkers. "Three more of the same," she announces, putting the Buds on the ledge and picking up the empties. One of the women reaches two fingers into her snug pocket, finds a bill, and wiggles it seductively. She whispers something in the server's ear. The girl accepts the money with a different kind of smile and sashays back to the bar. We all watch her exit. Except Jan, who is watching me.

"Enjoying the sights?"

"Huh? Oh. Uh, yes. What about you, honey. Are you having a good time?"

Jan complains her wine is cold from refrigeration. She also isn't happy about having to stand. I take a gulp of my unfamiliar drink and then another. The rum wraps around my head, muffling Jan's voice.

"Maybe I should put our purses in the car," I say.

"Uh-uh. But yours is small enough to fit in mine."

Jan stuffs my thin clutch into her bag and secures it to her shoulder. I reach down to hold her hand. My eyes feel kind of droopy.

"You should try a sip of my rummin Coke. Ish pretty good."

"You've got a buzz."

"I don't think so," I say indignantly. "How d'ya know?"

"You've got a goofy grin, and you're slurring your words. Let me taste that thing."

I hand her my drink and watch her take a sip, then another.

"Umm. It's strong, but it *is* good," she says, and the silly grin finds its way to her face.

A DJ, in an elevated booth near the bar, plays a nice mix of Motown, current pop favorites, and disco. The ledge throbs with the output of the giant speakers. "Open Your Heart to Me," Madonna pleads. Whitney calls out, "I Wanna Dance with Somebody," and Billy Ocean promises, "No more love on the run."

One or two couples venture to the star-splashed dance floor, but when no others join them, run out of steam, and trail back to their seats, or perch at the wall shelf. The rest of us sip, chat, and watch the room for another half hour, until The Pointer Sisters', "I'm So Excited," pulses the woofers. As if on signal, women emerge from the club's perimeters and swarm the center. I offer my palm to Jan, and she takes hold.

When I dance I get lost in the music—arms raised, spinning, oblivious to others. But I'm a virgin to the terpsichorean ways of a lesbian bar, so I watch, and learn.

The dancers are enthusiastic, raucous. Certain moves elicit automatic ooohs and ahhhs, and I name them. They include "the sandwich" where one gyrating girl is encased front and back by two other gyrating girls, and the "backfield in motion," which involves grinding, thrusting, or any kind of touching of your partner's rear end. I also note that line dancing is a crowd pleaser.

A catchy, upbeat, country music tune replaces the pop music.

Jan and I return to our spot on the ledge, marked by my jacket and her vest, to observe the club's regulars line up, six in a row, to step, cross, tap, and turn in syncopation. Our server returns, and we order rum-less Cokes. They arrive garnished with a lime. I suspect citrus is a code we are novice drinkers.

"They're basically doing the Electric Slide," I say to Jan. "It's easy to follow. Come on, let's get back out there."

"No, you go ahead," she says.

The beauty of line dancing is you don't need a partner. It's a communal experience. I imagine the practice dates to humankind's earliest societies, where members of the clan, or tribe, joined to shuffle and bounce to a rhythm made by striking a rock upon another or banging a hand on a hollow log. The group might be invoking the good will of God or celebrating the first harvest or preparing for war, but the individuals were a collective, moving as one, intent on a single purpose. Tonight, we dance to affirm we are women who love women.

I blend into the last row. The routine has a couple of extra kicks, some of the dancers have thumbs stuck into their belt loops, and there's also the tipping of an imaginary hat, but I catch on quickly. I wave at Jan, and she waves back. On the next song, I'm keeping up. I look toward Jan. She's talking to the woman who was sitting solo at the bar, but now is leaning on our ledge. I stay with the line through the end of the song then head back to Jan. The woman retreats as I approach.

"Who was that?"

"Her name's Cutter."

"Cutter? What kind of damn name is that?"

"Honey, are you having a good time?" Jan asks.

We stare at each other a moment, and soon I'm joining her in laughter. Our first visit to a gay club is winding down. I help Jan into her vest. She dips into her handbag to retrieve my clutch.

"No. Not now."

"Don't you want the car keys?"

"Hold onto them until we get outside."

"Okay, but a purse isn't the only reason you won't pass for butch. You're going to have to lose those highwater jeans and Buster Brown-looking shoes."

I roll my eyes at Jan. She laughs heartily.

We skirt the edge of the now-full dance floor and head to the exit. We pass Cutter, who gives Jan a nod and turns away under my gaze. I think Cutter's jeans aren't much better than mine, but her denim jacket is kind of cool. I place my hand gently at the base of Jan's back, imitating the way I've seen others claim their date for the night. At the door, the lady-in-black gives us a smile. "Have a good night. Be safe," she says.

We step out to the lighted parking lot, and Jan slips her arm through mine.

"That was fun," she says.

"It was."

"Now back to reality."

"Wouldn't it be wonderful if this was what's real? Just being able to be ourselves."

We get into my car and lean across the console for a long kiss. Over the years, we will visit other lesbian clubs. But our foray into The Crossing is a bellwether, an appropriate moniker for our first step into the out-in-the-open life we want to share.

Definitely a Habit

by Jamie Anderson

In 1975, lesbians in Phoenix, Arizona, either played softball or went to The Habit. Lois, my first girlfriend, excitedly told me about the bar. At first, I didn't jump at the opportunity because I was sure my parents would end up hauling my underaged ass home from some seedy jail. I wasn't a jock, so softball was out. Curiosity won out, and at the tender age of eighteen, I showed Lois's ID to the bouncer at The Habit. Lois was six inches shorter and looked nothing like me, but with a license that had done several rounds with a washing machine, who would know? Heart pounding, I stepped inside the smoky bar full of laughing women and loud music.

Lois didn't have to show her ID, since by that time, she was a regular. I followed her around like a lost puppy and smiled nervously when she introduced me to her friends. I'd already been given the heads-up on how to dress—androgynously in a flannel shirt, jeans, comfortable shoes, and for God's sake, don't wear a bra. I was warmly welcomed; it was the first of many visits. Soon, I got to know the whole cast of characters in this inviting yet dumpy tavern.

Big Jan was aptly named: several inches taller than my five-eight, missing a couple of front teeth, and recently out of prison. She always had a beer in her hand, a sly look, and you didn't want to fuck with her. Crazy Jan shared a first name but was shorter and more femme. While Big Jan was predictable in a tough butch kind of way, you never knew what Crazy Jan was going to do. One night she showed up in a Girl Scout uniform and five hats. Five. All mashed on her head. Looking out on the dance floor, you could always pick out her unique dance style, alternately twitching and then marching, all to a beat only she could hear.

There was the old-school butch, nattily dressed in chinos, button-down shirt, and sporting a duck tail. Her femme wore slacks, a pretty blouse, and had hair that defied gravity. Lord, could they jitterbug. As soon as the band struck up "Rock Around the Clock," they'd clean up the dance floor. I wish I could remember their names now.

Bon was a friend of mine, a hippie in torn jeans with a smile both playful and evil. I'm not sure why we called her Buns except it sounded like her name. Kathy was her girlfriend, otherwise known as Kung Fu, because she once took a martial arts class. Much sweeter than her nickname implied, she was usually found somewhere in Buns's wake. Buns was known for doing stupid stunts like riding her motorcycle after dropping acid, so maybe Kung Fu thought she could keep her safe, or maybe she was simply so in love she couldn't bear to be away from her.

Doc was often at the bar. He was an amiable, older guy with slicked-back hair who used to be a pharmacist; hence the nickname. If you were broke, Doc would buy you a drink. The only other man in the crowded bar would be one-half of the straight couple who ran the place. They owned a laundromat before this, so we were next in their scheme to make a living. One of the bartenders complained to me that the owners watered down the drinks. They were welcoming, though, and the place felt safe, so we didn't care much. It's not like we had too many other hangouts. We would've been kicked out of the straight bars, and it was rare to see women in the men's clubs.

There was a friendly feminist bunch from the university. Most were white and dressed in the requisite flannel shirts and jeans; they were in their twenties and thirties and were great dance partners.

Sometimes there were ladies of the evening who came in after working. They stood out because they were often the only women with makeup and in dresses. The Habit was a safe place for them because the men didn't bug them. And the rest of us didn't mind. Maybe they were lesbians. I never asked.

Barb sported a few more wrinkles than some of us. After slouching onto her favorite bar stool, she'd regale everyone with her stories, sprinkling them with hipster speak like "cool" and "groovy." It didn't matter if you met her five years or five minutes ago, she was your buddy.

There were lots of other regulars, too, faces I'd recognize

but didn't always remember their names. I flirted with the butches and gossiped with the femmes. Most were older than me. One night I was excited to find another eighteen-year-old. We confided in hushed tones about how it was to be the babies in that place. Funny, since "old" to me then was anyone in their twenties or later.

There was always something happening at The Habit. On Sunday there was a free buffet after the afternoon softball game at a nearby park. Tuesday night featured a solo musician. She was a skinny little thing with a big voice and acoustic guitar who blasted through covers by Phoebe Snow and Janis Joplin. Cheap beer on Thursday nights drew a huge crowd. Friday and Saturday nights featured the Indavana Blues Band. They weren't really a blues band. "Indavana" stood for "in the van of" because the guitarist and her drummer girlfriend drove a blue van. Along with Tuba on bass (her nickname because of the low sound of her instrument) and Rochelle "Roch" on harmonica and percussion, they banged out back-to-back songs great for shaking your booty or slow dancing with your sweetie.

On Donna Summer's "Love to Love You Baby," Tuba nailed that thundering bass line as the rest sang the refrain over and over, building to an orgasmic crescendo as the mass of sweaty bodies on the dance floor writhed to the beat. Another favorite was "London Homesick Blues." We raucously sang on the appealing chorus, dancing in a huge circle and conga line to the Jerry Jeff Walker favorite.

Before them, I'd never seen a woman behind a set of drums or playing an electric guitar. I had a mad crush on the guitar player. Her given name was Janine, but no one called her that. NeeNee wielded that axe like she'd been born with it. Her lover, Penny, sat behind the drums. A petite femme, the ring of drums and cymbals made her look even smaller. Tuba had beautiful olive skin, luminescent brown eyes, and jet-black hair. When she really got into a bass part, she'd kneel down and nod to the beat. Every butch in the joint wanted her. Roch was the youngest member of the band, a curly headed Latina who'd stomp back and forth as she wailed on her harmonicas. When she wasn't doing that, she added congas or tambourine, the counter to Penny's driving backbeat.

I wasn't sure how to make friends so I started baking cookies and bringing them to the bar. Rumor was that I baked with weed and while that made me feel badass, it wasn't true. They started calling me Cookie Lady. Barb shortened it to Cookie. I always made sure the band had some of my treats. Roch loved them and often had a stack on the small table that held her instruments. NeeNee didn't like cookies, so one night I brought her an avocado. Later there were other band members. I even thought of auditioning on bass when Tuba left the group, but I chickened out.

These bar women were my community and my family. They gave me courage to be an out lesbian at a time when no one else did. I thought of Big Jan when I was scared, the butch/femme couple when I danced (I can still do a decent jitterbug), Crazy Jan when I dressed (only one hat, though), and when I picked up my guitar, NeeNee. Years later, I toured nationally, performing for lesbians. It all started in a dinky bar populated with a cast of characters no screenwriter could make up. They were a habit I'm glad I didn't break.

****

Some of these nicknames aren't the kindest but it's what we used back then.

Except for the older couple, we didn't use "butch" and "femme" because we thought that was antiquated and patriarchal. However, looking back, it's clear to me that there were roles. I wore the androgynous uniform, but I was careful to have matching jewelry and flannel shirts in pretty colors. I could see subtle behaviors and ways of dress that differentiated the others, too. And there will always be a tender place in my heart for a handsome butch.

I tried to keep up with these women, but most have faded to memory. Roch went on to front several successful bands. NeeNee hung up her guitar and went to work for a natural foods company. I heard Barb passed away of cancer a few years ago. Lois and I reconnected after a twenty-year absence, and we see each other when we can. As for the others, I'd love to hear from them: jamie@jamieanderson.com.

The Territorial

by Lee Lynch

It wasn't possible in those days to be young and gay in NYC and not go to bars. One night I ended up at a place in Harlem called The Territorial. It greeted customers in the manner of prohibition speakeasies, with eyes peering through a window in a wooden door.

I was with Sophie, my first girlfriend, and by that time, my ex. Her lover Nadine Wallace—Wally in the bars—was there, too, a tough-as-nails, old-school butch who'd been Sophie's original connection to the gay world. Wally had given me a very hard time when I was still in high school because she wanted Sophie. We were white and Herm, also white, was our escort, a nice gay boy who was a regular, with his slight, funny, darker-skinned boyfriend, at The Territorial.

When I think back to the nineteen-year-old me boldly clubbing on 125th Street with this crew, Wally and Herm only slightly older than Sophie and me, it's no wonder the night ended the way it did. Sophie and Wally were high school dropouts who had a long way to go before they got where they needed to be. Herm didn't live with his boyfriend, but with his mother, in a small apartment in the Bronx.

This was a "bottle club," like The Stonewall Inn and many other illegal gay bars in the 1960s. You paid a cover and bought a setup, which consisted of overpriced mixers, ice, and glasses, to go with your own bottle. It was my practice to cash two-dollar checks at a grocery store to get me through a week at college, so if I managed to bring ten dollars with me, I probably spent it on dinner and the subway. Someone, probably Wally, paid my cover and bought the vodka.

At the time, I knew no other gay people. I had a sort of girlfriend at college, but she knew no one either and was probably out with her boyfriend that night. What can I say; it was the sixties and everyone was experimenting. Except me. I only wanted to be queer, be with queers, in queer places.

My problem was, as isolated as I was at school, I didn't belong with Herm and Wally at all. Sophie moved into their orbit after I left for college. I had a foot in both worlds, but there was no solid ground under me.

The Territorial was a huge high-ceilinged space, probably a former warehouse, possibly owned by organized crime. The management kept the lights low, and what light there was spiked the dark like flame. People sat on a balcony above us and across from us. It was typical of the hellish pits allotted to gays.

In those days, I experienced depressions so bad I could barely move. Light disappeared from my vision. I don't know how I kept from killing myself. I'd been prescribed tranquilizers called Milltowns, so I had the means, and I frequently mixed them with alcohol. By this, my sophomore year, I'd added marijuana and hash and speed to the mix. I like to believe some kind of higher power kept me alive so I could perform good works for my people, for gay people, so I could be one of the people to put our world on paper with words.

That night it was vodka and Milltowns. It was also fear—what was I doing so far uptown and with my nemesis, Wally, and two strange men? I'd lost my ability to connect with Sophie, or perhaps Wally intimidated her enough that she had to shut me out. I was lost, so lost, and no one was looking for me; no one even knew I was gone.

I drank the vodka straight, tipping the bottle up and pouring it down my throat. I was trying to quench my fear and confusion, trying to douse the conflagration of my unmoored blazing soul with this flammable liquid. I got blackout, out-of-control, drunk. Wally told Sophie to let me, if I needed to, when I took another and another draught. I'd hated the times my father came home drunk and my mother raged at him, but like him, I knew of no other solution. I didn't even know what I was trying to solve.

Gay people are kind. In the end, we take care of one another the best we can. That night it was Wally who nursed me when I was sick in the wreck of a bathroom. That night, it was Herm who skipped whatever romantic plans he had with his boyfriend to, I don't remember how, take me home, get me past his mother, give me a bed where I could sleep it off.

Goodness knows what would have happened if they'd let me loose in the post-midnight city, sent me off to Grand Central to catch a train back to school.

Goodness was what it took for them to keep me safe from a world that might not be kind to one more, nearly wasted, gay kid.

One Night Through My Lens

by Shawn Marie Bryan

A Point On The Wave

She hefted a case through the doorway. It was early; the bar wasn't open. I was let in to set up the camera. They even agreed to let the two just-shy-of-legal members of my volunteer crew join me. The work-around was to supply them with name tags, which was why I was sitting at the bar waiting to retrieve them while the intended recipients finished with the gear. I didn't mind. It was nice to tangibly feel a part of my community, rather than covering it, so to speak. It didn't matter that the joint was empty. In fact, it was better, more akin to the Zen I'd feel just knowing it, and a few others, existed any time I might need a relatively safer space to be among a greater family of strangers, bonded by a need of acceptance that couldn't be found elsewhere.

Well empty, save us, a few staff members, and the woman stocking the bar. She was beautiful, and that beauty extended to her strength and determination. I had seen her before. Not just here, but around in a few other bars and even at the helm of a music festival. Our community hosts the third largest Pride in the country—not a gigantic town, but a true heart-beating, growing, supportive one for the often exiled "us."

When you spend your spare time as a member of the cheekily named "Community News Team" for the second-rated PBS channel in the region, (but the only state to support two PBS stations...where in the world am I? Hint: each subtitle contains a lesbian bar name and this same PBS station hosted a music video show titled FMtv, which MTV had to pay off to name themselves...but I digress), you tended to see similar faces, especially a select few who were at the apex of making things happen or, more importantly, keeping the community together, even if they couldn't see that was part of their magic.

I wanted to talk to her. She fascinated me in all the right ways. Stop it! Yes, that was a right way, and yes, she set off my attraction alarm, no question, but I wasn't having lascivious thoughts.

For starters, I wasn't single, and I was working, and I didn't have nearly as much nerve as people thought I did. And I had tried—a few different times. When she organized an event, or opened a club, I would try not only to speak with her, but to capture an interview on film. She always referred me to her assorted partners in crime: her co-producers, co-owners, and actual co-partners. As I sat at the bar, watching her, a vague memory of me possibly handing her a card was interrupted by the bar opening and the manager appearing simultaneously.

"Turns out we don't actually have any name tags."

We agreed to keep my underage crew in the pool room with me, and she would send the fundraising organizer in as soon as she saw her. Not the woman behind the bar, the other organizer, naturally.

The segment was shot and the equipment repacked within a half hour. My young, yet almost adult, unit and I had a brief conversation on the sidewalk underneath the bar's unlit marquee. We discussed my assignment sheet for the night: a beer bust, a royalty pageant, a drag king (yay!) show, and getting b-roll of line dancing. All of this needed to be done in order to meet friends at the bar farthest across town to mark one friend's birthday before I dropped off the segments I edited the night before in time for the live newscast. Then if I wasn't too exhausted, I would join my regular group to wind down. They expressed envy for all the places I could get into. Perhaps they were too young to grasp how taxing a night it could be. I shared that I would rather hang out and talk with them, though they didn't believe me.

As we hugged our thank-you's and goodbyes, the lights for the sign flickered on. My young volunteers headed for their car. I turned to make my way to mine when I saw the woman from behind the bar peek out the door, look up, and nod with satisfaction that the lights under the sign had indeed turned on before she dipped back inside. I wondered when I might see her again, or a little more daringly, when we might actually speak, or even become friends.

Misdirected C Curls Crash

I was sitting at a bar, again. I didn't want to be. Was it ironic or just pathetic that I didn't actually drink? Having made it to the bar miraculously before my friend's birthday party had begun, I had no choice but to wait for them.

The night had gone typically, yet smooth overall. I was turned away from the beer bust because I am a woman, even though they invited the Community News Team to cover the fundraiser for a local AIDS foundation. Unfortunately, I was used to this treatment from that bar. It didn't matter that I was actually a lesbian (Queer Femme if you are into super specifics) and there to cover the event, not to participate. No women allowed at that gay bar. I explained for the umpteenth time that I was the "Street Team" and chances were if you invited us, you'd get me. Also, I would in no way be in front of the camera and would even edit and assign the story to the male anchor, but all to no avail.

Oh well, it freed me up to drive about twenty blocks across the longest continuous avenue in the contiguous United States (that's another location clue!) to capture some fantastic line dancing b-roll for a story about recovery. This particular bar was not without its controversies and prejudices, but at least they let everyone in. And it had divided itself so that whatever your music of choice might be, one side of the bar just might be blaring it.

A slight backtrack and perpendicular turn got me to the pageant with perfect timing for the crowning. It wasn't one of the highest titles, rather the lowest on the rung: Mr. and Ms. Gay Pride. Apparently their responsibility was to raise money for the awareness and inclusion of The Royal Court in the Pride parade and festivities. If there was anything left over, the money would go to The Center. (Too easy, many cities have a Center!)

The reactions I received while covering events for the Community News Team were as varied as the members within the rainbow, LGBTQQIAA, alphabet. Most weren't quite sure what to make of me. A few got excited to see me. A smaller percentage even embraced my seemingly nonsensical approaches to getting a clear picture to help tell a full story:

always get the kiss, and I stood firm that the lighting in the bathroom was the best for that queer-core band gearing up for Ladyfest Out West. (Ohhh, it was only called that in one town...) Luckily, they agreed. Some of the reactions were simply steeped in the patriarchal stereotype—that a woman was only supposed to voice the weather report, certainly not be operating the camera and setting it all up and hauling it back and forth in heels and (at that period in time) a corset top!

I think that's why the reactions from the Royalty crowd have remained my favorite. Mind you, and for those who may not have known, Royalty courts and their communities are comprised of a drag status quo. Yes, they perform, but it is more a way of life rather than just a show. Therefore, the men perform their gender expression as women and the women as men. So, it follows that the men couldn't get enough of me—until I stepped behind the camera and they quirked their heads in confusion. Whereas the women didn't have any time for me or even notice me until I stepped behind the camera. Then they, too, quirked their heads in confusion, not from doubt of my place or ability, but from my attire, as if they were saying, "Of course she can do that, and in heels, but why would she?"

Drag was a fairly big portion of the stories we shot for the show, not only because their presence among us was widespread, but also it was cinematic and fun! And no longer our secret gem. The mainstream, heteronormative society had been flocking to see the drag shows as well. At least for the queens. The kings didn't garner as much appeal from the masses. Which is a shame, because more often than not, the talent and the showmanship of the few king shows often outshone that of the more readily available queens.

Such was the case this evening, after I wrapped the crowning and headed out to film one of the scarce drag king shows. A mere few blocks farther south along the Way we call Broad, brought me to a bar I would have liked to spend more time in. Every time I went, I thought I would go back on my own when I wasn't working, and then life pulled me everywhere else. Maybe that was the case for lots of us, for this night's crowd was sparse. Great for me for camera angles and clearance but not so good for attendance, and therefore continued shows and support.

And the performers deserved that support—the show was fantastic! Now, admittedly, my first performer crush was on Fred Astaire and I am attracted to masculinity (as long as its core is all woman) so I might be a bit biased as to what turns my head. But I also come from a long life and education of theatre, so qualitatively, I feel rather confident in my enthusiasm for this show. Those who sang didn't miss a note; those who lip-synced razzle-dazzled above and beyond. And they all looked incredible. I remember smiling all the way to my next bar destination.

That high stayed with me, too, until I remembered why I wasn't so fond of the bar in which I currently sat. It isn't entirely fair that I put it all on this bar, for it was a prevalent vibe throughout this particular community during this particular time. This bar did become a symbol of it for me as I faced the majority of it here. The "it" I am speaking about was the active perception that femmes were not to be trusted. Apparently, there was a belief that femmes were actually straight, and that they just used butches and broke their hearts. Given that, it was a clear fact that butches could only trust and, therefore, only date or marry other butches. It was at this bar that a self-proclaimed butch shared this with me, pretty much verbatim as to how I've described it. I had heard similar theories and felt resultant chills throughout the bar scene. The activist in me wanted to scream a reminder of the butches, femmes, and drag queens who fought back at Stonewall. My Judy Butler-, Joan Nestle-, and Leslie Feinberg-wired brain wanted to get all theoretically practical up in here.

Instead, I remembered why we all sought these bars in the first place, why there were stories and events to cover in the first place: our shared need for tactile compassion, a home where our one commonality didn't incite rage, disgrace us, or cause us to be shunned or ignored. For even with these offshoots, I, too, still needed these establishments and, believe it or not, every member of the community they served.

As I created my own warm fuzzies, I took a look around. The butch who shared the distasteful (and in my opinion, inaccurate) Untrustworthy Femme Theory was sitting at a table with a femme! My gaze continued and caused my newly acquired smile to cease quickly when it landed on my ex. Not just any ex—the ex who swore I saved her life, that I was the absolute only one for her. The ex was sitting with her girlfriend. I'd like to say "new girlfriend"; however, she was really her longstanding girlfriend, the one she neglected to tell me about the entire time I was the only one for her.

Have we come full circle?

Luckily, my friend and her entire birthday party arrived and I was whisked away into the merriment. Toward the end of the celebration, the birthday gal's partner asked me why I had such a perplexed expression on my face when they arrived. I shared my ex's presence and that I only wished my current girlfriend were here to show I hadn't been squandered. Yes, we both laughed and recognized it was petty, and surely we were mature enough and solid in our feminist beliefs to know it was an invalid thought. Our worth comes from so many better places. Nevertheless, she guided me up and onto the dance floor with her hand on my lower back—swoon—and twirled me around with such pride for all the world to see. We waltzed and two-stepped and laughed, and I danced in my head all the way to my last bar of the night.

Detour To A Sustaining Home

When I think about the bar scene, and specifically my time within it—or rather, when I needed it—I'm very aware of how fortunate I was to have a handful of bars to choose from. And further, how lucky I was, and felt, to find the one that resonated for me the most.

For me, it wasn't an immediate fix or oasis. I had heard about this bar for years, but my sanctuary was always the library and activism, even when I shared these activities with no one. And, as I've mentioned, I didn't drink, so going to a bar never really entered my consciousness.

Then, the library underwent renovations, and I had just started writing a new play. I vaguely remembered that this bar was open for lunch, so I popped in, and continued to pop in during the day to write and sip a Dr. Pepper.

One evening out with a friend, she asked if I fancied a

game of Scrabble and drove us there to play. There I was in this bar, at night, playing a word game with a friend, sipping a Dr. Pepper, and it hit me: a feeling of complete ease. I didn't have to drink, I didn't have to cruise or be cruised. More important, I could simply be who I was without judgment or shame.

This was why we sought these places. This was why they were important and safe. They were home, even if just for a few hours one night (or day) a week. That was exactly how I felt walking into this—my—bar to unwind from a busy night before I could complete my scheduled to-dos. Meeting my chosen gang, breathing in the air of a shared space, with, at the very least, an underlying, even if unknown, purpose.

I was not immune from some drama or unpleasantness. I was stood up, swindled, almost punched. I was also applauded, welcomed, and experienced an eye-opening romantic encounter that has forever changed me. There were even times when I acted like a petulant child when friends wanted to go to another bar!

Incidentally, I didn't ever film or cover a story there. I could write there because that was how I dreamed. I could play, I could talk, and sometimes even sing. But not work. This bar was too important to me to bring work in. A sanctuary is only as pure as you keep it, and the happiest of hours aren't always designated by drink specials or certain times of day.

I didn't fully understand all of this on that night all those years ago. I knew I was happy to almost end my night there. I knew I would tip the server, with whom I had become friends, and because I didn't order alcohol, would tip one hundred percent. I knew once I got home after delivering the edited stories to the newsroom, that I would sleep well and not even be tired the next day because I had this bubble to process within, and that always made a difference.

As the years went on and the world evolved, these bars, including mine, were co-opted by other communities, rendering them effectively ineffective. The Community News Team disbanded. Young interns would try to teach, or tell, me how to be gay. I had several straight friends invite me to their favorite lesbian bar, completely unaware of the irony and the condescension.

We demanded safe, respecting spaces from a need as legitimate as bleeding and breathing. We paved the road for this expansion all the way to a point where we could leave these bars behind. Too bad the (unintentional, I hope) condescension couldn't be left behind as well. Actually, upon reflection, we didn't leave them behind, we carry them with us. In much the same way one might carry a passport or a green card. And the friends and connections we made during those years have morphed into an unspoken family. One we would (will) have to wrap around ourselves when we need that safety, that bubble, that autonomy, for as depressing as it sounds, you can never go home again. Especially if that home, that bar, my bar, is now a 7-11. (That is the last location clue.)

A Follow-Up (Because I'm still a reporter!)

That family, the one I wrap around myself, is real. (Those two underage interns hanging with me in the pool room? They got married and are still my very close friends.) A few years ago, people I met during my personal Happy Hour refuge and those who experienced it with me, started mentioning a person I needed to meet. This person's name kept coming up in several different circles as someone they were shocked I didn't already know, and that, Yes! I needed to meet her.

Remember the woman stocking the bar?

Enter the woman stocking the bar!

When we did "officially" meet, the power of our shared community sealed our friendship forever. Now she and I marvel at how we never quite met back then. We also, rightfully, refer to each other as our wonder twin. Then, a year or so into our twinship, she found in her possession that very calling card I had thought I might have managed to present to her. She even sent me a photograph of it for proof.

That happened. It all happened. It was a need. It was real. It will live on with all of us as its legacy. As long as we rise to the challenge.

Sharon's Lookout

by Anne Laughlin

1983

Sharon stood in the middle of the dance floor, a microphone dangling from her hand, resplendent in her custom-tailored tuxedo. The audience leaned toward her with expectant faces. There was a crackling tension in the air. She kept them waiting as she smoothed her ducktail and lit a cigarette from the silver case kept in her jacket pocket. Finally, she brought the microphone to her mouth.

"And the winner of the Fifth Annual Sharon's Lookout Talent Show is...Miss Lulu Lux!" The crowd roared as a vanishingly thin drag queen wearing a shimmering silver gown wound her way through the crowd and onto the dance floor. Sharon handed her an engraved plaque for her impeccably lip-synched performance of Donna Summer and Barbra Streisand's "No More Tears (Enough is Enough)." The audience was effusive in their love of Miss Lulu, but not particularly surprised. She was the best drag queen in town and had won the contest two times before. It was hard for the lesbians to compete with the queens. Their best act that night had been a trio of dykes singing Chris Williamson's "Song of the Soul" in perfect three-point harmony. It was frustrating.

Kelly swung her stool around and faced the back bar, a landscape as familiar to her as home. Perhaps more so. She'd gotten to Sharon's Lookout early that day and had one of the best seats to watch the show. When you arrive at three for an eight o'clock start time, there isn't much competition for the bar stools. Whenever possible, Kelly sat on the same stool, three seats from the end of the bar. From here she had a commanding view of the pool table, the dance floor, and the tables surrounding it. Sharon once threatened to install a brass nameplate on the back of it. She was the owner of the only gay bar in Cedar Rapids, which made her a powerful person. If you violated her code of conduct, or she turned on you for whatever reason, she'd 86 you, and that could end your social life. Fighting, for instance, was a violation, but you usually got one pass. If you fought a second time, you were out. Kelly knew of one man who bounced a check, fell off his bar stool, and got into a fight all in one week, and Sharon showed him the door. There wasn't much news of him after that.

The quiet in the bar lasted only a minute before the disco ball dropped and more Donna Summer blasted from the speakers. A woman climbed onto the stool next to Kelly, ordered a shot of tequila, and tossed it back with the practiced hand of a dedicated drinker. Kelly looked her over. She was familiar, but the city was small and the gay and lesbian community tight knit. Everyone, at the very least, looked familiar. The woman returned her gaze and gave her a crooked smile.

"Like what you see?"

For someone who'd been drinking for the past six hours, Kelly sounded remarkably sober. "I know I've seen you before, but I can't quite place you."

"Same here." She lit a cigarette and motioned to the bartender for a round. She was stocky with a strong, handsome face and more muscle than fat. "I don't get into town that often."

"Where do you live?" Kelly was a little interested. Not a lot.

"I have a farm out by Mount Vernon. I come here about once a month." It sounded positively Amish, like she drove the wagon into town on market days.

The bartender plunked their drinks on the bar. She was an enormous woman wearing a muscle tee with a labrys hanging around her neck on a thick chain. Kelly picked up her beer bottle. "It seems like we must have had a conversation or something, because I feel like it was more than just seeing your face. My memory's not that great." That was an understatement. She considered herself lucky if she woke in the morning and could remember whether she'd done anything horrible. "I'm Kelly, by the way."

"Denise." They were quiet for a while, staring straight ahead, tending to their cigarettes. "Did we sleep together?"

That hadn't occurred to Kelly, but now she wondered. She had no memory of it, but that didn't eliminate it as a possibility. She was encouraged by the fact Denise didn't seem to know either. "I don't think so. If I slept with you, I'm sure I would've remembered." This seemed the most diplomatic approach.

She laughed. "Maybe. Anyway, it's nice to meet you." A petite woman came up and put her hand on Denise's shoulder. "C'mon, sweetheart. We've got to get going." Denise immediately climbed off the stool and threw some money on the bar. "This is my girlfriend, Penny." Kelly nodded at her. "We're going to have a big camping weekend at our farm this summer. We'll barbeque some of our chickens and roast a pig. I'll make sure you're invited." There was still too much Chicago in Kelly for her to ever understand a pig roast, but it wasn't the first one she'd been invited to since moving to Iowa. It was part of the cultural landscape, like going to Scotland and eating haggis.

She looked at her watch. It was only ten. She saw a group of her friends sitting at a table and thought about joining them, but she was starting to fade. Sharon was standing at the end of the bar and motioned her over.

"Take this," she said and slipped a miniature bottle of cocaine into the front pocket of her jeans. "You look like you could use a pick-me-up."

"Thanks." As she turned toward the bathroom, Sharon put her hand on her arm.

"Are you going to the pot luck tomorrow?"

"Aren't they mandatory?" Kelly said. There was a lesbian pot luck almost every weekend, hosted by a rotating group of women who owned houses large enough for the thirty or so dykes who showed up.

Sharon kept her hand on her arm. "Listen, there's a new girl in town and I want you to introduce her to people, make her feel comfortable."

Kelly was shocked and a little flattered. "Me? That's a surprising choice."

Sharon laughed. "You'll be fine. You're actually a pretty nice person, behind the swagger, that is. Maybe you could promise to not make a pass at her." She took a slip of paper out of her pocket and handed it to Kelly. "Here's her number. Offer to pick her up."

She knew she'd been given orders, like a lieutenant

sending a squad out on a patrol. She wasn't that comfortable with new people, particularly when she was sober, but it wouldn't kill her. Maybe the girl would be cute. "Okay. I'll call her in the morning."

"I knew I could count on you," Sharon said. "We've got to look out for our own."

Kelly smiled without really meaning it. She just wanted to get to the bathroom to do some coke. She waited in line for the one-seater bathroom to open up. Someone tapped on her shoulder, and when she turned around, her friend Grace wrapped her in a hug. She was one of Kelly's best friends, the kind that would help her out with anything and never expect a thank-you. She worked as a laborer on a construction crew, and her standard apparel was T-shirt, jeans, worn seed cap, and a wallet secured to her back pocket by a wide, metal chain. The only difference between her daytime and nighttime wear was she put on a clean version for the evening. They didn't have a lot in common other than drinking and being lesbian, but that was plenty.

"I got laid off today," Grace said. She got laid off a lot. It was the nature of the construction business.

"That stinks. Can you hook up with some other site?"

"There's not much construction going on right now. Fucking recession." She lit a cigarette with her Zippo and squinted at Kelly through the smoke. "You know my tools got stolen the other day, don't you?"

Kelly gasped. Having tools stolen was a very serious matter. You were expected to have your own when you signed up with a crew. It was like a musician having a violin stolen, and nearly as expensive. "Oh, Christ." She didn't know what to say, so she passed Sharon's coke to her. It was the least she could do.

Grace handed it back. "Thanks, but I got to stay away from that for the moment."

Surprised, Kelly stuck it back in her pocket. "What are you going to do?"

Grace sucked on her cigarette. "Sharon's going to let me do cleanup after closing time, at least for the next month while Jamie's gone."

"Oookay. That means you have to stay sober until closing time." Kelly knew she had a look of horrified sympathy on her face.

Grace laughed. "I think I can manage it. I'm grateful for the work."

The bathroom opened up and Grace went in first. Sharon didn't allow two people in the bathroom at once. Kelly went in when Grace was done and cut up four lines on the top of the toilet tank. When she looked in the mirror to make sure she didn't have any powder on her nose, she saw a thin face with long, red hair and glasses, a little blurry eyed, but not much the worse for wear. She was proud of having inherited her father's hollow wooden leg. She could drink for hours and not show her drunkenness, at least in her opinion. Perhaps others thought differently.

The coke roared through her bloodstream, which usually made her want to party and talk. Mostly talk. But she didn't feel like it tonight. She said goodnight to Grace, returned the bottle to Sharon, and headed home. She lived three blocks from the bar in the basement apartment of a three-story office building. She must have been drunk when she rented it. The entire apartment had knotty pine paneling and old, stringy carpet. On the sunniest of days she had to turn on all the lights in order to see anything. It was depressing beyond belief. She got into bed, propped herself against her pillows with her last beer of the day, and picked up *Middlemarch,* the novel she'd been reading for months. The coke allowed her to focus on the words, while the alcohol guaranteed she'd forget everything she read the next day.

****

Her duties at Sunday's pot luck as social conduit for Sharon's newbie lasted about ten minutes. Gail was in her late twenties and knew how to socialize. As soon as they walked into the crowded living room, she disappeared from Kelly's side, apparently not the least bit interested in her. By the time Kelly left a half hour later, she saw Gail sitting on the giant bartender's lap, shrieking with laughter. She trotted to her car, anxious to be away from people. It was an entirely different thing being around people in a bar—you could talk or not talk, engage with people, or stare at the back of the bar. Parties forced her to be on her social game from start to finish, and she had no social game today. She didn't feel well, she was cranky, and the alcohol didn't seem to be doing its job of making all well with the world. She applied more alcohol to the problem when she got home but remained out of sorts until she passed out.

Now it was Monday, the most dreadful day of the week. Kelly pulled on her work clothes—a skirt suit, pantyhose that dug into her beer belly, and a white blouse with a foulard at the collar. She felt like the drag queens must—transformed by costume. Her apartment was across the street from the law office where she worked as a paralegal, a job she really liked despite the horrible clothes. She researched, assisted at trial, interviewed witnesses, digested information, and whatever else her boss dreamed up. They gave her a lot of autonomy and responsibility. She chucked her coat and bag into her office and climbed the stairs to see what he had in store for her that day.

Tim White had the biggest corner office in a small firm of five lawyers. He was the name partner, the experienced trial lawyer, a fat, self-satisfied man. He actually liked to say in front of a jury that he was "just a simple country lawyer," as if anyone would believe that. His office door was open and he waved her in.

"We've got that hearing at ten, and I want you with me. Then I need your help on a couple work comp cases." He often dispensed with the pleasantries.

"What cases are those?" Kelly was already looking past the courtroom appearance, which usually entailed carrying stuff for him and not much else.

"The Mitchell case, in particular. We have a hearing in a couple days, and I want you to check him out, figure out if he's faking his injury."

Kelly loved assignments like that. She often did investigative work—checking out accident scenes, interviewing witnesses, tracking down documents, and spying on plaintiffs suspected of malingering. It got her out of the office, and she took full advantage of the freedom. At two in the afternoon she left in the new Mercury Zephyr Tim co-signed for her and drove to Hiawatha, a tiny town on the northern border of the city.

The file identified the injured worker as John Mitchell. She knew a John Mitchell from the bar. He was one of the lesser drag queens, a bit too masculine to pull it off well, but everyone loved him. No way could it be the same John Mitchell, though once she thought about it, she had no idea what he did for a living. That was part of outside life, which tended to disappear when you stepped into Sharon's Lookout. That was where you could be your true self, independent of the role played to fit in with the straight world. People didn't talk much about their jobs or their difficult families. Sharon's was its own world, with its own rules, its own sensibility, its own population glued together by the one thing they all shared. Being gay was the only requirement for admission. The few straight people who came in, many of them sightseers, were not made to feel welcome. It seemed only fair that for once gays could move the shoe to the other foot.

Kelly pulled up to a tiny ranch house. The town was run-down and so were all the houses on the block. Some had rusted cars up on racks in front of the garages, toilets in the front yard, wooden porch stairs gray with weathering and listing to one side. The Mitchell house stood out like a gem. It had a green, uncluttered lawn, painted trim, attractive curtains, paved driveway, newly planted flower beds. She parked one house up from it and made herself as comfortable as her hangover would allow. Not the worst she'd ever had by a long shot, but it seemed disproportionately bad for her minor drunkenness on Sunday. The day was sunny and mild, a harbinger of spring finally arriving. She tuned into the Cubs game on the radio and settled in.

Fifty minutes later Mitchell appeared in the front yard with a lawn mower, which he proceeded to push up and down the yard with apparent ease, no sign of the back injury he claimed to have sustained in a work-related car accident. The bigger surprise was that he was the John Mitchell she knew from the bar. He wore slim blue jeans and a tight T-shirt, as if he were headed to Sharon's right after the lawn was done. She took some photos of him pushing, pulling, bending, and lifting. She had a job to do, but she felt bad her evidence was going to torpedo his claim, maybe lose him his job. He was a really nice guy, one of the gay men who spent plenty of time with the lesbians at Sharon's. She felt disloyal.

The best thing about investigation assignments was her boss never knew how long they were going to take. At three-thirty it felt like time to knock off for the day. She drove home to change and walked over to Sharon's, where her seat was waiting for her. Sharon had her beer on the bar before she sat down.

"How'd it go yesterday?" Sharon asked. She never came to the pot lucks; she said after six days of being around homos she wanted peace and quiet.

"It was fine. I hardly spent any time with Gail. She made twenty new friends in five minutes."

Sharon looked proud, as if she'd sent a child off to college. "Some people are like that. Natural extroverts."

Kelly drank from her beer. "I'm not one of those."

"No, you're not. And yet you spend all your time around people in this bar."

Kelly put her beer down, and a hot flash of shame coursed through her. "Is that a problem?"

"Not at all. I was simply pointing out the irony." Sharon served another customer, one of the older gay men who came in during the afternoons. When she returned, Kelly had a scowl on her face. "Come on. You're not pouting about what I said, are you?" She laughed. "You need to get over yourself."

Kelly felt shaken, as if an earthquake was rumbling beneath the house she grew up in. Some kind of foundation was in danger. She ordered a shot of vodka, and Sharon poured two. They knocked them back and slammed the glasses on the bar, as was the custom. Kelly decided to change the topic.

"Something weird happened today. I'd like your advice on it."

Sharon poured them two more shots. "I'm listening." She was good at listening. She acted as confessor to the hundred or so gays and lesbians who came regularly to the bar.

Kelly told her about seeing John Mitchell cheating on his work comp claim. "I have photos of him mowing his lawn. There's no denying he's faking his injury."

"But there would be deniability if there were no photos?" Sharon leaned toward Kelly over the bar.

"For now, I guess. But if he keeps stretching out the weeks of his workers' compensation, they'll send me out again."

"John's a nice guy," Sharon said. She came around the

bar and sat on the stool next to Kelly. She pulled it in close, invading her personal space.

"He is that."

"Remember when Andy Wilson broke his femur a few months ago? John moved in and took care of him until he could get around on his own. He's that kind of guy. An important part of our community."

"I know. That's why I was a little surprised he's pulling this scam." She leaned away from Sharon and downed the shot of cold vodka.

"Well, you know what to do." Sharon looked at her steadily.

She felt a chill at the back of her neck. "I do?"

"You have to get rid of the photos you took today. I'll call John and you drive back out there and get some shots of him with a cane or walker, or whatever he's using." She put her hand on mine. "He'd do the same for you."

"I don't even know him that well." Her voice sounded like someone was pressing on her vocal cords.

Sharon squeezed her hand. "Do it for me, then."

"I don't know. I could get into trouble."

Sharon squeezed harder and looked Kelly in the eye. "It'll be fine. Just do what I say, and no one will know a thing about it."

She stayed silent, trying to find a way around Sharon without running straight through her. There didn't seem to be one. Sharon took her little bottle out of her shirt pocket and handed it to her. "Why don't you go in the bathroom and get yourself straightened out. I'll call John." She got off the stool and went around the bar to the phone.

Kelly did three or four lines of coke and scrubbed her nose clean without looking in the mirror. As the coke hit her system she went from feeling jangly and afraid to confident and in control. Why wouldn't it work? There's no reason her boss wouldn't believe the rigged photos. She joined Sharon at the bar.

"Did you get hold of him?"

Sharon turned from the phone with a smile. "We're all set. I told him you'd get there in about half an hour. If you park in front of his house, he'll see you and come out the door with his walker."

"Okay. I'll head out now."

"First thing though, and don't forget this, you need to expose and get rid of the film you already shot. Got that?" Sharon looked at her like a coach sending a kicker out into the field.

Kelly walked back to her apartment. Her only anxiety now was to get the mission accomplished and return to the bar to start drinking. She picked up her camera, opened the back, and removed the film, destroying all the images on it. She reloaded the camera, headed out to Hiawatha, and parked in front of John Mitchell's house. Soon he came out the front door, stepping gingerly behind a walker and slowly making his way to his car. He didn't look toward her. She took as many photos as would do the job and drove away. The first rush of coke was easing up. She stopped at a Quick Mart to pick up a can of beer for the drive back.

Sharon was waiting for her and had a beer and a shot on the bar as soon as she walked through the door. "Did you get it done?"

"Yeah. It's done." She drank the vodka and started on her beer. "I'll give my report to my boss tomorrow morning and have the film developed."

Sharon looked pleased and poured Kelly another shot. "Good girl. Drinks are on the house tonight."

Kelly proceeded to take full advantage of the offer. Several trips to the bathroom with Sharon's bottle of coke kept her going until closing time, that terrifying time of the night when all that was left was the weaving walk home to her empty apartment. At one point in her life she'd loved being alone. Now it meant there was no distraction from the fact that she was stinking drunk, just as she was most days of the week. If she was lucky, she immediately went to bed and slept like the dead. If she was wired from coke or simply unable to stop, she drank more beer in her dark, silent living room. She could feel her heartbeat, almost hear it. Eventually she'd pass out in her chair.

Tuesday was almost unbearable. Her hangover was one of the worst ever. If a normal person felt that bad, they'd call an ambulance. But Kelly was used to it; she knew she'd somehow live to drink another day. She dropped the new film off to be developed and went immediately up to her boss's office to report on her John Mitchell surveillance. She felt detached, as if she were in an audience, watching another Kelly onstage, glibly telling him that Mitchell seemed quite injured. He took it in stride and handed her the file, asking her to summarize the medical records and prepare it for the work comp hearing.

"You don't look very well," he said. "Are you feeling all right?"

"Not really. I feel sick to my stomach." She wasn't lying. He gave her the rest of the day off, a salvation. She walked quickly across the street to her apartment, where she threw up, changed her clothes, grabbed a beer from the fridge, and collapsed on her small sofa. The beer would normally settle her stomach and make her feel better, but today she could barely drink it. It was a hangover that topped all her hangovers. She didn't touch a drop after that first sip of beer.

The next day she sat at her desk and tackled her backlog of work. She felt a million times better than the day before, but still a little off. By late afternoon she was caught up and looking forward to going to Sharon's after work. Her boss called her up to his office. Kelly had nearly forgotten the whole John Mitchell caper, until she heard his voice on the phone. She sat in one of the chairs in front of his desk and didn't see anything in his face that alarmed her. "What can I do for you, boss?"

"Do you have those photos from yesterday? I'd like to take a look at them."

"I picked them up at lunch." She ran downstairs to her office and grabbed the photos. So far so good. Tim looked at them for some time before looking up at her.

"You personally took these photos yesterday?"

Something lurched in her midsection, as if she'd hit a particularly strong pocket of turbulence. "Of course."

"It's a puzzle, then. I just got off the phone with the general counsel's office at the insurance company. He got a report from someone at the company Mitchell works for that makes these photos very peculiar."

Kelly's heart rate accelerated. She couldn't believe what was happening. She stayed quiet as Tim went on. "Seems his sales manager saw Mitchell at the Walmart yesterday, stacking huge bags of planting soil and mulch into the trunk of his car. He confronted Mitchell, who basically admitted he'd been faking his injury, at least for the last few weeks." He looked sad as he stared at her. "Tell me what happened here."

Her skin felt on fire and she couldn't think straight. She knew there was no way out of this.

"The thing I don't understand," he said, "is why you did it. Is Mitchell a secret boyfriend of yours, a cousin? What does he have on you that would make you do something so stupid? And wrong."

She had no answer for this either. If she told him John Mitchell was an acquaintance, she'd look even more stupid. She stood there mute until Tim did what he had to do.

A half hour later she walked into the bar and saw Sharon brushing down the pool tables. Wednesday was the weekly pool tournament, a big night for the lesbians. She sat on her stool and fiddled with a coaster. Sharon came around the bar and stood in front of her.

"They found out about Mitchell," Kelly said. She was straining to maintain her composure.

"I don't understand," Sharon said. She looked concerned but perfectly calm.

"I got fired. I lost my fucking job helping John Mitchell." Her face crumpled and she started to cry. "Now I'm in real trouble."

Sharon grabbed a box of tissues on the back bar and put it in front of Kelly. "Let it out, honey. That's a bad shock." She patted her on the arm.

"A bad shock? I've never felt so humiliated in my life." She couldn't bear it. Tim had seemed nearly as sad as he was angry, said she'd betrayed his trust. She put her hands to her face. "What am I going to do?" The thought of trying to find another paralegal job made her ache. She'd searched a long time to find the one at Tim White's office. No one wanted the cost of a paralegal, not in Cedar Rapids.

"It's all going to be okay," Sharon said. She reached down and pulled out a beer. "At least you know one thing. You're not an alcoholic. We've talked all this time, and you haven't even asked for a drink."

That was good to hear. For a second it trumped her sorrow. She'd wondered if she was alcoholic, and it was a huge relief to hear she wasn't. Sharon would know. She'd seen plenty of drunks. She took a drink from the bottle. "I'm really scared. I don't have any savings."

Sharon passed her the perpetually full bottle of coke. "You need a little something extra, I think." She could feel her accelerated heartbeat, the tightness in her chest—probably not the best condition in which to snort coke. She just wanted this awful feeling to go away. When she returned to the bar she passed the bottle back to Sharon. A shot of vodka was waiting for her, and she drank it down.

"I know you went out of your way to help someone in our community," Sharon said. "Now I'll help you the way you tried to help John."

Kelly looked at her with a blank face. "How's that?"

"You'll come to work here. Day shift. I've been thinking for some time that I should be here more at night, to keep an eye on things. It'll take about fifteen minutes to show you the ropes."

Kelly felt stunned. Too much was happening at once. Did she want to work for Sharon? Did she have a choice? There was something appealing about having a reason for practically living at the bar. At least until she could figure out what to do. She nodded her head.

Sharon's face lit up with a smile. She had a devastating smile, one that made you believe you were the most important person to her, that her happiness could inspire your own. "Excellent." She dropped two shot glasses on the bar and poured more vodka. "Why don't you start tomorrow?"

Poem for the Queer Spaces
Where Love Blooms in New York

by JP Howard

Some days I have no words,
just memory of her scent
as she leaned in to kiss me.

My bar stool melted,
the club became a spinning wheel and
everyone around us disappeared.

The beat beat beat of house music,
her lips fire against my neck, when she whispered:
I've dreamed about kissing you every day since we met.

I repeated that line to lovers in New York clubs over the years.
It was true, each time I whispered or begged or texted,
I've dreamed about kissing you every day since we met.
Oh how I've always loved the scent of womyn in clubs;
sweaty bodies drenched with Egyptian musk.
Rhythm of DJ's helped us forget the world beyond those club
doors.

ROLL CALL:
I remember all the New York ladies' clubs, each one a new
adventure.
I kissed beautiful womyn in the Clit Club, Cubby Hole, The Box
and
on the second floor of Crazy Nanny's, in the back, by the bar.
I once kissed my secret lover in a public corner windowsill of
Henrietta Hudson's on Halloween eve.
A lavender skeleton dangled above us, she slid her hand under
my shirt and
I whispered, *I've dreamed about kissing you every day since we
met.*

We were young and free, all our bodies sexy.
We pushed up against one another on dance floors,
butches in oxford wingtips and femmes in stilettos,
swirling until the music stopped.

The Treasure Chest

by L. K. Early

The day after I sold my grandmother's bar, I went in person to give my cousin, Chris, her share of the profits. I don't know why I went in person. Perhaps I felt like I owed Chris something, though I hadn't seen her since I left Buffalo for NYC ten years ago. Perhaps I felt like it was the right thing to do, like my grandmother would've wanted it. Perhaps I just wanted to see the place one more time.

It was early winter, and the sun was just setting in the sky like a cat settles in for a cozy afternoon nap. I stood on the opposite side of the street, staring at the hole-in-the-wall dive for a long time before I decided to go in. The outside looked just like I'd remembered it: old wood paneling, a heavy wooden door, a single broad window with the name hand-painted across it in old-fashioned gold lettering, *The Treasure Chest*.

As I crossed the street to get a better look at the place, I couldn't help but feel a twinge of remorse. But then I noticed the way the paint was chipped and faded and in need of retouching. And when I pulled open the front door, the little bell smacked impotently against the door frame rather than ringing out like it used to. The effect was less than inviting. Even less inviting was the dusty, defunct jukebox that sat under the window.

I knew I had made the right decision.

The place was nearly empty, save for a single customer, a woman in her forties sitting at the far end of the bar. She looked up, raised her beer to me in salutation, then went back to texting on her phone. Chris was nowhere to be seen. I stepped inside, and unzipped my coat, and walked without thinking toward the wall of framed photographs.

I could have described them all with my eyes closed, but I wanted to see them anyway, for old time's sake. The photos closest to the door were the oldest and the fewest. They were my favorites, perhaps because there were only four of them: a charming woman in a military uniform; a lanky bartender in the widest necktie I'd ever seen; a long line of women in suits and fedoras, all facing the camera with cigars clenched between their teeth; and finally, a photo of my grandmother herself, in a poodle skirt and fuzzy sweater, laughing at the camera in a startled sort of happiness. Someone had written in pencil in the bottom right corner: *Dotty at The Spot.*

I remembered how my grandmother would linger before these four photos on slow afternoons just like this one.

"My treasures," she'd whisper to herself.

I often asked her about the picture of herself, "Where are you? What is The Spot?"

"Here, silly," she'd say. "This place used to be called The Spot a million years ago, before I bought it."

"Why'd you change the name?"

"No reason..."

"Who took the picture? What are you laughing at?"

"No one in particular," she'd say. "And it doesn't matter anyways. It was the happiness that mattered, wasn't it? That's the part *they* couldn't stand."

A darkness would settle over her face, and she'd make herself busy with work again. I never asked her who *they* were, but as I grew older and learned my queer history, I could guess.

I straightened the frame that always seemed to hang at a slant. The photos spanned the entire length of the wall. The people in them wore the mini-skirts and beehives of the sixties, then the plaid and silk of the seventies, then the leather and denim of the eighties, and so on. And closest to the bar, there were pictures of us, Chris and me, back when we were young and fresh out of the closet and finding ourselves. Luckily, we didn't have to look much further than the family business.

"I don't have much room to speak," I said, smiling.

But when I looked up, she was leaning against the back of the bar with her arms crossed. "Why are you here, Eileen?"

I swallowed. "It's done."

She nodded and pursed her lips—apparently less than pleased, but also less than resigned to the fact. "Since when?"

"Since yesterday."

She nodded again. "Okay."

She turned curtly away and began to unpack the crate as if the conversation were over.

"I brought your share," I said after a beat.

"Could have just put it in the mail."

"I know, but I thought—I guess I wanted to take a stroll down memory lane."

She scoffed and shook her head. "Good for you."

"Look, Chris. This is just business. It's nothing personal."

"How can you say that?"

"Take a look around!" I said. "This place is falling apart."

"It needs a little work, that's all," she mumbled.

"That's not what the contractor said, and you know it. The plumbing, the floors, the tiles in that filthy bathroom. How long has it been since that jukebox played a song?"

At that she was quiet.

"Look, this place is an investment with no return. Better to sell now and get a little bit of cash than to let it fall into complete disrepair and get nothing. Besides, not many people are buying in this market. We're lucky we got what we did."

"That's easy for you to say."

"Come on, Chris. I've helped you as best I could up until now. But I can't keep this place floating for much longer, and neither can you. Take the money and be happy. That's what Grandma would have wanted."

"You don't know that."

"Fair enough, but it's not like we can just call her up and ask her, can we?"

My words were a little harsh, and I regretted them immediately.

"What if I *am* happy?" Chris said. "What if this isn't just some memory for me? This is my life, Eileen. This place *is* my happiness."

"And mine!" The woman at the end of the bar raised her glass in a toast and took a long swig.

"And Doreen's!" Chris continued. "And many other people's. This isn't just a bar. You know that. There's history here. A lot of it. This place means a *lot*...to a lot of people."

I looked around the room. "And where are they? Where are all these people?"

"It's still early," she said.

"Yeah," Doreen chimed in again. "Just wait till happy hour. That's when the business gets good."

"I'm sorry to say it, but it would take more than one good night to save this place." I reached into my bag and pulled out an envelope. I pushed it across the bar. "Take the money, Chris. You've earned it."

She glanced at the envelope then picked up the empty crate and headed for the hall. I guessed the conversation really was over, so I grabbed my coat and made for the door.

"Where are you going?" she called after me.

"I thought I'd worn out my welcome."

"Well, Margie called out sick tonight. So why don't you put an apron on and get your butt behind the bar?"

"All right," I said. "For old times' sake."

But no sooner had I stepped behind the bar than we heard a loud crash down the hall, like an anvil had dropped and then shattered into a million pieces (if anvils were made of glass, of course.). Chris nearly dropped her crate, and Doreen almost fell from her stool.

"What now?" Chris grumbled as she headed down the hall.

I watched her shadow on the wall. She stomped sullenly toward the sound, then paused, then set the crate down.

"Everything okay?" I called.

"Eileen, I think you should come see this," she called back.

I looked at Doreen. She saluted me and took another swig of beer.

I found Chris standing over the enormous mirror that had hung on the wall by the bathroom for as long as I could remember. And now here it was, leaning like a drunk against the wall, the glass shattered all over the floor, and the frame broken and twisted from the impact of the crash.

"Look," Chris whispered.

It was the whisper that raised the hairs on the back of my neck, even before I saw what she was looking at. There in the empty space where the mirror once hung, was a little metal door. It was about the size of a medicine cabinet and set into the wall. On the right side were two rusted metal hinges, and on the left was a little screw-sized hole.

"What is that?" I took a step closer, crunching the

glass beneath my shoes.

"Looks like a safe," Chris said.

"Did you know about this?"

"No way."

"What do you think is inside?"

"How should I know?" she said.

Doreen called from the other room, "Everything okay?"

"Yeah!" Chris called back. "We'll be out in a minute!"

We returned our attention to the safe, leaning really close, so close that our heads were almost touching. I probed the little screw hole with the tip of my finger.

"This thing looks old," I said. "And where's the handle?"

"Probably rusted off ages ago."

"Do you have a screwdriver or something like that?" I suggested. "Maybe we can pry it open."

Chris darted down the hall to the office and returned with a toolbox. She pulled out a flathead screwdriver and inserted the tip between the edge of the door and the brick wall, right next to where the handle would be, but it wouldn't go in more than a quarter of an inch.

"This thing's too thick," she said.

She scraped away at the mortar between the wall and the safe, and after a few minutes, she shoved the screwdriver in again, this time managing to get it deep between the metal door and the brick. She pushed hard against the handle of the screwdriver, and the old metal door began to warp, bulging out toward us. But something was keeping it closed. Chris moved like she was about to throw her weight against the thing, and that's when I heard it.

RING! RING!

The bell on the front door chimed brightly.

We both paused.

"Maybe we should do this later," I said. "We should clean up before any more customers arrive."

"Doreen can take care of them." Chris grunted and threw herself against the screwdriver. "We're...so...close."

Her face turned bright red before she gave up and took another breath.

RING! RING!

I heard the bell again.

Strange, I thought. I could have sworn that thing was broken.

I heard laughter and women's voices—lots of them.

"Doreen?" I called.

All at once the jukebox kicked on, playing some old-timey song that I didn't recognize.

"Do you hear that?" I asked Chris, but she was lost in concentration, peering closely at the edges of the safe.

"Maybe I should unscrew the hinges instead," she muttered to herself.

The smell of cigar smoke drew me out of the hallway. "Doreen? There's no smoking in here—"

I froze as soon as I got to the main room. Even if I had wanted to move, where could I go? The place was packed door to door with women! Black women, white women, women in skirts, women in suits. The tables had been pushed up against the walls to clear a space for dancing, and, boy, were they dancing! Or maybe waltzing was a better word for it.

A crowd of women in lovely knee-length skirts and gorgeous sweaters huddled around the jukebox, which was now, somehow, in perfect working condition. They giggled to themselves and glanced over their shoulders toward the bar. I followed their line of sight.

I gasped! It was just like the photo—a line of women in suits and fedoras, smoking cigars and sharing ashtrays. The woman in Doreen's seat turned toward me, but she was definitely not Doreen. She regarded me with more than a fair share of suspicion. She nudged the woman next to her. "Look what the cat dragged in."

"Where's Doreen?" I asked.

"Ain't no Doreen here, sweetheart."

I glanced around the room. Doreen was nowhere to be found. "Well...you can't smoke those in here."

"Since when?"

"Since always."

"News to me," she said, shrugging as she bit down on her thick cigar.

The doorbell chimed again as more women pushed into the room. I didn't think it was possible! They stopped just inside the door where a little table was set up. The young woman behind the table pointed to a sign that said, "Save The Spot!" The women happily pulled out their cash and tucked it into the glass jar before pressing farther into the crowd in search of an open table.

"What's going on?" I said, mostly to myself.

"It's a fundraiser, sweetheart," Not-Doreen said, puffing her smoke in my face. "Everyone has to do their part to keep The Spot up and running."

"The *Spot?*"

She looked at me kind of sideways, tipping her fedora as she said, "Are you sure you're in the right place, darling?"

I took a step back, waving away her smoke. "I don't understand."

I headed back down the hall in search of Chris, but she was gone. Even more troubling was the fact that the heavy mirror was back up on the wall, all in one piece, like it had never fallen at all. Stunned, I checked the floor anyway.

No glass.

No toolbox.

No Chris.

This doesn't make any sense!

I stepped right up to the mirror. I grabbed the bottom of the thing and lifted, but I could tell right away that it was too heavy for me. The last thing I wanted was for it to come crashing down again.

"What's your big plan, kiddo?" someone said behind me.

I turned slowly, nonchalantly. "No plan. Just straightening it out, that's all."

"Straightening it out?"

The woman behind me wore an old military uniform, like the woman in the photo. Wait. That was a poor choice of words. The woman behind me didn't just look *like* the woman in the photo, she *was* the woman in the photo, and she was even more attractive in person—if not a little intimidating.

"Y-yep," I stuttered. "Drives me crazy when things are crooked. But it looks good now. And totally secure."

"Then I suggest you move away from it."

"Sure," I said. "No problem. Gotta pee anyway."

"Mm-hmm."

I felt her eyes on my back as I entered the bathroom. I went into a stall and closed the door, if only to have a moment to think. I leaned back against the wall and took a deep breath.

I'm not losing my mind. I'm not losing my mind.

I heard someone pacing in the stall next to me, muttering to herself under her breath, "This is really happening. This is really happening."

"Chris?" I whispered. "Is that you?"

I heard the stall door whip open, and whoever was in there was suddenly pounding on my door. "Eileen! Open up!"

I opened the door.

"What the hell, Chris?" I whisper-shouted. "Where have you been?"

She slipped inside with me and closed the door. "Where have *I* been? Where have *you* been?"

"I've been looking for you."

"Something weird is going on," she said.

"No kidding. Who are all those people out there?"

"I don't know."

"I recognized one woman," I said. "But I don't think you're going to believe me."

"The officer? From the photograph?"

"Yeah."

"I saw her, too."

"How is that even possible?"

"How should I know? One minute I was digging in my toolbox, looking for something to pry that safe open with, and the next thing I knew the mirror was back on the wall and you were gone."

"That's exactly what happened to me."

"Good."

"Good?"

"Then that means we're not crazy."

"How do you figure that?"

"Well, we can't be, because we're both here. And if we're both here, then we can't both be losing our minds."

"Right," I said. She made everything sound so reasonable.

"So, this must really be happening."

"Right," I agreed. "But what *is* this? Time travel?"

"You said you saw the woman in the military uniform, the one from the photo," she said. "Did you see anyone else you recognized?"

"I saw the row of women with cigars. They're all lined up at the bar, just like in the picture."

"Okay. Did you see the bartender? The skinny one?"

"I don't remember. I didn't have a chance to look. You?"

"No." She rubbed the back of her neck and looked down at the ground. "Not yet."

"So that just leaves the photo of Grandma."

"Yeah," she said slowly.

"You don't think—" If I could have, I would've backed away, but there was nowhere else to go in that tiny stall. "You don't think she might be here?"

Chris shrugged.

Just then the bathroom door swung open. Two women walked in. One went into the stall beside us, and the other waited at the sink. Chris and I listened, frozen in place.

"What a party," the woman in the stall exclaimed.

"I know! I've already gotten so many good shots."

"You and that camera. Why don't you give it a break for a while?"

"I can't. It's for posterity. You know, just in case The Spot does end up closing after all."

The woman in the stall flushed the toilet, opened the door, and walked to the sink.

"Keep taking pictures like that, and you could end up in jail," she said. "Or worse, you could put others there."

"Oh, Karla, don't be so dark."

"Didn't you hear? Shorty's got raided last month."

"No..."

"Just don't be pointing that camera at me. The last thing the world needs is physical proof of my *perversions*." She exaggerated the last word, and they both laughed.

"All right, all right," the photographer said with a hint of melancholy in her voice. "Do you really think they'll raise enough money to keep this place open?"

"I sure hope so. It would be a pity for it to close."

"Yeah. Then where would we go?"

"Oh, honey, there will always be other parties."

"You're right." She sighed. "It was just nice, you know, having a place to call our own...like our own little hideout."

"Our own private island..."

"Our own private island," the photographer mused. "I like that. And these—we heard the subtle click of the camera shutter—are my little treasures."

"Dotty! I thought I told you not to take my picture."

Dotty!

I pressed my face against the stall door and tried to catch a glimpse of the women through the crack. They were young— teenagers—that much I could tell. The one with the camera wore a poodle skirt and fuzzy sweater, her hair pulled back into a tight ponytail and tied with a pink ribbon. The one next to her wore high-waisted pants and a sleeveless white blouse that complemented her dark skin. But from where I stood, I couldn't get a good look at either of their faces before they bolted for the door. "It's for posterity!"

As soon as they were out of the room, Chris yanked open the stall door.

"Where are you going?" I said.

"To talk to her," she said.

"To who?"

"To Grandma."

"Are you sure it's her?"

"Of course, and you are, too. I can see it in your eyes."

"Even if it is her, what do you plan to do?" I asked.

"I'm going to find out if she wants us to sell the bar."

"That's it? That's the first thing you think of? Settling a grudge?"

"You said today that she would want us to sell it. Now's our chance to ask her."

"You can't just ask her something like that. She'll have no idea what you're talking about."

"I guess I'll just have to explain the situation to her."

"You can't."

"Why not?"

"You'll mess with the space-time continuum."

"Take a look around, Eileen. I'm pretty sure the space-time continuum is already messed up."

She had a good point. "Fine. But we absolutely *cannot* tell her who we are or what we know about the future."

"Sure thing," she said, pulling open the bathroom door.

We found Dotty—I wasn't quite ready yet to call her Grandma—standing with her friend, Karla, by the bar. Dotty had the camera raised again, which made Karla blush and turn away. Undeterred, Dotty touched the bottom of Karla's chin, gently nudging her face back toward the camera. Their eyes met, and for one protracted moment, they held each other in a passionate gaze. I felt as though I'd stumbled upon a secret love letter, written long ago. I knew I shouldn't read it, because the words weren't meant for me, but I couldn't look away.

Then Karla snatched the camera from Dotty's hands, and in an instant, she had the lens turned back on the photographer. Dotty eyes went wide in surprise as Karla snapped a photo.

"For posterity," Karla said with a smirk.

Dotty smacked Karla's arm before leaning forward and planting a little kiss on her lips.

A cocky Karla turned to get the bartender's attention, but the bartender was at the other end of the bar, leaning into a conversation with the woman who managed the collections table by the front door. A metal cashier box was passed between them, which the bartender quickly slipped out of sight onto a shelf under the bar. She was headed our way when Chris tapped Dotty on the shoulder.

"Excuse me, Dotty Booth?"

She turned and smiled. "That's right."

"Who's asking?" Karla said with a scowl.

Chris hesitated. Clearly, she hadn't thought this conversation through.

"We're f-family friends," she stuttered.

Dotty's smile quickly faded into suspicion. "I don't have many family friends."

"Uh, she didn't mean blood family," I said. "She meant *family*." I draped an arm around Chris's shoulders and squeezed her in a sideways hug. "Right, Chris?"

She put on her best smile. "That's right."

"Oh." Dotty sighed in relief. "Well, we're all family here at The Spot."

She turned back to the bar and raised a hand to get the bartender's attention. Chris wasn't about to give up, though. She squeezed herself into a space next to Dotty and also raised a hand, as if she, too, were waiting for a drink.

"This place is great, isn't it?"

"Of course it is," Dotty replied.

"If it were up to you," Chris asked, "if you owned the place, would you let it close?"

"If I owned it?" Dotty said with a flustered smile. "I don't know if I could ever own a place like this."

"Why not?"

"I don't know one thing about running a business."

Chris pushed on. "Still, it's fun to think about. One day this might all be yours. You could spend your days surrounded by family. You could hang all your pictures on the walls."

"Not unless she has a death wish!" Karla interrupted. "Has everyone lost their minds tonight?"

"It is a wonderful fantasy, though, isn't it?" Dotty said, her eyes sparkling. "Then we'd always have our own little island."

"Exactly," Chris said. "Your own little treasure chest."

I elbowed her in the ribs and shook my head in disapproval. She shrugged and waved me off. "So? If it were up to you, what would you do?"

"Well..." Dotty thought for a long moment. We all leaned a little closer, Karla included, waiting for the answer. "I guess I would do whatever I could to keep it open."

Chris smacked a hand down on the bar. "That's exactly what I thought."

"However," Dotty continued to say, "a bar is just four walls. It's the memories that matter, and the people. That's why I take pictures. No one can take your memories away."

"Don't be too sure about that," Karla said, turning suddenly toward the window.

We all looked up and saw the silent red swipe of a police light.

"Police!" someone shouted.

In an instant, everyone jumped into action. Couples separated on the dance floor. Cigars and cigarettes were extinguished. The bartender reached below the bar and grabbed not one, but three, metal cashier boxes.

"Heads up!" she shouted before she slid them down the bar in our direction.

The woman in the military uniform grabbed them up without a word and disappeared down the back hallway just as the police busted through the door. Chris and I looked at each other.

"The safe," we whispered in unison.

The police barged in with flashlights raised. "Everyone, hands up!"

We all moved away from the bar in a panic, until we stood with our backs against the wall, watching as one police officer grabbed the jar from the table. He smirked to himself as he took the cash out and shoved it into his pocket. The other officers pressed forward, asking to see identification.

"Dotty, get rid of that damned camera," Karla whispered, "before it's too late."

Pale as a ghost, Dotty pulled the strap from around her neck. She hid the camera behind her back. I felt her tremble beside me.

"Give it to me," I whispered.

"What? No!"

"I'll hide it."

She hesitated. I grabbed it anyway. She held on, begging me silently not to take the camera away.

"I'm sorry," I said.

With tears in her eyes, she relented.

As soon as the camera was securely in my hands, Chris shoved me toward the hallway. "Go! I'll take care of these guys."

I slipped down the hall, and there, in front of the bathroom, I 'wasn't surprised to find the woman in uniform already closing the safe door. She bent to pick up the mirror.

"Wait!" I said. "There's one more."

She flinched when she heard me, and for one terrible moment, I thought she'd punch me right in the face, but then she saw the camera.

"Hurry up." She pulled open the safe door.

Once the camera was inside, we worked together to set the mirror back on the wall. It was so heavy, I thought I'd blow a gasket. When it was in place, I slouched against the wall, my thighs shaking like Jello.

"By the way," she said, "you never saw this."

"Saw what?" I panted.

She smiled. It was the same charming smile as the one in the photograph.

"I've been dying to know," I said between breaths. "What's your name?"

"Gretchen," she said, tipping her little hat. "It's a pleasure, ma'am."

Just then, two flashlights flooded the hall. "Who's back there?" a man shouted.

I grabbed Gretchen's hand. I pulled her close. "Quick! Kiss me."

"Yes, *ma'am,*" she said as she pushed me up against the wall and planted her lips on mine in a not-so-spontaneous act of passion that stopped the officers in their tracks.

"That's enough, ladies!" one officer shouted. "You've had your fun. Now it's time to come with us back to the station."

Gretchen let me go, smiling and licking her lips. She turned to the officer, her wrists outstretched. "It was worth it."

My heart pounded as one of the policemen approached. He pulled out his handcuffs, but I wasn't ready to be arrested, especially not in this decade. With nowhere else to go, I ducked into the bathroom, headed straight for the stall, and slammed the door shut, expecting the police to barge in after me. I braced myself against the door as my heart pounded in my ears, over and over, until finally it slowed and the room became quiet.

I listened for a long time until I was absolutely certain.

No police.

No women.

No music.

I opened the stall door and stepped out. Someone was shouting out in the hall.

"Chris? *Chris?* Customers are getting kind of impatient out here..."

It was Doreen. *It was Doreen!*

I whipped open the bathroom door, and when I stepped out, glass crunched beneath my shoes. The mirror still slouched like a drunk against the wall, and Chris was kneeling down on one knee, prying at the safe with a crowbar.

"Where did you get that?" I asked.

"Next door."

For a moment, I was indignant that she'd thought to go find a crowbar before she thought to check on me. For all she knew I could be locked up in a 1940's jail cell. But then—BANG!—the latch on the safe popped and the little door slammed open and shut, and open again.

"Jackpot!" Chris shouted.

We'd expected to find the three cashier boxes and the camera, but the safe was stacked from top to bottom with cashier boxes, shoe boxes, old tins, and even a dusty porcelain piggy bank. Chris pulled out a round coffee tin and ripped off the lid. It was packed with fat rolls of cash. And I'm not talking dollar bills, I'm talking twenties and fifties and higher.

"Why would Grandma rat hole so much money here?" Chris said. "What is it for?"

I picked up the dusty camera and pointed it at Chris.

"For posterity," I said as I snapped her photo.

A Menacing Look

by Darryl Denning

Ah, the Seventies,
Wild and open.
The Hayloft,
Studio City,
Stand up bar.
Movies for gays—
"Auntie Mame,"
Judy Garland,
Kitschy musicals.

Conversation starts.
Just my type—tall,
Blond, V-shape,
Paul Newman eyes,
Sexy Austrian accent.
A drink at his place?
Of course I said yes.

His cozy front room.
Clothes strewn all over.
The real scene of action—
His dimly lit bedroom.
I'm thinking this could
Really go somewhere.
Then a menacing look,
A shiny straight razor
In a smooth Arian hand.
"First I'll shave you,
Then you shave me."
Holy crap, this guy
Could slit my throat.
Calmly he says, "I'll
Get the shaving cream."

An opening to escape.
Bolting down the hall.
Grabbing things on the run.
Into the December cold.
Naked as a jaybird.
Hiding in the bushes.
Heart racing.
Teeth chattering.
Butt freezing.
Porch light flicks on.
A terry cloth robe.
"Where are you?
Where'd you go?"

At last he gave up.
I dashed for my car
At bare bullet speed.
Duds clutched like laundry.
How many people on
Laurel Avenue, between
Sunset and Hollywood, saw
Everything I had to offer?

A screeching wheely.
Right on Hollywood.
Quick left on Curson.
Wattles Park one side,
Ritzy houses the other.
Raising on my haunches,
Levis on first, shirt next,
Hell with the shoes.
That was a close one.

Found out later that my
Auto scene in the buff
Was directly opposite
Elsa Lanchester and
Charles Laughton's place.
Had I known, I would have
Taken more time dressing.
Might have nabbed a

Movie role or two.
You know what they always
Said about Charles Laughton.

All I Never Said

by Patrick Coulton

"Well," Joey said, "I guess just...thanks for everything." Smirk.

His smirk bounced around in my visual field like a flashbulb for a while afterward, fading slightly with every new blink. As I drove out of Fishtown and back to my own sweltering, summer-drenched apartment in Center City, I wondered if I'd ever see Joey again. His words echoed on a slow playback tape in my mind, "Thanks for everything."

I remember the first time I saw him, behind the bar at Key West. It was early fall, and the large floor-to-ceiling windows were open in the downstairs lounge. Cool breezes wafted the smell of cut grass and burning firewood under our noses. The bar was filled. So were the seats in the lounge area, as it always was for happy hour, or any hour, really. In the early nineties, the gay bars were where I found friends who became Family. More than just a sexual stomping ground, the bars were a place where we could all find each other, not just for sex, but for mutual support.

For me, they were a place where I felt an energetic sense of relief, some respite from the stresses of the hetero everyday world. Back then, many of my friends were not yet out to their families and certainly not out at work. Their affections for other men would have to remain private once they left the familiar and protected space of the gay bar.

The man of *my* affection that day was busy polishing glasses, scanning the room, making drinks, etc. Joey was medium height, a tad shorter than myself at six-foot-one, and he had a decent build. He had dark brown hair, his eyes a deep chestnut brown. Through his white T-shirt, I could make out his square chest, sightly hairy, just the way I liked it. He was cute, but shy, which made our subtle flirting all the more fun. It was the quick, harmless kind of flirting that one does when in a committed relationship, which I was at the time. Our mild flirtation would start when I'd first arrive, then we'd always nervously fall back into our respective roles of customer and server. When in doubt, pile on the societal armor, the safety. Sometimes our hands touched when I would pay for my beer. He'd do a half-smile smirk thing, glance my way just until it felt uncomfortable, and then quickly pull back and put the money in the drawer of the register. I, too, would quickly draw my hand back and smile.

"See ya later!" I'd say.

Months of flirting, two times a week, and this is about all I could ever put up with. I didn't know his schedule; I was just lucky enough to walk in and always see the same shy, cute Joey, smiling and flirting and waiting for me to give it right back.

Around this time, the relationship I was in for the previous eight months started to fizzle. Mich, the man I was seeing, was adorable: blond hair, well-toned, tan body, blue eyes, killer smile, affectionate, and sexually perfect. The downsides were that he lived in Millville, New Jersey, quite a ways outside of town; he required more of my time than I had to spare for even myself; and he, too, was an habitual flirt. Throw in strained conversation that would only cover machinery work, cars, and sex, and the recipe for disaster was complete.

He ended it over the phone after admitting he was too lonely without me there every night. He further admitted that one night he stopped being so lonely and stopped being alone. He had already found my replacement while cruising his favorite leather bar, and with that, we were done. Neither of us turned out to be what the other needed; I required more time to myself to study and make art, and he needed more of me than I was willing to give. I was single, yet again.

After the breakup, I spent a few weeks out of the scene altogether. Whether you were queer, lesbian, gay, bisexual, or pansexual, there was one similarity that always sucked: the dating game. Back then, at the age of twenty-six, I had seen my share of pitfalls and personality clashes with many a man, such to the extent that I knew one thing: I had to regain my strength of self before going out and attempting to traverse the gay bar scene. *Again.* I was struck at odds with the notion that as much of a haven as I had felt the bars to be, there was more than a small amount of anxiety just thinking of the prospects of trying to meet a guy, strike up a conversation, get a number, go on a date, etc. How could these places be a sigh of relief and at the same time be the cause of the anxiety in the first place? I took my time grappling with this paradox, utlimately deciding I would take it slow getting back out there.

After a good three weeks, I had rebuilt my self-confidence and was on the prowl, enjoying the visceral energy I felt from the chase. I went out on a Saturday night, hopping and searching from bar to bar, before ending my night at Woody's bar and dance-floor area, to no avail. "Patrick's Law" (think Muphy's Law, but gay) was working against me. "If you go out searching for something, you won't find it." Doesn't matter if you were looking for someone to have forever, or someone to have for just now. If you did so seek, you would not find.

I had encountered this encumbrance on numerous occasions when I really wanted to meet a new guy. I had decided to just give up (secretly in the hopes of the sex finding *me*). I slunk downstairs at Woody's to finish my last beer and watched the other last call-ers look around for a friend to make their bed warmer for the night. Just then I caught a gimpse of someone out of the corner of my eye, staring at me quite deeply.

It was Joey from Key West Bar.

Months of flirting with him, and now here he was standing in the shadows, working me with that irresistible half-smile/smirk thing. The expression he wore with the smile wasn't smug, rather sort of a James Dean thing, only a little darker. Utterly adorable. We both just stood there, flirting like we were still at Key West Bar and still keeping our distance. For me, this was too innocuous, too safe. So I broke the ice.

"Nice to see you outside of work." I slowly passed my eyes up and down his body, so he'd know I was interested.

His shy *façade* faded into a lustful grin, and all of his social defenses melted away with it. He smiled, now uncautious, and came over to me. He placed one foot between my legs, gripped the rounded edge of the top of the bar on either side of me, and gave me the once-over I just gave him. I wondered for a moment if he was drunker than I thought, as he careened back and forth. His eyes traced the front of my body, and he pulled himself closer into me; the outer fibers of our clothes barely touched at first.

"Nice to see you, too," he said.

He moved in closer to tell me something, his hip pressing against mine as he put his mouth next to my ear.

"I want to go home with you," he whispered.

Sweat and heat and electricity pinged up my body. He kissed me behind the ear quickly, and as he pulled away, I caught a lingering scent of Jack Daniels. It didn't faze me.

Once that ping of desire hit my brain, I wanted to go home with him, too.

****

Now normally, this is the part where one might find all of the diverse details of our sex together. Normally. What can be said? Two bodies were naked, entwined, engulfed. Consumed. My describing it to you wouldn't help me paint a better picture of who Joey was. Afterall, the sex wasn't that important.

It was wonderful, don't get me wrong. It was just what I was looking for, and we had a very good time. *Very.* That wasn't the true reason behind why we met. So many people go into gay bars for so many other purposes, and sometimes when they thought they wanted or needed sex, there was something else they were trying to get from each other.

What is sex anyway? What goes on after the physical gratification? I knew my own answers to this, of course. I didn't always know so clearly what sex and love were, and in my younger years, the two were very much muddled together. I knew what I felt, and I could tell after just one kiss with someone whether sex would be able to happen or not. I knew that I had an energetic rapture with another man's skin, and I knew it was sometimes a chore to find a man with the kind of energy that was compatible with my own. I'd always experienced sex like this, as an intimate exchange of energy. Bath houses and glory holes were never my twist. I needed to see the eyes and feel the soul of the man who I was going to pop off my root chakra with, one-night stand or not. I passed these things over in my mind while standing there in my bathroom, taking a whiz in the afterglow of Joey and me.

"Where'd you go?" he called from the other room.

I smiled, remembering how adorable he was, huddled under the sheets in the amber light, and I wished I could pee quicker to get back there sooner. As soon as I was done, I found my way through my modest one-bedroom apartment in the dark, through the living room, and back to the bedroom. I struggled to see in the low light, and after my eyes adjusted, I couldn't make out his shape amidst the sheets. Had he left that quickly? Did I hear him wrong? Did his voice instead say, "Well, I'd better go?"

I started back through the living room on my way to the front door, hoping to catch him before he was down the stairs and out the front door of the building.

"Hee, hee, hee," I heard from directly behind me in the living room.

From the orange streetlight streaming through the living room window, I could now make out a shape crouched low, behind Mom-Mom's comfy old puke-green chair.

"Whatcha doin' back there?" I asked.

He was naked, squatting down behind the chair, looking up at me. He didn't move.

"I just wanted to see if you'd have missed me."

****

Joey and I would spend a few more nights together, as well as some endearing lunch-time chats. I learned that Joey was the child of a single mother, and he was born terribly and painfully gifted. Joey's mother had an intuition to have his IQ tested when he was young, at six years of age. Every parent in the world has had the hope that their child would really be somebody. She was a single parent raising her son by herself, working in a local factory. Joey scored so high on the IQ test that he qualified for a full scholarship to a local, well-established boarding school for boys.

His mother's sacrifice of not having him home all of the time was immense, and one she told him she hoped she'd grow accustomed to over time. Joey never did. She explained to him that when the pain of his separation grew nearly intolerable for her, she'd play a game of sorts while she was hunched over the large industrial sewing machine at work. She envisioned that she was sewing Joey into the seams of his own successes. She watched as each stitch from the machine traveled out and away from her, and she imagined each one as a new accomplishment.

Stitch. Joey learning the flute.

Stitch. Joey composing a quartet.

Stitch. Joey teaching and laughing and smiling and disappearing off the edge of the sewing machine onto the pile of parachute material on the floor. "Practice makes perfect," she heard herself tell Joey time and again. This was her practice, her way of removing the talons from the distance.

****

After a month or so of dating, Joey and I assessed our situation: he was in his junior year as a music composition major (already collaborating with world-renowned composers) and would be going back to college in a month, before the end of summer. Given the situation, we agreed to take it easy with our interaction, and we agreed to stop sleeping together. It just made sense not to make anything more difficult emotionally down the line. Keeping things on a level of friendship was the prudent choice and the one that we decided on together.

Two weeks before Joey was due to return to college, I got a phone call.

"Hi...um...it's me."

Of course, I instantly knew who it was. He sounded different, though. Like he had either just got done crying, or was trying to keep from crying.

"I hate to ask you, but you told me if there was ever anything I needed, to call, so..."

"Sure. What's up?"

"My mom's in the hospital, and I kind of need a ride up there. I have some things I need to bring her."

"Sure, of course. Just tell me what time."

"Okay." He sniffed. "Meet you in half an hour?"

"Okay."

****

Less than one week later, Joey's mother died.

I had never met her, was never privy to the interactions of their life together (aside from the stories Joey told me). I never heard their fights or witnessed any of their hugs to make up. Oddly enough, it wasn't until the very end of our time together that I learned why he hid from me in the living room that night.

Eventually, during our afternoon chats, he told me about the problems he encountered growing up without her. Life was hard enough growing up without a father, and then to have his mother—his entire *world* at that time—send him away to school at such a young age, it did something. It caused many rifts, many bitter tides that would never turn back.

Joey said he spent much of his youth wondering why he was left to his own devices. He never really understood why until he was grown and his mother's actions became so much clearer to him. But as a child, he didn't know any of this. His mom had to erect many walls to shield herself from the pain of having her one and only child not be with her. Joey lay awake many nights wishing to trade in his gifts just to know and have back the mother he remembered as a small boy. He wanted the woman without walls. The woman whom he watched doing crossword puzzles, licking her upper lip, deep in thought. The woman who made all the pain of not having a father go away with a grilled cheese sandwich, a kiss, and a hug.

His mother lay awake at nights knowing deep in her soul what he would become. She envisioned all of the lives of people he would touch with his gifts, and this in turn was *her* gift to him. She felt this about him early on, felt his ability to make and channel and create and breathe things into life that she could only imagine. He couldn't know this at six years old, and he wouldn't know this at sixteen years old.

She never knew if she'd ever find a way to express to him why she sent him to school the way she did, and how much she loved him for all that he was. Though these words escaped her for much of her life, she always hoped one day he would know it. That somewhere along the way, all that she never said would be told to him, so he could know deep in his heart and soul how much she really loved him, and so he would forgive her for creating and keeping such distance.

****

I picked up Joey a few days after his mom died, which was also his last day in Philly. He asked me for one last favor: a ride to his old home in Fishtown. He needed to close up his mom's house, gather some things, and say goodbye. While he was taking care of the house, I waited in the car thinking about my own mother. She hadn't become the woman I had hoped or needed her to be, and our distance grew. I struggled for many years to let that woman from my childhood go: The woman I went bowling with because I was too young to be in kindergarten with my brother and sister (we were too poor for daycare). The one who loved my sea-green-colored seagull drawings. The one who gave me my very own kissey-spot back where my hair stood up in a cowlick, (she called them bunny ears). The woman who yelled at me to get out of the apple tree that was too close to the power lines.

I tried in vain to keep that woman from vanishing, but because of our circumstances, she did. We do see each other every so often, sometimes twice a year, exchanging stories from her world and mine. This was how it was supposed to go with our mothers, for Joey and me. I knew what I wanted to say when he got back in the car that afternoon. I wanted to tell him I understood some, but not all, of the pain he was going through and tell him how deeply I thought his mother really loved him.

Just then his knuckles rapped at the window before he pulled the door open. The momentary blast of intense August heat fogged the windows as he smiled and slumped inside.

We didn't say much as I drove him back to his place to finish packing, and all of a sudden, I didn't know how to say any of the words I'd been thinking.

We chatted lightly about this and that, more conventions of safety to keep things from becoming a bawl session. All the words that I never said became stored away somewhere deep inside. All that I never said would come out months later during a journaling session in the lounge at Key West. During that car ride back to his apartment, part of me could relate to what his mother must have felt, seeing him go away and flourish and not knowing what would become of him.

I looked over at him when I stopped the car and gave him a quick kiss behind the ear to say goodbye.

"Well," Joey said, "I guess just...thanks for everything."

Smirk.

The Pulse

by Michael Ward

It could've been me
I've burned rubber on I-4 many times
Kissed under Orlando skies
Laid my heart down on dance floors
Felt my pulse, thump thump thump and bump with the boom
boom bass
I've been knee deep in love in
Sweet sticky Orlando
Who knew a war zone would erupt on the dance floor?
On that June night—Latin night—
Where mi familia
Laughed till their bellies hurt
Enjoyed a rare freedom to be us unabashedly
Fell over and over for the cute guys staking ground on
the dance floor
Breaking our hearts every time they traveled into
their lover's arms
Danced the last steps of their short lives snuffed out by bullets
No, none of you—my extended family—
Expected to be martyrs or victims or survivors
Racked with guilt of why your life was spared
At such an unimaginable cost
I'd like to check on you
Have us speak heart to heart
No need for words
Our eyes can read the pain in one another
the tragedy we've endured
Day after day
Raped by vultures of reporters
Night after night
In our lives, in our homes, in our dreams
Hoping if just for one solitary moment
We'll once again feel whole, feel alive, unafraid
Feel the same old pulse

My Nose Pressed Against the Glass of History

by Karin Kallmaker

The bookstores were my bars.

In my late twenties, I finally found my way inside Lioness Books in Sacramento, and it was an explosion of possibilities. That was my moment, the one so many women speak of about coming out: What the mirror reflected and who I knew I was were not the same thing. Truth became a clamor I was certain other people could hear ringing inside me.

When I stood inside women's bookstores, everything I could become swelled against the constraints of the world outside the doors. Though these were scant hours, they were lived by the woman I wanted to be. Every time I left, it was with the sense of shrinking to fit into the confinements of my day-to-day world.

Several years after that fateful first bookstore visit, I screwed up the courage to go to a San Francisco bookstore for a reading. The store, Old Wives' Tales, was legendary, and I was eager to see it for myself. The author appearing was also my editor. Too shy to introduce myself ahead of time, I finally did so after the event and she promptly invited me out for a drink.

So the first woman who took me to a lesbian bar was Katherine Forrest. It sounds slightly illicit, but for both of us, it was a research venture. She had heard about the famous lesbian bar Amelia's, a sister bar to the even more famous Maud's, and she was eager to see it for herself.

By then Maud's was already closed. I had never heard of either, having only recently moved to the Bay Area, but when Katherine asked if I knew of it, I lied through my teeth and tried for an air of sophistication. A freaked-out imp in my head was screaming, "You're having a drink with Katherine Forrest! Don't dribble down your front!" I was certain that in her experience and wisdom she would expose me as a lesbian bar imposter. (In the years since, I've realized that even if she had discerned that I was a clueless newbie at the bar scene she was far too gracious a person to ever point it out.)

I watched Katherine watch the bar. I didn't know what she was looking for. Only later, years later, would I piece together that she was seeking out what she'd read about in books: the dance of butch-femme, the free-to-be-me space, that slice of lesbian life captured in our literature. Her own fictional creation, the titular Nightwood Bar, was inspired by what Amelia's and Maud's, The Palms and Connections had once been. As fuddled as I was, I still sensed that Amelia's in 1992 was not what she expected.

Perhaps she was aware that she was too late. And she looked around the bar the way I would be looking at Boadecia's Bookstore the night it closed, years later. Mourning as the time and tide washed our present into the community's past.

****

Something magical happened to me every time I went to a woman's bookstore. Because of that, I knew that the bars had been a lifesaving magic to generations of women, including THE generation. That first generation that defied all strictures of propriety, risked arrest, loss of jobs, housing, families, children. The generation of women who created a lesbian bar scene even without a place to call their own, congregating for "Ladies' Nights" when owners gave them permission to enter without a man and still treated them like criminals.

In that narrow, dark world, they thrived. They were the first generation that said, "We govern ourselves and do not need your permission to do so." A butch lighting a cigarette for a femme was an act of bravery in a world of unrelenting menace.

Because of those women, the bookstores existed for me to find. The bookstores became LGBT centers, and then nightclubs and online circles. My gratitude is profound for the courage of all those who found enough air and space to plant our revolution.

Over the decades, as firsthand accounts and treasured photographs crept into online archives, my secondhand experience of bar culture only deepened. Fiction gave way to fact. Pictures captured women leaning into each other. They were laughing together. Singing, dancing, defiantly loving. I'm left with the feeling of looking in on a sacred place I can never really know.

I'm nostalgic for a past not my own. Immensely privileged to know of it without having to experience it.

****

I've been raising a queer daughter — she is the new queer. Where generations before her sought to nail down an identity the world said we couldn't have, she seeks not to be nailed down. To be fluid in everything except a commitment to inclusion. She and her generation have hoisted a massive umbrella. All queers are welcome to shelter.

Her far-flung community does this especially in cyberspace, creating safe zones for people to be who they are. To me it seems much like the bar culture without the booze and neon.

We are stronger together. My daughter knows it, I know it, we all know it in our guts. If that weren't enough, all our books of faith, religious and secular, remind us of that truth. From the mouths of our sheroes and heroes, we have heard those words in infinite variety in the cause of resistance.

We shall overcome.

Sisterhood is powerful.

We're here, we're queer, Get used to it!

The Pulse Massacre at one of our safe spaces, a queer nightclub, was a gut-punching reminder. Yes, we are stronger together. Sometimes it's not strong enough. When it's not strong enough, we need each other more than ever. My daughter comforted friends online. I despaired that safe spaces are still an illusion.

And I reminded myself: Safety for our kind was an illusion in the 1950s, and yet we thrived. It was an illusion in the 1960s, the '70s, the '80s... And yet we thrived.

We thrive.

Herizon Nights:
When We Knew We Mattered

by Bonnie J. Morris, Ph.D.

While I was in graduate school, between 1983 and 1989, I belonged to a private lesbian social club called Herizon. It was a bar, and more than a bar: a woman-only space with dues-paying members, similar to the London Gateways Club, which as historian Leila Rupp describes, "... got around restrictive licensing laws by functioning as a membership club, and word of mouth served as a means of recruitment."[*] This membership ranged from 200-300, although on any given night, only a few women might be present, requiring that all of us rotate through the week as volunteer host bartenders (I often did graduate work at the bar).

Without requiring anyone to subscribe to a political outlook, beyond an assumed, pro-choice feminism (several members were staff of the local abortion services clinic), most of us shared an interest in cultural representations of our own kind. And because Herizon was in a university town, some of those who were professors and students in the membership used scholarly resources and skills to detect evidence of lesbian life in the historical past and in present-day media.

Why did some of us turn bar nights into fierce archival work toward our own cultural validation? Why were some of us taking notes on our own lives, filming or journaling or tape recording the club's business meetings instead of drinking Genny Cream Ale and Labatt's Blue Light?

At Herizon, two women in particular, our media specialists Faith Rogow and Del Brown, took the lead in monitoring and recording the increasing images of lesbians and/or feminist figures on television and in film. When any innovation occurred, such as the unexpected lesbian kiss on *L.A. Law,* we used a primitive but effective tool called a "telephone tree" to spread the word. (You called two households, they called two more, and so on.) Not everyone could afford the still-new and costly item known as a VCR, which allowed a lucky few to capture and replay a microsecond-long televised kiss or inside joke. Prior to Internet conveniences like Twitter, we used bar nights and our telephone tree lines to spread news of our own existence in mainstream media.

"Did you see that?"

"Did you hear about that?"

"Come over next week; we'll watch it together."

We had discussions about whichever films had any lesbian characters; we showed those films at the bar; we hunted down and shared information about both mainstream and alternative entertainment events featuring lesbian characters: Lily Tomlin on Broadway, women's music festivals in summer. But we also kept track of Herizon's own success story as a space for visiting performers, speakers, and guests whose work affirmed a lesbian sensibility. A lesbian *intelligence.*

The irony was that while Faith, Del, and I were at an excellent public university in a liberal state, no one was positioned to mentor our scholarly interest in our own lives as subject matter. There were budding gay studies programs elsewhere, and certainly Faith and I were gaining doctorates at one of the only Ph.D. programs in *women's history* in America; but no one was teaching lesbian history or showing us how to get grant money to fund the very real work we did on our own time. Our lesbian lives were neither historical, yet, nor recognizable as part of a community within the local community. Though Binghamton had five bars catering to lesbians or lesbians and gay men, the recreational lives of a still outcast minority did not register as subject matter in the eyes of our own (straight) professors.

At Herizon, we knew we were more than a bar. We were— as twenty-somethings, remember—doing something absolutely extraordinary: creating a woman-only space for the express purpose of allowing the local lesbian community to thrive, safe from harassment. In that space we saw ourselves, with all our personal and class baggage, take on roles of leadership, invention, and decision making. We might be drinking and shooting pool, but we were also directing plays, offering restaurant and talent nights and rock bands, and hosting holiday rituals for those unwelcome at their own family tables. A range of events affirmed personhood and called on the varying skills of the membership. No one was expected to be passive or silent. We partied as a lesbian nation. No man's permission was necessary or sought in our self-appointed agency.

Now that almost forty years have passed, the journals, films, photos, business-meeting notes, and material ephemera that a few of us saved carefully are cultural proof of a time when lesbians were self-aware of autonomous self-raising. Not every bar was like Herizon; I found, in other bars, my journal marked me suspect: an informer? But in my twenties, I was peculiarly alert to my ability to record my life while living. I felt a holy obligation to write our good nights down; to disprove homophobia by chronicling our best selves; to mark the ways community saved lives; to preserve, like Sappho's fragments, lyric line notes on a culture where the women loved each other—bold, apart.

*Leila J. Rupp. *Sapphistries*. NY: New York University Press, p. 188.

Author Biographies

Jamie Anderson:

Jamie Anderson still loves a comfy flannel shirt. Her writing has appeared in a plethora of periodicals, from *Sinister Wisdom* to *SingOut!*. "Plethora" is her favorite word. She is the author of a memoir, *Drive All Night*, and is currently working on her second book, one about women's music of the seventies and eighties. Her popular blog, jamiebobamie.wordpress.com, has had over 470,000 hits. When she isn't writing, she's performing and recording her original music in the US and Canada. She lives in Ottawa, Canada, with her wife and two cats. www.jamieanderson.com

Nashon Anderson:

Nahshon A. Fuentes is a Transgender writer and filmmaker. Nahshon attended California State University, Los Angeles. At age 19, Nahshon survived an attempted murder, which inspired the short manuscript, "Shooting Range," which won a 2014 BRIO Award from Bronx Council on Arts. A recipient of grants from The Actors Fund of America, Episcopal Actors Guild, Mayer Foundation, National Arts and Disability Center, and Robert Rauschenberg Foundation. Nahshon is a grants advisory panelist for the New York State Council on The Arts. Nahshon is a member of SAG-AFTRA, a 2015 VONA and 2016 Lambda Fellow currently writing a memoir.

Ann Aptaker:

Ann Aptaker's "Cantor Gold" crime series celebrates her favorite themes: dangerous women, crime and mystery fiction, New York City's fascinating history and its rich pre-Stonewall outlaw LGBTQ culture. Her debut novel, *Criminal Gold*, book one in the series, was a Goldie Award finalist. The series' second book, *Tarnished Gold*, was both a Lambda Award and Goldie Award winner, the only book in the Mystery category to win both awards. *Genuine Gold*, book three in the series, was released in January 2017 from Bold Strokes Books. Ann resides in her beloved hometown, New York City.

Rachel E. Bailey:

Rachel E. Bailey has been published in *Words 57, The Finger, The Stonesthrow Review*, on *Yahoo!Voices,* in *Amative Magazine, Writing.com 2014 Anthology*, and *My Favorite Apocalypse.* She's had short plays—*The Big Opening* and *Messenger*—performed for stage and screen. Her novels, *Dyre: By Moon's Light* and *Dyre: A Knight of Spirit and Shadows* (and *In Shining Armor*, under the pseudonym E. L. Phillips) were published in 2016. She's currently working on a novel about (mostly) LGBTQIA superheroes and the (mostly) LGBTQIA supervillains who loathe them, set in a fictional, futuristic city. She can be reached at: The.Real.REBailey@Gmail.com

Renée Bess:

Renée Bess is a former teacher whose 1994 short story, "At the Beauty Parlor," won first place in a Philadelphia area literary contest. Two of her other short stories are in Canadian LGBT anthologies, "Piece of My Heart" and "Ma-ka: Diasporic Juks."

Her five novels, *Leave of Absense, Breaking Jaie, Re:Building Sasha, The Butterfly Moments,* and *The Rules,* were published by Regal Crest Enterprises.

Renée is committed to writing stories with multi-ethnic casts of characters, timely social themes, strong character development, and well-crafted language. Read more about her here: www.reneebess.com

Beth Burnett:

Beth Burnett is the Director of Education and the head of the writing academy at the Golden Crown Literary Society. She teaches women's empowerment classes, runs a Lansing women's networking group, and gives seminars on open communication. Beth has published four books with Sapphire Books Publishing and is expecting her fifth in about nine months. In her spare time, Beth reads, walks with her geriatric dog, and works on perfecting her riffs and licks.

Shawn Marie Bryan:

Shawn Marie Bryan is the radio host for Women A'Loud! and Be(h)n's Book. In addition to being a writer, she is a playwright. Her one-woman show has been produced at political festivals, theatrical venues and even at libraries. Shawn enjoys working with all media, especially editing and producing audio and video and narrating/producing audiobooks. She is the general manager for Network Listen and has recently partnered with Recognized Publishing. Despite both being redheads Shawn Marie and her love live in the California desert.

Lisa Carlson:

Born and raised in Brooklyn, Lisa Carlson currently lives in New Jersey with her husband Kurt and her two children. She earned a B.A. degree in English at Rutgers University and later became a National Writing Fellow at Kean University. Her work has been published in *The National Writing e-anthology, Skinny Poetry Journal, The Da Da Poetry Journal* "Maintenant," and a number of Six Word Memoir books including *Crush*. She spends her free time reading, writing, listening to music and relaxing at the Jersey Shore. Asbury Park holds a special place in her heart.

Ian Cassidy:

Ian Cassidy lives in Lichfield, UK and is a graduate of the famous Curtis Brown Creative Writing School. His comic novel *The Unsinkable Herr Goering* was published in 2013 by The Cassowary Press. He has published many short stories including "Never Said a Word," in "Roads Ahead," Tindal Street Press. Under the pseudonym Daisy Cains, Ian's work has been published in many LGBT anthologies including; *Personal Pronouns, Trans*, and the magazines *Hyacinth Noir Magazine*, and *HCE Magazine*.

Patrick Coulton:

Patrick Coulton lives in Philadelphia, PA, but would love to move to Toronto on a temporary or long-term visa. He draws upon his 27 years of loving, working, and living in the City of Brotherly Love and Sisterly Affection, as inspiration. He writes fiction, creative non-fiction and poetry with the occasional and welcome "help" from his three cats Tom, Lila, and Zoe.

Karen Di Prima:

Karen Di Prima is a freelance writer who has previously written for *The Philadelphia Business Journal, The American Lawyer, NJ Lifestyles Magazine*, and others. As a fiction writer, she has completed three (unpublished) novels, one of which was awarded Honorable Mention in a contest conducted by Riverside Books. One of her short stories was recently published in the *Broad River Review*. Karen and her wife live outside of Philadelphia.

Darryl Denning:

Darryl Denning was first published at the age of 12, when he won a prize in the Los Angeles Examiner's "Bill of Rights Essay Contest." Most recently (2016) his work was published in poet Lorene Delaney-Ullman's *Saved Objects* project. In October 2017, his poetry will appear in Flashpoint Publications, *Our Happy Hours – LGBT Voices From the Gay Bars*, in Offbeat Magazine, and in The Curious Element. Mr. Denning is the Facilitator of the Senior Writing Class at the Los Angeles LGBT Center.

Katherine E.K. Duckett:

Katharine Duckett is a writer who lives in Brooklyn. Her fiction has appeared in *Best of Apex Magazine: Volume I, Wilde Stories 2015: The Year's Best Gay Speculative Fiction*, and *Interzone*. Her nonfiction has appeared on *The Toast* and *Tor.com*.

L.K. Early:

L.K. Early is currently enrolled in the Golden Crown Literary Society's Writing Academy. She has a passion for sci-fi, romance, and ghost stories, though not necessarily in that order. Her short story, "Lucky Strike," can be found in *Haunting Muses* (Bedazzled Ink, 2016).

Katherine V. Forrest:

Katherine V. Forrest's sixteen works of fiction, in translation worldwide, include the lesbian classics *Curious Wine*, *An Emergence of Green*, her nine-volume Kate Delafield mystery series, and *Daughters of a Coral Dawn*, the first novel in her award-winning lesbian-feminist utopian trilogy.

Her numerous awards and honors include five Lambda Literary Awards, the Golden Crown Literary Society's Trailblazer Award, a Lifetime Achievement from the Publishing Triangle, the Pioneer Award from the Lambda Literary Foundation, and a profile in *USA Today*. She is president emeritus of the nation's premier LGBT literary organization, Lambda Literary.

Senior editor at the storied Naiad Press for ten years, editor of hundreds of lesbian novels over a span of more than three decades, she is currently supervising editor at Spinsters Ink and Bella Books.

She and her spouse of 25 years and their two feline companions have made the beautiful Coachella Valley their home for the past six years.

Angela Garrigan:

Angela Garrigan was born in Liverpool, England in 1955, the second of seven children in an Irish Catholic family. A long time advocate for equal rights, she came out in 1981 after a disastrous attempt at marriage. In 1986 she moved to London where she met her lifelong partner of thirty years and counting. She now lives in the west of Ireland where she was passionately involved in the recent campaign for Marriage Equality. She has co-authored two lesbian amateur sleuth novels and is now working on the third.

Cheryl Head:

Cheryl A. Head had a fulfilling career in public media before turning to writing, and she is inspired by storytelling in all forms.

Head's first novel, *Long Way Home: A World War II Novel,* is a book about personal courage, race and sexual identity. It was a 2015 Next Generation Indie Book Awards finalist in the African American Literature, and Historical Fiction categories.

Her second novel, *Bury Me When I'm Dead* (Bywater Books), was honored as a 2017 Lambda Literary Awards finalist. The book is the initial installment in the Charlie Mack Motown Mystery series.

Brian Heyburn:

Brian Heyburn is a third year Ph.D. Student in Disability Studies at the University of Illinois at Chicago, where he also received his Master's Degree. He is a member of the Program on Disability, Arts, Culture, and the Humanities. His research interests include the invisible labor of the lived experience of disability, inspirational narratives of disability, queerness and disability, and representation of disability through photography.

JP Howard:

JP Howard is the author of the debut poetry collection, *SAY/MIRROR* (The Operating System), a Lammy finalist. JP is featured in Headmistress Press' 2017 Lesbian Poet Trading Card Series and is a 2017 Lambda NYC LGBTQ Writers in Schools author. JP is a 2016 Lambda Literary Emerging Writers Award winner. She is a scholar-facilitator for Humanities New York and has received fellowships from Cave Canem, VONA/Voices, and Lambda. JP is a Pushcart Prize nominee. She curates Women Writers in Bloom Poetry Salon, a forum offering women writers a monthly venue to come together in a positive and supportive space.

Heather Jane:

Heather Jane was born in southeastern Pennsylvania and lived in the area of the Pennsylvania/Delaware border most of her life. Her love of writing and poetry began in high school, where she studied the classics and worked as the assistant editor on the literary magazine. She majored in Anthropology and Latin American Studies at the University of Delaware.

Heather wrote her collection of poems, *Turn Forty With Me*, in the two years prior to Pennsylvania granting the right to gay marriage. The struggle for this decision to come through and the continuing fight for LGBTQ civil rights are ever present in her writing. Heather currently lives outside of Portland, Oregon with her wife Jeanine Hoffman and their family of pets.

Karin Kallmaker:

Karin Kallmaker has always written about lesbians and love and isn't likely to change. Her nearly thirty novels include *Painted Moon, Captain of Industry,* and *Maybe Next Time*. She's also written more than five dozen short stories and novellas. She has won three Lambda Literary Awards and is a Golden Crown Literary Society Trailblazer. Learn more at kallmaker.com or search social media or your favorite book sites for "Kallmaker." There's only one.

Clay Kerrigan:

Clay Kerrigan is a poet, writer, teacher, and ritual artist who lives in Los Angeles. He received his Master's degree at the California Institute of the Arts. Clay's writing has been featured in *Entropy Magazine*, in the inaugural issue of *Yes Femmes*. He has produced chapbooks for Darin Klein's Box of Books VIII and The Earthfire Institute Wildlife Sanctuary. He is currently a writing instructor at both Los Angeles City College and Glendale Community College, and a manuscript editor for Litmus Press.

Anne Laughlin:

Anne Laughlin is the author of five crime novels published by Bold Strokes Books. The most recent, *A Date to Die*, will be released in October 2017. She has won four Goldies and been short listed three times for a Lammy. Her short stories have appeared in many anthologies, with *It Only Occurred to Me Lately* a finalist in the Saints & Sinners Short Fiction Contest. Anne has been accepted into residencies at Ragdale, Vermont Studio Center, and others. In 2008 she was accepted into the Emerging Writers Retreat by the Lambda Literary Foundation. She lives in Chicago with her wife, Linda Braasch.

Mercedes Lewis:

Mercedes Lewis is a dreamer who is living the dream. Mercedes retired from the military and is making up for lost time. A poet now, with her lesbian, and writer legs firmly beneath her, she is thankful to be a part of this project. Mercedes writes mostly short stories for anthologies and poetry. Her first complete book of poetry, "Glimpses of a Fractured Soul," will be released in April 2017. Mercedes is also a proud member of the Board of Directors of the Golden Crown Literary Society, a non-profit organization for the promotion, education and recognition of lesbian literature.

Lee Lynch:

Lee Lynch's most recent book is the award-winning novel Rainbow Gap from Bold Strokes Books. She is the recipient of Golden Crown Literary Society awards for her books: Rainbow Gap, The Swashbuckler, Beggar of Love, The Raid, and An American Queer, and was designated a Trailblazer by that organization. The Lee Lynch Classic Award was named in her honor. Lynch is a recipient of the Dr. James Duggins Outstanding Mid-Career Novelist Prize, the Alice B. Reader Award, and has been inducted into The Saints and Sinners Hall of Fame. Her stories and essays appear in many anthologies. Originally from Queens, New York, she lives in the Pacific Northwest with her wife Lainie Lynch.

Kitty Kat:

Kitty Kat lives with her family on the beautiful west coast of Scotland, where she enjoys walking in the hills that overlook the snowy peaks of Arran to the south and Bute to the north. Stepping outside, she can breathe in clean fresh air, a mixture of countryside and the salt of the sea, perfect inspirations for a writer. An interest in history and politics as well as a background in Social Services influence her writing.

Kitty is an avid reader and reviewer and regularly updates her blog. https://kittykatwordpresscom.wordpress.com.

Liz McMullen:

The NYC Nightlife was a lifeline as Liz McMullen came out. It provided support and a place where she could joyously celebrate her gender expressions and passion for dancing. Escuelita is a Latino Club known for its glamorous Drag Shows. If what happened at the Pulse Night Club had happened at Escuelita, Liz would have lost members of her chosen family or perhaps been murdered herself. "The Remix" is a love letter to those who made her who she is today. Liz is an award winning novelist. She and her co-author, Shelia, won a Goldie for *Finding Home*, the first book in "The Finding Home Series."

Penny Mickelbury:

Novelist, playwright, journalist, teacher Penny Mickelbury writes the Mimi Patterson/Gianna Maglione mystery novels which are set in Washington, D.C. Mimi is the city's top investigative newspaper reporter and Gianna is a police lieutenant who heads the Hate Crimes Unit. As do many cops and reporters, they have conflicts. Mimi insists on the public's right to know, Gianna insists that too much information hinders her investigations. Their immediate and powerful attraction to each other adds another problem. How does love grow when hate is always center stage? Two of the four Mimi/Gianna novels are Lammy finalists. Penny and her partner live between Atlanta and Los Angeles.

Martha Miller:

Midwestern writer Martha Miller is the author of: *Skin to Skin: Erotic Lesbian Love Stories*, *Nine Nights on the Windy Tree: a Bertha Brannon Mystery*, and *Dispatch to Death*, by New Victoria Press; *Retirement Plan,* and *Widow: a Bertha Brannon Mystery* by Bold Strokes Books. Characters from "Motordrone Molly" originated in Miller's *Tales from the Levee by Herrington Press*. Her stories, reviews and articles are widely published. She's won both Academic and literary writing awards. Martha, a retired English instructor, loves to read and watch basketball. She lives a quiet life with her wife, Ann, two dogs and two cats.

Sallyanne Monti:

As far back as Sallyanne can remember, the collision of an overactive mind and a warped sense of humor left her feeling misunderstood by most. When the dust settled, it left a pile-up of colorful words in its wake, telling an explosive story of witty absurdity and unexpected outcomes. Since then, her fiction and non-fiction short stories, articles and poems have appeared in numerous anthologies, magazines and newspapers.

In her spare time, Sallyanne plays the guitar, composes music, produces fundraising events and writes her memoirs. She lives in Palm Springs, CA with her wife, Mickey, and their doggies, Sola & Zorra.

Jennifer Morales:

Jennifer Morales is a poet, fiction writer, and performance artist who lives in rural Wisconsin. *Meet Me Halfway*, her collection of short stories about race relations in Milwaukee (University of Wisconsin Press, 2015,) was selected by the Wisconsin Center for the Book as 2016 Book of the Year. Recent publications include poetry in *MAYDAY Magazine*, *Glass Poetry Journal*, *Kenning Journal*, *Stoneboat*, and *I Didn't Know There Were Latinos in Wisconsin*, and fiction in *The Long Story* and *Temenos*. "Knickers" is an excerpt from *Junction*, an unpublished novel addressing the new frontier of queer divorce.

Bonnie J. Morris:

Bonnie J. Morris, Ph.D., is a women's history professor and the author of 15 books; including three Lambda Literary Award finalists. She's best known for her work with women's music festivals and lesbian culture (*Eden Built by Eves; The Disappearing L.)* She also lectures for Olivia Travel and the Library of Congress.

Dontá Morrison:

Dontá Morrison is a Los Angeles based author and HIV advocate who hosts a weekly podcast titled "The Dontá Show". A veteran of the U.S Air Force and graduate of Pepperdine University, his motivating spirit has influenced the lives of many; especially, the numerous young gay men he has mentored over the years. As a dedicated change-agent, he aspires to one day eradicate the HIV related stigmas impacting the lives of those infected and affected by the virus and build a bridge between the LGBT community and those who misunderstand them most. Dontá Morrison www.dontamorrison.com

Merril Mushroom:

Merril Mushroom is an old-timey butch bar dyke. Her writing has appeared in many of the lesbian publications that proliferated during the last third of the 20th century.

Richard Natale:

Richard Natale is a Los Angeles-based writer/journalist. His stories have appeared in such literary journals as Gertrude Press, the MCB Quarterly, Chelsea Station, Hollywood Dementia, Wilde Oats, and the anthologies, Image/Out, Men in Love and Off the Rocks. His novels include, *Love the Jersey Shore, Café Eisenhower,* which received an honorable mention from the Rainbow Book Awards, *Junior Willis*, the YA fantasy *The Golden City of Doubloon* and the short-story compilation, *Island Fever*. Natale also wrote and directed the feature film *Green Plaid Shirt*, which was shown at twenty-five film festivals around the world.

Joan Nestle:

Joan Nestle is a self-described seventy-seven-year-old fem, writer, archivist, created by old time lesbian bars and old time activist movements—all knowledges of resistance needed now more than ever.

"The Bathroom Line," written by Joan Nestle, is reprinted by permission from *A Restricted Country*, (© Firebrand Books, 1987.)

Steven Reigns:

Steven Reigns is a Los Angeles-based poet, educator, and was appointed the first City Poet of West Hollywood in October of 2014. Alongside over a dozen chapbooks, he has published the collections *Inheritance* (Sibling Rivalry, 2011) and *Your Dead Body is My Welcome Mat* (Burning Page Press, 2001). He holds a BA in Creative Writing from the University of South Florida, a Master of Clinical Psychology from Antioch University, and is a nine-time recipient of Los Angeles City's Department of Cultural Affairs' Artist in Residency Grant program. He edited *My Life is Poetry*, featuring his students in the first-ever autobiographical poetry workshop for LGBT seniors, and has taught writing workshops around the country to LGBT youth and people living with HIV. Currently he is touring *The Gay Rub*, an exhibition of rubbings from LGBT landmarks, and is at work on a new collection of poetry. Visit him at www.stevenreigns.com.

Cindy Rizzo:

Cindy Rizzo is the author of three novels of lesbian   fiction: Gettiing Back (2015, Ylva Publishing), Love Is Enough (2014), and Exception to the Rule (2013) which won the 2014 award for Best Debut Author from the Golden Crown Literary Society. Her short story, *The Miracle of the Lights*, appeared in the award-winning anthology, Unwrap These Presents (Ylva Publishing.) She was the co-editor of a fiction anthology, *All the Ways Home*, (1995, New Victoria) whichi ncluded her story *Herring Cove*.

Cindy lives in New York City with her wife, Jennifer. You can contact Cindy here: cindyt.rizzo@gmail.com, via Facebook www.facebook.com/ctrizzo, or on Twitter @cindyrizzo.

James Schwartz:

James Schwartz is a poet, slam performer, and author of *The Literary Party: Growing Up Gay and Amish in America*, and several poetry collections, chapbooks and anthologies from Writing Knights Press. He resides in Michigan. He can be contacted here: literaryparty.blogspot.com Twitter @queerspoetry.

Jen Silver:

Jen lives in West Yorkshire with her long-term partner whom she married in December 2014. Reading, writing, golf, archery, and taking part in archaeological digs all form part of Jen's everyday life. Her novels, published by Affinity eBook Press, include the Starling Hill Trilogy: *Starting Over*, *Arc Over Time*, and *Carved in Stone. The Circle Dance*, and *Christmas at Winterbourne* are standalone books.

For the characters in Jen's stories, life definitely begins at forty, and older, as they continue to discover and enjoy their appetites for adventure and romance.

Earlon Sterling:

Sterling is a first generation northerner who grew up in Chicago. She spent her childhood sneaking into museums and hiding in bookstores. Sterling is an avid reader who is working on becoming a writer.

Rae Theodore:

Rae Theodore is the author of *Leaving Normal: Adventures in Gender* (Regal Crest, 2nd edition, 2017,) a big butch memoir that takes a hard, humorous and sometimes heartbreaking look at living outside the gender margins without a rulebook. *Leaving Normal* was shortlisted for an award for creative nonfiction by the Golden Crown Literary Society. You can read about Rae's musings on that middle space where boy/girl collide at: middleagebutch.wordpress.com. Currently, Rae is working on a book titled *Love Is Like Tiny Cheeseburgers: Musings from a Butch Romantic*. She lives in Royersford, Pennsylvania, with her wife, kids and cats.

Ardy Tibby:

Born into white middle class privilege during WWII, Ardy was raised in Compton in Southern California. From the mi- 60's to the 70's she was a (closeted) teacher. On becoming a Radical Lesbian Feminist Activist in the mid '70s, she "dropped out of the patriarchy." Performing as a storyteller and living in several communities over 25 years, Ardy has been politically/culturally/ socially active everywhere. Now 75 years old, she lives happily in Melbourne, Australia and makes occasional return visits to the U.S., often coinciding with OLOC gatherings. You can contact her at: ardyke@yahoo.com

Shelley Thrasher:

Shelley Thrasher, a retired English professor, has been a consulting editor for Bold Strokes Books since 2004. She has written three novels—(*The Storm* (2012), *First Tango in Paris* (2014), and *Autumn Spring* (2015,) published by Bold Strokes. *Autumn Spring* was a Lambda Literary finalist. In late 2016, Sapphire Press published her debut book of poetry, *In and Out of Love.* She loves traveling abroad and working in the yard of her new home in East Texas, where she and her wife, Connie, live with their dogs, Hillary and Holly, their parrot, Bratus, and their polydactyl cat, Toesie

Johnny Townsend:

Johnny Townsend earned an MFA in fiction writing from Louisiana State University. He has published stories and essays in The Washington Post, The Los Angeles Times, The Humanist, The Progressive, Glimmer Train, and in many other publications. His collections of unorthodox Mormon short stories have been named to Kirkus Reviews' Best of 2011, 2012, 2013, 2014, and 2015. He has written one non-fiction book, an account of the arson at the UpStairs Lounge, where 32 people died in a French Quarter gay bar on Gay Pride Day in 1973. He is also an associate producer for the documentary "Upstairs Inferno."

Michael Ward:

Michael Ward is an Atlanta-based poet and journalist. His work has appeared in *Black Gay Genius: Answering Joseph Beam's Call* (Vintage Entity Press, 2014) and The Counter Narrative Project. Previously he worked as a digital contributor for UPTOWN Magazine.

Rebekah Weatherspoon:

Raised in Southern New Hampshire, Rebekah Weatherspoon now lives in Southern California where she finally found her love for writing romance. Her BDSM romance, *At Her Feet,* won the Golden Crown Literary Award for erotic lesbian fiction and most recently her novella, *FIT* (#1 in the FIT Trilogy,) won the Romance Times Book Reviews Reviewers' Choice Award for Best Erotica Novella. You can find out more about Rebekah and her books at www.rebekahweatherspoon.com

CPSIA information can be obtained
at www.ICGtesting.com
Printed in the USA
BVOW08s0114161117

500483BV00027B/1418/P